Shaping the Future of Power

China's rise to power has become one of the most discussed questions both in International Relations theory (IRT) and foreign policy circles. Although power has been a core concept of IRT for a long time, the faces and mechanisms of power as it relates to Chinese foreign policy making have reinvigorated and changed the contours of the debate. With the rise of China and other powers across the global political arena comes a new visibility for different kinds of encounters between states, particularly between China and other Global South states. These encounters are made more visible to IR scholars now because of the increasing influence and impact that rising powers are making in the international system. This book shows that foreign policy encounters between rising powers and Global South states do not necessarily exhibit the same logics, behaviors, or investment strategies of Euro-American hegemons. Instead, they have distinctive features that require new theoretical frameworks for their analysis. *Shaping the Future of Power* probes the type of power mechanisms that build, diffuse, and project China's power in Africa. It is necessary to take into account the processes of knowledge production, social capital formation, and skills transfers in Chinese foreign policy toward African states to fully understand China's power-building mechanisms. These elements are crucial for the relational power framework to capture both the material aspects and ideational people-centered aspects to power. By examining China's investments in human resource development programs for Africa, the book examines a vital, yet undertheorized, aspect of China's foreign policy making.

Lina Benabdallah is Assistant Professor of Politics and International Affairs at Wake Forest University.

Shaping the Future of Power

KNOWLEDGE PRODUCTION AND
NETWORK-BUILDING IN
CHINA-AFRICA RELATIONS

Lina Benabdallah

University of Michigan Press
Ann Arbor

For questions or permissions, please contact um.press.perms@umich.edu

Published in the United States of America by the
University of Michigan Press
Printed and bound by CPI Group (UK) Ltd, Croydon, CR0 4YY

First published July 2020

A CIP catalog record for this book is available from the British Library.

Library of Congress Cataloging-in-Publication data has been applied for.

ISBN 978-0-472-07454-9 (hardcover: alk. paper)
ISBN 978-0-472-05454-1 (paper: alk. paper)
ISBN 978-0-472-12689-7 (e-book)

To mom and dad
Nadjia and Mohsen Benabdallah

Contents

Digital materials related to this title can be found on the Fulcrum platform via the following citable URL: https://doi.org/10.3998/mpub.10194365

Abbreviations

AFRICOM	US Africa Command
ANC	African National Congress
AU	African Union
BRI	Belt and Road Initiative
BRICS	Brazil, Russia, India, China, South Africa
CCP	Chinese Communist Party
CCTV	China Central Television
CGTN	China Global Television Network
CIs	Confucius Institutes
ECPC	Ethiopia-China Polytechnic College
FOCAC	Forum on China-Africa Cooperation
G77	Group of 77
IMF	International Monetary Fund
IR	International Relations
IRT	International Relations theory
MOFA	Ministry of Foreign Affairs (China)
NATO	North Atlantic Treaty Organization
PKO	peacekeeping operations (United Nations)
PLA	People's Liberation Army
PMC	private military companies
PRC	People's Republic of China
PSC	private security companies
ROC	Republic of China
SACE	Sino Africa Centre of Excellence
TUTE	Tianjin University of Technology and Education
UN	United Nations
UNESCO	United Nations Educational, Scientific and Cultural Organization

Acknowledgments

This book was long in the making, and it is my pleasure to acknowledge the many debts I incurred along the way. During the six years it took to complete the research and writing, I was privileged to be surrounded with amazing networks of friends, professors, colleagues, students, and family. First, a special word of thanks goes to Badredine Arfi who gave me a lot of confidence to find my voice but also strongly critiqued my work and pushed me when I needed it. I am indebted to Aida Hozic for sharpening my thinking about critical theories and for pushing me to always question everything. Laura Sjoberg graciously read several drafts of the manuscript. Her feedback helped make this book better and I am thankful for her patience and support.

I am grateful to Les Thiele, Dan O'Neill, and Ben Smith for providing me with advice, mentorship, and feedback. I was also very fortunate to have found a very supportive community of Africanists at the University of Florida's Center for African Studies. Brenda Chalfin, Leo Villalón, Fiona Mclaughlin, and Agnes Leslie all gave me a home in the Center. My research would not have been possible without their generous support. I must also thank Liu Haifang who welcomed me in her Peking University office in the summer of 2014 when I had just finished my dissertation prospectus and popped up unannounced and feeling out of place. Haifang opened many doors for me. Thanks to her continuous support, I had wonderful opportunities to make excellent contacts and attend several events in Beijing that became key to my research. Her friendship and mentorship are invaluable.

While the book has its roots in my dissertation work at the University of Florida, it developed significantly during my time at Wake Forest University. I am thankful to Betina Wilkinson, Sarah Lischer, and Michaelle Browers for reading several of my chapters and providing me with excellent feedback. I am also grateful to Nate Plageman and Katy Harriger, for their support of my research. I would be remiss not to acknowledge the brilliant conversations I had with students in my China-Africa Encounters class. Their curiosity and stimulating discussions sharpened my thinking in more than one way.

Several chapters of this book were presented at International Studies Association meetings and invited talks. I am thankful to Kim Dionne for wonderful feedback on my prospectus when I was visiting Smith College in the spring of 2018. I also thank Dr. Liu Yawei for inviting me to several roundtables and consultation workshops. I learned a lot about foreign policy making thanks to such events. The book benefited greatly from the methodology workshop organized by ISA-Northeast and from feedback provided by Patrick Thaddeus Jackson. I am also thankful to Deborah Brautigam for the invitation to participate at the conference of the China Africa Research Institute, and the chance to present the core arguments about knowledge production and norm diffusion in China-Africa relations. I am thankful to Palgrave MacMillan for allowing me to use adapted parts of the article: "Explaining Attractiveness: Knowledge Production and Power Projection in China's Policy for Africa." *Journal of International Relations and Development* 22 (2): 495–514, which appear in chapter 5.

I am indebted to Oumar Ba for his unique camaraderie and friendship that took shape during grad school and continued through figuring out the many ins and outs of early-career faculty experiences. I also thank Yoon Jung Park and Daniel Large for the many conversations about research and publishing, and for being up for chatting about China-Africa matters for hours. At the University of Michigan Press, Elizabeth Demers deserves particular thanks not only for taking a chance on my book but also for her guidance and patience through the process. My thanks also go to Danielle Coty and Mary Hashman for their hard work with my book. I am grateful for three anonymous reviewers for offering several pages of helpful feedback. I owe them many thanks.

Last but certainly not least, my loving thanks to my family. I could not have finished this without their moral, emotional, and financial support. Mom, despite being thousands of miles away, has been with me through every step of the process. She shared all the highs and lows I experienced writing this book. I am forever grateful for her sharp critiques and boundless love. My dad's comforting embrace always gives me courage and security in the midst of many challenges that come with living abroad. I also want to thank my sister Meliza, my brothers Assil and Wael, and aunts Nadia and Naima for their love and support. Being home with them, however short, is comforting beyond words.

CHAPTER ONE
Introduction

IN 1978, THE PERCENTAGE OF China's population living under extreme poverty was 90. By 2014, that number had been reduced to less than 1 percent.[1] By any measure, China is an economic development success story—if not a miracle. Any developing country would look to China's example and envy the fact that China lifted hundreds of millions of people out of extreme poverty in such record time. Even more, while doing so, China became the world's second largest economy, and now has the world's largest middle class. The list of superlatives could go on, but the point is that this unprecedented success inspires many leaders and political elites in developing countries to view the Chinese experience as a more attractive model for their own development than the often-failing prescriptions from the International Monetary Fund and the World Bank. Political elites in several countries, particularly African countries, are interested in learning from China's state-led, centralized development model. This is especially true for African countries that have existing affinities with China's governance system, social values, and economic structures. Many African leaders' skepticism toward capitalism, neoliberal conditionality structures, and democratic governance puts them in a position to look for alternative models to learn from and adopt.

Ethiopia is an example of a country that has expressed a strong preference for modeling its development path after China's. The Ethiopian government has openly discussed its strategy of learning about China's development model from Chinese politicians, economists, development experts, and party strategists. As many policy experts have noted, Ethiopia has been one of the most eager countries to adopt and adapt China's development model.[2] It is not surprising, then, that members of Ethiopia's ruling party, the Ethiopian People's Revolutionary Democratic Front (EPRDF), welcome

Chinese government-sponsored professionalization trainings. Delegation after delegation, members of the EPRDF are hosted by the Central Party School of the Chinese Communist Party (CCP) for seminars sharing the CCP's poverty alleviation techniques, social media management, party organizational structure, and cadre education. For example, in April 2017, at the invitation of the CCP, a study group of the EPRDF visited China for ten days (China International Department 2017). Two months later, another delegation led by the EPRDF's minister of rural politics, Tefera Deribew, visited China for another period of ten days.[3] The training seminars for party elites represent a space where the appeal of China's development and governance model is intertwined with the networking and connections between political elites on either side.[4]

Ethiopia's EDPRF is nowhere near the only example of a ruling party in Africa with close ties to the CCP. Several others across the continent either have strong ties to the CCP going back to the 1950s or have been cultivating them more recently (Eisenmen 2018a, 2018b). South Africa's ruling party, the African National Congress (ANC), has a very close relationship with the CCP. Immediately before the 2019 South African elections, the ANC enhanced its party-to-party interactions with the CCP by seeking to learn lessons on how to manage the public relations and messaging side of the elections. To this effect, in the summer of 2018, upon returning from a top-party level visit to China, ANC secretary-general Ace Magashule announced that the CCP will train three hundred cadres over the next five years (Kgosana 2018). The CCP's networks with South Africa's party elites can also be observed in its support for the development of the ANC's own party school in the outskirts of Johannesburg (Findlay 2014). Officials stated that the school would be modeled after the CCP's Central Party School in Shanghai, where "party members and foreign guests attend classes on 'revolutionary traditions,' learning everything from Marxist theory to media management" (Findlay 2014). In addition to China's development model, which is attractive to many leaders in the Global South, China's governance model (including the party school system) is also a source of attraction.

A similar pattern can also be found in Kenya. Since the recent launch of the Jubilee Party of Kenya, China's CCP has been providing party member trainings to several delegations (Wanga 2016). Given how new the party is, there is obviously a lot of capacity-building work that needs to be done for the party to get stronger and gain political traction. The CCP has been hosting delegations of no less than fifty members to provide seminars on party management, cadre formation, and organizational structure. During a training debriefing meeting attended by several top CCP party members to share strategies with the Jubilee Party, a top party official emphasized the CCP's people-centered development approach as a key to its successful diplomacy in Africa. The officer also highlighted poverty elimination as a big area of overlap with the majority of African countries. According to his remarks, the CCP's goal is to eradicate poverty in China by 2020. This emphasis on poverty elimination and the creation of economic growth opportunities for rural areas is of great interest to Kenya's Jubilee Party members. Attending the seminars allows the party elite to learn directly from their Chinese counterparts on how they approach poverty eradication. The party's secretary general, Raphael Tuju, observed that "in 1961, Kenya's GDP per capita was four times higher compared to China's. Today, the GDP per capita in Kenya is $1,450 while in China it is $8,875. China's GDP has gone up more than 50 times, while in Kenya, it has gone up only three times. We should find out the focus that China took in the last 40 years" (Mutethya 2018). Tuju's remarks show how China's development success story is attractive to several party leaders and political elites. Professionalization trainings in fighting corruption and better public-resource management were of particular interest to Tuju.

For China, its development model, and its governance practices and norms, become more legitimated when they are adopted, mimicked, or at least received positively by the international community. China is positioned in a way that allows it to make choices about *if* and *how* it interacts with states interested in emulating its development or governance model. Especially in cases where Beijing promotes the China model as an alternative for other states, the Chinese government sponsors a variety of elite trainings and interweaves social relations with business investments. China's competitive advantage in a race for influence and attractiveness is built around expanding social capital, professional networks, and relational power with African elites. This book is about how and why social capital and network-building matter for shaping the future of power in global politics.

In particular, this book explores the interwoven roles of social relations, knowledge production, and power in China's foreign relations. It revolves around a central yet complex question: Do all major powers project their influence and power in the same way? Or does China project its power and influence differently than other major powers? I argue—in contrast with conventional approaches to International Relations theory (IRT)—that social networks and people-centered relations are a core factor for the (successful) conduct of Chinese foreign policy even in the areas where traditional IRT would expect materialism to dominate. Whereas it is more feasible to geo-code China's port investments in Africa, for instance, or count how many stadiums and highways were built by Chinese firms, it is equally important to understand the social fabric and network-building even if they are not as readily visible. Social capital and social networks here are meant in the sense that webs of personal and professional relations and social networks are what enable actors to be powerful. Accounting for the role of relations both empirically and theoretically is indispensable for understanding how China is becoming such a major power and to understanding China's shaping of the future of power.

On September 3, 2018, Beijing rolled out red carpets for over fifty African state leaders and officials hosting the seventh Forum on China-Africa Coop-eration (FOCAC). For days after the Forum, pictures of African presidents shaking hands with Chinese president Xi Jinping at the glamorous Great Hall of the People decorated with African nations' flags flooded Chinese and international news outlets. This FOCAC meeting, like its predecessors, is a space for cultivating social capital, forging people-to-people bonds, and building strong personal connections between African delegations and their Chinese counterparts. FOCAC meetings are not just about the one or two-day overmediatized summits, they include a variety of functions from busi-ness summits to press conferences, from private meetings among heads of states to dinner banquets.

China became the continent of Africa's largest trading partner in 2009, overtaking European and Western powers, which have long been the most influential outsiders in African economies.[5] China has also become the des-tination of the largest number of African students seeking university degrees outside of the continent. Over the course of the last two decades, China matched and even eclipsed European powers' influence in Africa without fighting wars, wielding military power, or using what are traditionally un-derstood as aggressive tools of "great power" diplomacy. China's foreign policy toward African states is very diverse in scope with a variety of means deployed. One way that China's foreign policy toward Africa is conducted is forum diplomacy, through FOCAC, which is organized to chart multilateral relations between China and African states. The Forum—which takes place every three years—outlines the agenda and scope for the upcoming three years. Given the numerous and high-profile actors involved, organizing FO-

CAC is very complicated logistically. By the time government representatives arrived in Beijing in September 2018, most aspects of the agenda were already negotiated and ironed out. The meeting itself was not the place for negotiating the agenda or scope of China-Africa relations. Rather, it was an opportunity for the Chinese government to exercise the art of social relations under the spotlight of major international media outlets. The media attention was an opportunity to project to the world a brand of China-Africa relations focused around presidential handshakes, embraces, agreements, and solidarity. Yet China's summit-diplomacy through FOCAC or other platforms is about more than media optics: China's art of diplomacy by social relationships goes beyond camera lenses and extends beyond Africa.

Relations and relationality are central to China's foreign policy and diplomatic conduct generally and in Africa specifically. The China-Africa Forum cements and institutionalizes the practice of cultivating social relationships, but it is neither its beginning nor its end. The forum is a place where discourse meets practice about the centrality of relationality and exchanges of favors, support, and, in the words of Mayfair Yang, it is a place for the "cultivation of personal relationships and networks of mutual dependence; and the manufacturing of obligation and indebtedness" (Yang 1994, 6). Building social relations and manufacturing obligation in China-Africa relations is most evident in FOCAC, which concludes with the release of action plans that outline the multilateral pledges made. In the latest action plan (following the 2018 FOCAC meeting), of eight major initiatives announced as part of China-Africa relations between 2018 and 2021, people-to-people exchanges is one.[6] The word "exchange" itself appeared eighty-five times in the text, most of which is put in the context of high-level officials' visits, expert trainings, and academic and cultural exchanges.

In order to fully understand China's foreign policy toward African states and its importance in global politics, one certainly needs to look at the financial figures, foreign aid levels, and foreign direct investments. But those material factors and the capabilities that they reflect are not the whole story. It is as crucial to examine the investments made in people-to-people relations and human resource development in China-Africa relations. Especially when investment in human capital is not only becoming a hallmark of China's foreign policy in Africa but also with developing countries more broadly. To be sure, human resource development programs are—at the very base— about social relationships, exchanges, and increasing network and social power between Chinese hosts and participating parties. They are also about diffusing technical knowledge, norms, and ways of thinking about governance, development, and security, among other things, based on China's experiences. During FOCAC 2018, Chinese loans and grants to Africa declined compared to the sixth FOCAC in 2015. Yet, despite this decline in loans, the amounts of people-to-people exchange programs and professionalization trainings pledged significantly increased from the previous Forum announcements (Brautigam 2018). The word "training" appeared forty-three times in the action plan in the contexts of security, culture, development, and media. Some could see China's focus on people-centered diplomacy as a trivial detail, but that would be a misinterpretation of the contours of Chinese foreign policy-making.

HUMAN CAPITAL INVESTMENTS IN CHINESE FOREIGN POLICY MAKING

Chinese president Xi Jinping, speaking at the sixth Forum on China-Africa Cooperation in Johannesburg in December 2015, announced China's ten investment plans in Africa for the upcoming three years (2015–18). These plans laid out Beijing's continued "support of Chinese enterprises' active role in Africa's infrastructural development, particularly in sectors such as railways, roads, regional aviation, ports, electricity and telecommunications." He also announced financial investments to the tune of "US$5 billion in grant and zero-interest loans; US$35 billion in loans of concessional nature on more favorable terms and export credit line; and an increase of US$5 billion to the China-Africa Development Fund" (Xi 2015b). Yet another set of investments featured in Xi's speech pertained to "training 20,000 technical personnel, providing 40,000 training opportunities for African personnel in China, offering African students 2,000 education opportunities with degrees or diplomas, and 30,000 government scholarships" (Ministry of Foreign Affairs 2015a). Likewise, the summit's action plan announced that for each of the three years, China will sponsor "200 African scholars to visit China and 500 African youths to study in China and train 1,000 media professionals from Africa" (Ministry of Foreign Affairs 2015c). Three years later and at the seventh FOCAC, President Xi's speech laid out similar patterns for China-Africa cooperation for the period between 2018 and 2021. If closely examined one can see for example that although Chinese state loans and investments in Africa dropped by US$10 billion, opportunities for government-sponsored scholarships increased from 30,000 to 50,000. FOCAC 2018 announced another 50,000 scholarship opportunities, technical skill trainings through the China-based Lu Ban workshops, trainings for peacekeeping and police units, training of a hundred anticorruption officials, inviting 2,000 exchange students over the period of three years, and training health experts, agriculture specialists, and media staff. While investments in natural resources and infrastructure projects have declined, investments in human capital and people-to-people exchange programs have spiked since 2015. How can scholars of international relations and foreign policy explain this?

A substantial body of research on China's foreign policy suggests that China's power should be viewed through the lenses of economic prowess, natural resource extractions, and material capabilities. If that indeed were the case, how are we to make sense of China's increasing investments in human resource development for African states? Building on and going beyond extant literature on China's foreign policy in Africa, this book seeks to address this puzzle by examining how China is deploying social capital and relational productive power in Africa through knowledge production via human resource development and professionalization training programs. This book's central proposition is that by understanding power as relational and social, it is possible to see that China's investments in human resource development programs are central to China-Africa power relations for two main reasons. First, they expand China's network of connections with military officers, civil servants, journalists, and regular citizens. Second, they act as spaces for expert knowledge production, norm diffusion, and the interpellation of trainees. To elaborate on this argument, the book develops and then deploys a new theoretical framework to analyze and explicate the implications of knowledge production and skills transfers in foreign policy. The next section introduces the tools used in the framework.

POWER AND KNOWLEDGE PRODUCTION
IN CHINESE FOREIGN POLICY

There is a rich and diverse plethora of studies on China's investments in natural resources, infrastructure construction, and mega-transportation projects in Africa. However, not much work has been done on China's investments in human resource development programs and on their impacts on African participants as processes of knowledge production and skills transfers. This is not surprising since China's rise has by and large been examined from the perspective of mainstream IR approaches. Frameworks based on neorealism, neoliberalism, and rationalist theories broadly defined often interpret power as being material, compulsory, and military. Such approaches do not have room to analyze knowledge production and people-centered diplomacy *as power*. Many nonmainstream IR scholars, including critical theorists, poststructuralists, and development studies specialists, have recognized the limitations of mainstream perspectives on power and worked to reveal the role of knowledge production in governance practices. Still, emerging work on the power-knowledge nexus largely focuses its attention on North-South relations. In this work, Global North actors are taken as hegemonic generators of rules, norms, and producers of expert knowledge on development, governance, security, and so forth. These norms, rules, and knowledge are then understood to be internalized and normalized by Global South others who are viewed as consumers and not as producers of norms. Scholarship problematizing hegemonic configurations of Global North actors as experts and Global South actors as learners is urgent and important but still limited. It does not problematize the knowledge-power nexus in contexts beyond North-South relations, and therefore falls short in providing a satisfactory understanding of the case of China's foreign policy in the Global South and with African states as an example.

The above-addressed limitations open up opportunities to enrich the study of global politics and call for more studies to theorize power-knowledge in the Global South. This book is an answer to that call. It deploys a framework based on the concept of relational productive power to think of China's human development investments as spaces for the production of Chinese expert knowledge (e.g., on journalism, development, and security) and as fields for the diffusion of Chinese values (e.g., on journalism, development, and security) to African participants. In this pursuit, the book draws on Foucauldian conceptualizations of knowledge as power and power as productive of subjectivities and regimes of truths, and on relational network approaches to power building. I enrich this framework by deploying Qin Yaqin's treatment of the concept of *guanxi* in international relations and his relational theory.

RELATIONALITY IN INTERNATIONAL RELATIONS

A key argument of this book is that relationality is one of the most important aspects of China's foreign policy. By relationality, I mean the focus on people-to-people connections as the core concept and unit of analysis (whether one is considering foreign or domestic types of relations). This is in line with a great number of IR scholars who pay attention to relationality and view actors' identities and the roles they perform as determined in relation to other actors.[7]

In the specific context of China's foreign policy, scholars have linked relationality to the norm of *guanxi* (关系), which is a core Confucian concept that translates (reductively) as "connections" (Fang Yang 2011, 163). Guanxi implies a type of special network or a circle of relations through which the exchange of favors is expected in business, social, and political relations. Although the importance of personal connections and networks in business is not exclusive to China and is well known in European and Anglo-Saxon contexts and elsewhere, guanxi is a deeply ingrained cultural trait and part of China's business standard operating procedures (Shih and Huang 2015, 8). Cultivating a network of relations is important for the success of a business, for instance, because actors draw on their networks for support and for favors. Guanxi is equally as important domestically as it is to China's foreign relations in that it defines China's conduct with its neighbors and other states (Kavalski 2013; Shih and Huang 2015). Maintaining dependable relations and cultivating strong friendships are essential for the success of China's foreign policy. Chinese foreign policy makers pay a great deal of attention to nurturing people-to-people relations, whether this means elite exchanges, presidential official visits, or people-level exchanges, summit diplomacy, and so forth. Professional networks are valued, nurtured, and taken as assets for successful and prosperous foreign relations and reputation.

A thorough analysis of China's foreign policy in the Global South through the Belt and Road Initiative or with African states has to take into account the power of guanxi and China's investments in constructing networks of guanxi. Taking relations and relationality as a core characteristic of Chinese foreign policy conduct clearly shows that China's investments in capacity-building programs, trainings for military officials, media experts, and so on are endeavors that strengthen China's guanxi in the African continent. Investments in human resource development programs, as I explain in the next section, are just as important (if not more important) in the long term than material aspects of power.

POWER AND RELATIONALITY IN CHINESE FOREIGN POLICY

Most scholarship on China's foreign policy and its influence in Africa focuses on investigating investments in natural resource extraction, trade agreements, and infrastructure projects. The impact of investments in human resource development through professionalization training programs is an understudied aspect of these relations, and hence the overriding goal of this research is to shed light on them. Since the early 2000s, Chinese foreign policy makers have emphasized Africans' call for more programs that facilitate the trainings of skilled labor and promote opportunities for transfers of technology from Chinese experts to African recipients. For African elites, what has long been missing in Africa's relations to traditional powers is this very aspect of transferring skills. In their view, without training a strong workforce, Africa and Africans would continue being dependent on European elites and their expertise. The problem with this is that turning Africa into a huge market for European goods and technology comes at the cost of creating necessary conditions for local enterprises and companies to acquire skilled labor and trainings and operate independently of European expertise. For this reason, one of the ways that China markets its investments in Africa as different from the European powers is to emphasize vocational training programs. Yet, by the same token, one cannot take at face value that these trainings are necessarily going to lead to autonomy and independence for tech companies and high skill jobs on the African side.

To be sure, there is a high demand from African leaders and officials for more transfers of technology and transfers of skills to African workers. There is merit to transfers of technology and skills insofar as they have the potential to enable the host countries to have the resources to model themselves after the big firms and gradually work toward promoting local production. However, recognizing the importance of technology transfers in promoting industrialization and development should not overshadow the question of whose technology is being transferred and for what in return. In other words, can technology, expertise, and knowledge be neutral? Can technology, skills, and knowledge transfers be free of power dynamics? In this book, I start from the assumption that the answer to these questions is "no." The Chinese government offers routine training opportunities to civil servants, doctors, police forces, military officials, scientists, farmers, and university professors, among other occupations. Professionalization trainings also target, increasingly, media specialists since they are viewed as the painters of China's image in Africa. Media scholarships are given both to professional journalists who are interested in short-term training and to students of media and communications who are getting higher education degrees. As noted above, despite a decline in the overall volumes of Chinese investment packages in Africa in the seventh FOCAC meeting (2018), the numbers of vocational trainings and people-to-people exchange opportunities have gone up. This signals the importance of focusing our analysis and attention on this big portion of China's foreign policy conduct in Africa.

DATA AND METHODS

Why is China increasingly investing in human capital development programs in Africa even when it limits its loans and financial grants to African governments? To what extent do skills transfers and professionalization training programs promote China's development and governance model as a viable alternative to the liberal order? How is China's power manifested in its relations to postcolonial Global South states?

When I set out to examine these questions, I did not plan on "discovering" what China's power in Africa looked like. During my first research field trip to Beijing (in the summer of 2014), I initially meant to research FOCAC, explore China's foreign policy through the institutional prism of FOCAC, and ask about the organizational structure and negotiating power within FOCAC. During this fieldwork trip, I noticed a proliferation of professionalization training workshops hosted in Beijing for delegations of African political elites, civil servants, and occasionally cohorts dressed in military uniforms. I was able to attend some of them. As I did so, I remember feeling overwhelmed by how many of these events there were all over Beijing. In June 2014, while I was still in Beijing, the Chinese government hosted the second China-Africa media forum (under the umbrella of FOCAC), which I attended. Seeing dozens of government officials, ministers of telecommunication, journalists, and media staff from Africa in the audience of their Chinese counterparts sharing expert knowledge on journalism values, principles, and digital technology left me deeply curious about the workshops. During that trip, and thanks to several colleagues who granted me access to attend many of these workshops, I was able to talk to many African diplomats about the workshops and their impressions of them. I got very positive impressions from African invitees about China's development model, Chinese megacities, high technology, rapid trains, and so forth. There was a sense of admiration for and awe toward China's development model. As one diplomat from Rwanda said to me, "Whether we like it or not, the [Chinese] system works."[8]

I then started to refocus my research questions to learn more about Chinese government-sponsored training seminars, the impressions African participants had, and the goals/objectives from the Chinese side. In this pursuit, I conducted semistructured interviews with several agencies and actors in China. I had interviews with senior officials at China's Ministry of Foreign Affairs (MOFA), with African affairs specialists, with think tank analysts, former diplomats, and academics.[9] I also talked to several African journalists who were attending the Communication University of China on all-expense-paid scholarships offered to them by the Chinese government. In addition, several times I observed—without participating—groups of African trainees discuss how they should navigate journalism ethics, integrity, and being fully sponsored by the Chinese government. On a second fieldwork trip, I decided to speak with African diplomats in Addis Ababa, the home of the African Union headquarters (which, symbolically, China built for Africans). I was in Addis Ababa in February 2015 and got to speak to several diplomats at the Union about their experiences with Chinese-funded professionalization seminars and paid-for trips to China. Most of my interviews were conducted in English but a few were in French and some in Arabic.[10] The impressions on China's knowledge-sharing programs with Africans were overwhelmingly positive. In a conversation over dinner with a Nigerian diplomat who had participated in two delegation visits to China, he emphasized that the most important part about the trips for him was how African delegations were treated as equals, with respect and care, by their Chinese hosts.[11]

During my interviews at the African Union headquarters, I was told repeatedly that Africa is the youngest continent and that training the youth, preparing them for jobs, and teaching them Mandarin to get jobs with Chinese companies were all welcome developments from an economic perspective. Chinese know-how and professional skills were viewed as having a positive effect on employment rates. One diplomat expressed his intention to enroll in a "Mandarin for Business" course he saw advertised by the Confucius Institute at Addis Ababa University. This led me to visit the Confucius Institute—China's culture and language center—located at Addis Ababa University. I interviewed the director, several Ethiopian students who were enrolled in Chinese language classes, and the volunteers who were working there. I also visited the French and German cultural institutes just to get a sense of how they compared to China's Confucius Institute. In addition to these conversations in Addis Ababa, I also traveled to Kenya in March 2015 and conducted interviews with news anchors and staff at the Africa office of the China Global Television Network, formerly known as CCTV Africa.

I supplemented the data I collected from all the interviews with official documents, discourses such as China's Africa policy papers, action plans from the seven FOCAC forums, speeches by presidents and high-ranking diplomats, and other official China-Africa documents. I also relied on news media coverage both in Chinese news outlets and also prominent African and several international outlets. Additionally, I gained insights from several trips I took to China after my fieldwork period. During a trip in May 2018 I visited the Chinese peacekeeping training base on the outskirts of Beijing in Lafang and spoke, informally, to several trainers at the base. I was also able to tour Djibouti on an official delegation visit in August 2018 thanks to a workshop organized by the Carter Center. During the tour we saw the Chinese-built multipurpose port that is adjacent to China's military base, the special economic zone, Djibouti's data center, the Chinese-built Ethiopia-Djibouti Standard Gauge Railway, and so forth. Over the past six years of researching this topic, high profile and pedestrian, formal and informal, academic or policy-focused interactions have provided important insights for my analysis of China's foreign policy in Africa and African responses to China's influence.

This book looks to make sense of these very rich fieldwork observations both theoretically and empirically. Throughout my analysis of official documents and fieldwork observations, I have come to realize that the social bonds, connections, and networking opportunities were recurrent emphases of the people with whom I interacted. The trips I took, observations, and official documents led me to probe the links between foreign policy making, network building, knowledge production, and power projection. Beijing-sponsored professionalization trainings for Africans seemed to serve two main functions. First, they enhance people-to-people connections, expanding networks of relations among elites, public servants, foreign policy makers, and youth groups on both sides. Second, they serve as spaces for the diffusion of expert knowledge, skills, and norms about development, security, diplomacy, internet governance, and so on from trainers to trainees. The remainder of this book explores themes, theories, and findings of this research with an eye toward how they shed light on shaping the future of power in global politics. It is organized as follows.

THE STRUCTURE OF SHAPING THE FUTURE OF POWER IN GLOBAL POLITICS

In chapter 2, "Network-Building in China-Africa Relations: Past and Present," I lay out the context of China-Africa relations by examining important

patterns in Chinese foreign policy making and by tracing China's investments in professionalization training programs for Africans historically.
Putting into a historical perspective China's professionalization training
programs for Africans helps show that although these investments are not
new and have been part of China's foreign policy making since the era of
Chairman Mao Zedong, they have increased both in size and scope in today's context. The chapter also provides background information that is
necessary to understand the analysis developed in subsequent chapters.
Chinese foreign policy, for instance, is characterized by avoiding confronta-
tion and by rhetorically insisting on China's peaceful rise and friendly intentions. Chinese foreign policy is also characterized by playing a dual role,
identifying as a developing country while at the same time measuring up to
great power status. Explaining these aspects of China's policy is important
to my discussion of the theoretical frameworks for analyzing power relations in the Global South.

Chapter 3, "Relationality, Social Capital, and the Future of Power," develops the conceptual and analytical frameworks that I deploy in analyzing the
case studies of the book. The chapter develops step by step the core theoretical framework, which consists of three important concepts: relationality (via
guanxi), knowledge production, and norm diffusion. Of the different conceptualizations of power in IR literature, I argue for a productive relational
face of power. By drawing on Qin Yaqin's relational power, Michel Foucault's
insights on the power-knowledge nexus, and literature on institutions as
norms diffusers and socializers, I introduce a framework that enables us to
understand the role of social networks and relational capital in the foreign
policy making of emerging (super)powers. Understanding power from a relational perspective means that actors are as powerful as their social networks.
Measuring power or influence from this perspective is not done through
measuring material capabilities (military or economic). Rather, power and
influence are viewed from a social capital standpoint and social relations are
taken to precede power relations. When personal networks and social capital
become formal and institutionalized, they in turn become spaces for the
production of knowledge and the diffusion of norms, values, and ways of
doing things. Expanding networks of connections and promoting people-
to-people exchanges are central to China's strategy, and an appropriate
framework to analyze China's power building mechanisms has to account
for relationality. Therefore, this framework aims at explaining a big portion
of China's foreign policy practices, but it does not seek to argue that material

power conceptualizations are irrelevant to understanding emerging powers. It complements our understanding of power in global politics.

Chapters 4 through 6 are the case studies through which I explore the theoretical framework, relational productive power, the book presents. Together they examine three cases of Chinese government-sponsored professionalization trainings and people-to-people exchange programs. Each one of these chapters is organized into two main sections, one that looks at FOCAC discourses announcing the professionalization training programs across FOCAC's seven meetings, and another that examines the content of the trainings and their role in expanding China's social network in Africa. In chapter 4, "Guanxi in Military Diplomacy and Security Trainings," I analyze Beijing-sponsored trainings for high-ranking military officers, peacekeeping troops, and private security agents. The chapter begins by examining the articulation of discourses around China's security strategy in Africa and follows this by investigating the various security practices implemented through peacekeeping troops' trainings, private security trainings, and high-level military officers' meetings and exchanges. The chapter argues that security-related exchanges and trainings are opportunities for Chinese military officials to expand their connections and build strong personal relations with their African counterparts. Yet equally important is that military joint drills and trainings are platforms that serve to expand alliance-like ties between China and high-ranking African military officers.

Chapter 5, "Guanxi in Public Diplomacy and Trainings for Journalists," discusses Beijing-sponsored training programs and scholarships for journalists (professionals and academics) to experience living and studying in China. The recipients of long-term scholarships typically to get all expenses paid (airfare, tuition waiver, health insurance, accommodation, and a monthly allowance) and are enrolled in Chinese institutions to complete graduate degrees in journalism. Many China-trained journalists return to their respective countries and resume their reporting jobs. By examining a sample curriculum, I find that topics such as government-media relations, censorship, and social media's "red lines" are emphasized in seminars organized for African participants. In my interviews with some of the participants, I found that their impressions of China have positively changed since traveling and living in the country. Even when some journalists are not always impressed with China's restrictive journalism model, which includes many limitations when it comes to freedom of speech and reporting critically on the government, overall their experiences *of* China were positive.

Chapter 6, "Guanxi in Cultural Diplomacy and Confucius Institutes," examines the role of and the influence that Chinese cultural centers play in promoting China's self-image and shaping a brand around shared interests between the people of China and their African counterparts. The chapter examines these cultural diplomacy institutes as spaces for interpellation through knowledge production and the diffusion of norms about China's attractive development model. China's Confucius Institutes in African countries have as an audience both college students who study Mandarin and the community outside of the college, which is invited to participate in cultural events. Confucius Institutes also serve as network hubs and liaison between Chinese companies looking to hire local labor in Africa and African students who are studying Mandarin. Being a student of Mandarin, therefore, is branded as a path that leads to concrete jobs and better life prospects.

Finally, the conclusion, "Relational Power beyond China-Africa Relations," reflects on the research questions asked in this study and brings back the bigger picture of Chinese foreign policy conduct in Africa and the Global South. The chapter also suggests three lines of future research that this book's findings open up: broadening the conceptualization of power in IR to include post-Western interpretations and actors beyond the West; contextualizing China's conduct in Africa in the broader context of other rising powers' strategies in Africa; and contextualizing Africa in the broader context of China's foreign policy making toward other Global South states. These three approaches would help us further understand Chinese conceptualizations of power, order, and hegemony and how they differ (or not) from Global North or Western perspectives. Along these lines of research, the chapter concludes by offering a critique of poststructuralist IR scholarship, which assumes that power and domination in foreign relations are a result of "othering" where a superior "self" dominates an inferior "other." From my analysis of China's foreign policy in Africa, power seems to circulate and operate successfully precisely because there is no hierarchical othering. China portrays itself as another developing country, as African states' equal, and this—in my analysis—makes power relations less visible/confrontational and therefore more successful.

CHAPTER TWO

Network-Building in China-Africa Relations

Past and Present

DURING THE SEVENTY-THIRD United Nations General Assembly high-level meeting held in September 2018, twenty-seven African leaders made the trip to New York to participate. Earlier that same month, fifty-one African leaders showed up in Beijing to attend the seventh edition of the Forum on China-Africa Cooperation (FOCAC) (Dahir 2018). That twice as many African leaders were interested in attending FOCAC than the UN General Assembly can be due to several variables, but it certainly shows that the relations between the Chinese government and its African counterparts is such that to date, FOCAC 2018 holds the record for participation from African leaders in any multilateral platform.[1] At the 2018 FOCAC meeting, China pledged a financial package of $60 billion for investments, loans, and grants to be spent over a period of three years on the continent. By 2018, China was Africa's largest trading partner for the ninth consecutive year with trade volumes surpassing $100 billion by the end of the year. Robust financial ties and diplomatic relations between China and African countries are not a new phenomenon—they have been cultivated for several decades.

Soon after the establishment of the People's Republic of China (PRC) in 1949, the Chinese government formulated a foreign policy strategy with five pillars known as the Principles of Coexistence that would guide its conduct with other states. The principles include mutual respect for sovereignty and territorial integrity, mutual nonaggression, noninterference in each other's internal affairs, equality and mutual benefit, and peaceful coexistence.[2] As a national strategy, these principles were to work together toward the common goal of preserving China's independence, sovereignty, and territorial integrity. Between China and other states, these principles helped create a favorable environment for China's reform and opening up to the external world.[3] The principle of nonaggression and antihegemony is central to the overall conduct of Chinese foreign policy in the Global South. Despite China surpassing most developing countries economically, militarily, and in technological innovation, the Chinese government insists upon qualifying its foreign policy in terms of antihegemonism.

Within these principles, the core focus of Chinese foreign policy priorities can be divided into three main areas of interest: China's relations with major powers (particularly the United States), China's relations with its neighbors (e.g., Japan), and China's relations with developing countries (including other Asian states as well as African and South American states).[4] Nathan and Scobell (2012) explain that China's current priority is its relations with the US because it and China are the world's largest economies, and because resolving many global issues will hinge upon coordination between the two powers. Nathan and Scobell (2012) call this the first ring, which also includes Taiwan. In the second ring, the authors include Japan as well as China's other immediate neighbors and other Asian countries. The last ring includes no less than three-quarters of the world's countries, with the majority being developing countries. Yet despite the large group of countries included in this third ring, Chinese foreign policy had not systematically engaged this last ring until the beginning of the 1990s. This was partly because of its Maoist isolationist policy and partly due to ancient Sino-centric views that perceive China as the center of the universe and consider countries that are far away from the center to be barbarians and uninteresting.[5]

Understanding China's global strategy through the three rings is important for this book in two ways. China's evolving involvement in African affairs is rather recent when compared against the experiences of traditional (or colonial) powers. First, it still is in the making and much of China's recent strategy in Africa has followed an approach of "testing the water by feeling the stones." Second, examining Chinese foreign policy in Africa as a case of China's foreign policy in the third ring may allow us to deductively explain the main characteristics of China's foreign policy toward about three-quarters of the world. Although Africa is of a third-level priority for China's foreign policy, it does not make it less important for understanding China's rise to power. On the contrary, countries within the third-level circle reveal a lot more about China's power practices than do China's relations with the US or European powers.

In order to shed light on the history and trajectory of Chinese investments in human capital in Africa, this chapter is organized into three main sections. The first section provides an essential background to the main characteristics of Chinese foreign policy conduct since Mao's rule. Examples of such characteristics examined include China's dual identity both as a developing country and a superpower, and China's noninterference principle. The second section traces the origins and history of Chinese-sponsored professionalization training programs for Africans. Putting professionalization trainings in a historical background shows how they have always been a foundational aspect of China-Africa relations. The last section gives a brief overview of the current status of Chinese government-sponsored professionalization training programs. By surveying thousands of training programs provided by China for Africans, the section analyzes some trends on what the most recurrent topics/areas of trainings are and which countries are the top recipients of the trainings. The section gives a necessary primer on the current programs that are funded by the Chinese government to train Africans as a preparation for the empirical analysis.

Mao's China and Leading the "Third World"

Despite the late development of relations between China and other parts of the developing world, Global South countries quickly became an important part of Chinese foreign policy for three main reasons. Maintaining good relations with developing countries is necessary for increasing China's diplomatic support, market extension, and image building (Taylor 2006, 7). First, China was in need of diplomatic support in order to curtail Taiwan's independence claims. When the Chinese civil war ended in 1949, the PRC was ruled by Mao's communist regime whereas the Republic of China (ROC) or Taiwan was ruled by Kuomintang's Nationalist Party. Both governments claimed to be the "official China" yet Taiwan was the one that received official recognition from the international community (including the UN). However, that did not last long, as the PRC moved to take back the United Nations Security Council seat from Taiwan and began an international diplomatic campaign to delegitimize Taiwan as the official China (Cohen 2011, 56). In 1971, when the PRC successfully replaced the ROC as a permanent member of the Security Council, support and votes from the Group of 77 (G77) countries were crucial. Chinese government officials reiterate their recognition of the G77 support and have since then represented the voice and concerns of developing countries in a wide variety of contexts.

Second, developing countries represent a huge market potential for the sale of Chinese goods and products as well as a significant source of crude oil and other natural resources. China's trade volume with Africa reached $233 billion in 2014 whereas the trade volume was less than $1 billion in the 1970s. Maintaining strong relations with Global South countries increases trade interdependence and opens markets for Chinese goods, investments, and contractors. Third, China's engagement in implementing development projects that generate economic growth in developing countries promotes a positive image of China and its development model. Starting in the 1980s, Chinese foreign policy makers have framed China's interest in collaborating with the Global South under the South-South Cooperation platform.[6]

The South-South Cooperation guidelines formulated by the United Nations Development Programme are already deeply enmeshed with Chinese foreign policy mechanisms. Some of the principles include respect for national sovereignty, noninterference in domestic affairs, nonconditionality, mutual benefit, and equal partnership (United Nations Office of South-South Cooperation 2017). UN agencies and many developing countries have promoted South-to-South Cooperation vigorously, and China is increasingly becoming an innovator in terms of South-South Cooperation models and platforms. The BRICS countries[7] and the group of eleven countries expected to reach middle-income status by 2030[8] have expanded and revived South-South Cooperation through cooperation mechanisms such as triangular projects between two developing countries and a UN agency. For a number of years now, the majority of developing countries' partners have effectively been other developing countries. Foreign direct investment from and to countries in the Global South has been increasing, and high levels of economic and financial interdependence have drawn these countries closer to one another. Many scholars have questioned the merit of the popularized narrative on "Africa's rise" by assessing the impact of Brazil, India, and China on Africa's economies. A closer look suggests that while African economies have successfully grown out of their formal colonial ties and dependencies on developed countries, they have not really become independent. Instead, according to Taylor (2014), several African economies are diversifying their dependency, switching from relying on developed countries to becoming increasingly dependent on developing countries.

This is related to a central question I pose in this book: How do Chinese government-funded pledges like 200,000 professionalization training opportunities for Africans fit in the "Africa rising" narrative? Do they suggest further dependence with new actors to replace old colonial powers? In addition, what are the power dynamics and impacts of establishing Confucius Institutes to teach Chinese language and culture in African university and high school classrooms? In sum, is South-South Cooperation as horizontal in practice as it is in rhetoric, or what kind of hierarchies and power dynamics permeate South-South cooperation?

China's Dual Performative Role

Another unique characteristic of Chinese foreign policy making is that it plays a dual role, as a developing country and as a major power. Because relations shape actors' roles and performance as much as they are shaped by them, the role that the PRC assumes in different contexts varies from a role of an emerging power, to great power relations, to a leader of the developing world. The flexibility in China's roles and brands leads me to discuss another unique characteristic of China's foreign policy: that of being able to simultaneously assume a role as a global power and as a developing country (see Tang 2018). Beijing can exercise influence on developing states when trying to diffuse its own norms and values because it can play the role of a leading developing country to its advantage.[9] Chinese officials emphasize China's role as a fellow developing country when they express dissatisfaction with the West-dominated neoliberal order and call on reforming aspects of the international system that do not accommodate the Global South. To be sure, China is uniquely positioned to brand its position in the world as, in the words of Xi Jinping, "the world's largest developing country."[10] This is because China is still undergoing poverty eradication projects and development plans for the thirty million of its citizens who continue to live under the poverty line. Rural areas in China still suffer from considerable levels of poverty, air pollution, and health issues that need serious government attention. Branding China as a developing country that is still figuring out its development path makes it a compelling example for developing nations to model themselves after and aspire to.

Based on this dual role, Chinese foreign policy is following two strategies simultaneously. One is to actively support the international order to gain experience and legitimacy as a responsible power.[11] The other is to proactively design Chinese-made initiatives and promote them primarily in developing countries as programs that are intended to bring prosperity and growth to all participants (Benabdallah 2019; Bloomfield 2016; Clark 2012;

Fung 2016; Sohn 2012). These two parallel strategies echo China's dual role: both a developing country and a major power at once. Hence, the Chinese government is pragmatically situating itself in a central position by providing global goods through supporting various organs of the United Nations system, while also producing alternative platforms outside of the UN for developing nations to learn from China's expertise.[12] Therefore, the ebb and flow of China's rapprochement, so to speak, with developing countries in Africa and elsewhere is oftentimes issue-based depending on what role Chinese foreign policy is playing. Along these lines, experts project that as "China regains it former global status it is increasingly a conflicted rising power possessing a series of competing international identities that try to satisfy a variety of international constituencies." (Shambaugh and Ren Xiao 2012, 36–37). The diverse, flexible role-playing of China's foreign policy has a considerable effect on China-Africa relations. To some extent, no matter how strongly China defines itself as a developing country, it also remains a great power and it exercises, cultivates, and uses that power in nonconfrontational ways guided by the five principles of coexistence. At the same time, no matter how powerful China becomes, the history of camaraderie and solidarity that links the Chinese Communist Party (CCP) to revolutionary leaders in Africa still resonates with many people.

China's Noninterference Principle: Use and Limitations

The noninterference principle has long been an important part of Chinese foreign policy discourse toward its neighboring countries as well as toward countries with which it has business ties. Ever since Prime Minister Zhou Enlai outlined the Five Principles of Peaceful Coexistence in 1954, noninterference has been a cornerstone of the CCP's narrative of China's commitment to a foreign policy conduct that respects states' sovereignties, resulting from having endured a century of foreign aggression.[13] Chinese foreign policy officially articulated noninterference as a pillar in China's relations to African countries during the Bandung Conference (1955).[14] Starting from this principle, as far as Beijing is concerned, the question of secessionist movements in Tibet and Xinjiang, cross-strait relations with Taiwan, and more recently election frictions in Hong Kong and Uyghur human rights issues are all internal affairs that fall within the prerogatives of the Chinese government to handle. Not surprisingly, the principle of noninterference is always reiterated in the Chinese official discourse toward African states. For example, China's first Africa strategy paper states that the CCP

develops exchanges of various forms with friendly political parties and organizations of African countries on the basis of the principles of independence,
equality, mutual respect and non-interference in each other's internal affairs.
The purpose of such exchanges is to increase understanding and friendship
and seek trust and cooperation. (China's MOFA 2006)

The principle of noninterference is always evoked in China-Africa cooperation forums and officials' discourses about the relationship between China
and African countries. Yet it is paradoxical that China has intervened in African domestic affairs on more than one occasion and continues to do so today.
The rhetorical reference to the principle of noninterference, coupled with
foreign policy practices that do interfere with the domestic affairs of other
states, is another defining characteristic of China's foreign policy brand.

Since the early years of the People's Republic of China, China's interference in the internal affairs of African countries has been well documented.
China's People's Liberation Army helped train armies in Zanzibar, thereby
helping the island in its secessionist movement from mainland Tanganyika.
In the 1990s, Chinese navy patrols were vital in countering piracy off the
Somali coast. The patrols, which were very frequent and efficient, are techni-
cally an interference in Somali maritime territory. More recently, despite the
noninterference discourse, Chinese arms supply played an important role in
Sudan's conflict against South Sudan. Even more complex, Chinese-
manufactured weapons "sold to Sudan have been funneled to rebels in South
Sudan" (Ferrie 2016). The Chinese government was put in a more embarrass-
ing spot when a deal for multiyear arms supplies between South Sudan and
the China North Industries Corporation was made public (Tiezzi 2015). China's arms supply to South Sudan's government is in direct conflict with its
noninterference principle. The principle has many practical limitations, but
its rhetorical purchase continues to withstand the test of time. The cases of
Sudan and Libya are both a testimony to China's ability to adapt its noninterference principle.

China's noninterference principle was put to the test multiple times in
Africa (Large 2008b; Barber 2018). During many years of the Darfur conflict,
Chinese foreign policy makers kept ignoring African as well as US and major
EU states' calls to use China's economic and political leverage to stop the
conflict while arms sales between Beijing and Khartoum were ongoing. Afri-
can governments condemned China's silence and nonengagement in the
Darfur crisis while China conducted business as usual with Sudanese presi-
dent Omar Hassan Ahmad Al-Bashir and reiterated the noninterference

principle.[15] When the conflict in Sudan began to spill over to Chad, Chad's Ministry of Foreign Affairs appealed directly to Beijing's diplomacy to urge the Sudanese government to stop the violence, but to no avail. Beijing's nonaction had in fact provoked several international human rights and advocacy groups to call for a boycott of the 2008 Olympic Games in Beijing unless China took a stand on Darfur.[16] Such a diplomatic dilemma ended with the Chinese government putting pressure on Sudan to allow humanitarian intervention in South Sudan. China, after much reticence to interfere, became one of the first countries to recognize the establishment of the state of South Sudan with Juba as its capital and business as usual was carried on in securing oil exports to China (Junbo 2012, 8). However, in late 2013, violent fighting broke out between rival factions within South Sudan, and this time about 400 Chinese oil workers had to be evacuated and oil exports to China decreased. The Chinese Ministry of Foreign Affairs did not invoke the noninterference principle when it issued statements calling for an immediate cease-fire and asked South Sudan's government to protect Chinese nationals in the country.[17] The Chinese Ministry of Foreign Affairs (MOFA) played a proactive role in mediating negotiations between the warring factions in Addis Ababa in 2014 and by May 2014 China had contributed to the UN Mission in South Sudan with 314 troops (Tiezzi 2014).

Sudan is not the only place where China's principle of noninterference has shown practical limitations. In Libya, China had to improvise emergency evacuations of over 35,000 Chinese workers at the start of the civil conflict. By early spring 2011, several countries were calling for implementing the responsibility to protect norm with regards to Muammar Gaddafi's indiscriminate use of force in Benghazi. Despite China's rhetorical celebrations of the noninterference principle, it voted yes to UNSC Resolution 1970, which referred Gaddafi to the International Criminal Court.[18] By March 2011, the Security Council passed Resolution 1973, which called on member states to deploy all necessary means to protect civilians in Libya. This time China abstained from the vote on grounds that diplomatic solutions were not completely exhausted (Fung 2015). Since China did not use its veto power on Resolution 1973, the consequence was the North Atlantic Treaty Organization's irresponsible interpretation of the responsibility to protect in Libya. NATO's abuse of its mandate was a blow to China's solidarity rhetoric and a stain on its noninterference principle. During interviews I had with several policy makers and academics in Beijing in the summer of 2014, Resolution 1973 was clearly a thorn in China's reputation and Global South solidarity brand. The experts I spoke to all made two-pronged explanations of China's position. One is that Beijing had delicately cleared the voting decision with the Arab League and regional organizations before the vote. The other is that China was taken by surprise at how aggressive and beyond mandate NATO's intervention was.

Yet interference does not have to be as apparent as was the case with the UN Security Council approval of Resolution 1973, which led to a devastating humanitarian action in Libya. More recently, controversial loan terms from China to Zambia, Kenya, and Sierra Leone have raised skepticism around fiscal sustainability and the financial autonomy of African states as concerns their relationships to Chinese banks and loaners. Similarly, China's foreign aid to Africa (or foreign aid in general) has the potential to influence the political landscape and to impact regime durability and regime change. Typically branded as conditionality-free, China's foreign aid to Africa was estimated at about $15 billion in 2018. Essentially, China's aid is perceived by recipients to be swifter and more efficient when compared to traditional foreign aid because it "lacks socioeconomic and environmental safeguards required by traditional donors" (Swedlund 2017a, 128).

To illustrate the impact of foreign aid and investments on the political landscape, one can take the example of Zimbabwe.[19] President Robert Mugabe was controversial in his statements after concluding a $240 million deal in 2006 for military equipment and trainings from China and how those were intended to be used to put down any domestic opposition to his regime. Mugabe reportedly warned the opposition that "those who might harbor any plans of turning against the government: be warned, we have armed men and women who can pull the trigger. . . . The defense forces have benefited from the government's Look East policy [in reference to the close ties between his government and China] through which they have not only acquired new equipment, but also learned new military strategies" (Reuters 2006). Noninterference should not just be understood in the confines of military and security realms. It should expand to economic and cultural spheres. Influencing states' behavior to accept new norms and procedures still counts as interference whether the influence is carried out at gunpoint or in cultural institutes.

From the beginning of PRC-Africa relations, the discourse around the noninterference principle was never fully applied in practice and, in my view, it has had a performative function strictly. The principle is brought up in almost every official text between the Chinese government and its African

counterparts in order to brand China's rise as nonthreatening, and to distance China-Africa relations from the colonial legacies of European powers.
It is hard, indeed, to imagine that Africa's largest trading partner does not
interfere in African internal affairs. Chapter 4, "Guanxi in Military Diplomacy," provides another test area for the noninterference principle especially with regard to Chinese private security trainings of African security
agents. Before I discuss in what ways China's power is manifested and cultivated in its investments in Africa, I provide a brief overview of the disconti-
nuities and changes in China's prioritization of its relations to African states.
I divide China's contemporary diplomacy in the continent into three main
periods: the anticolonial period, the 1970s developmental period, and post-
2000 (first China-Africa Forum) period. These periods highlight China's foreign policy toward African states in terms of investments in human resource
development and how they have fared over time. While China's interest in
sponsoring professionalization training programs for Africans did not spark
all of a sudden in the last decade, the magnitude and scope of these programs have increased significantly since 2000. In addition, while Chinese
government-sponsored trainings in the first period (1950s) were very much
grounded in ideological anticapitalist motives, the surge in capacity-building
programs since the early 2000s has little to do with showing support to anticolonial revolutionaries. Instead, it has more to do with strengthening relationality between China's African counterparts and deepening the nodes of
the network. In what comes I explore these claims in more detail.

TRACING CHINA-SPONSORED PROFESSIONALIZATION TRAINING
PROGRAMS FOR AFRICANS

China-African relations have a long history of trade, exchanges, and cultural
encounters. Indeed, pre-Westphalian China (then known as Ming China)
was a trade, culture, and science hub. Ming was the central power of trade
routes along the ancient Silk Road, which reached Europe and Africa. Arche-
ologists trace the earliest interactions between China and Africa back to the
fourteenth century due to an excavation of coins from the Sung dynasty
(960–1279) found in Zanzibar and some coins found as far south as what today is Zimbabwe (Taylor 2011, 2). The coins are attributed to the explorations
by Chinese admiral Zheng He who became a symbol of China's ancient
peaceful outreach expeditions to other continents for cultural and trade exchanges (Prashad 2001, 6).

Zheng He's seven expedition voyages between 1416 and 1423 are often evoked in official speeches by Chinese government officials as China-Africa scholarship to manufacture a rhetorical/discursive narrative of China's encounter with Africa as one of an economic and cultural nature rather than aggression and colonialism (Musgrave and Nexon 2018). Chinese officials are adamant about using Zheng He to claim that China is far from a latecomer to Africa but that it differs from the traditional powers in that it did not make colonies out of African states (Taylor 2006, 16).[20] For example, the Chinese ambassador in Ghana expressed the following about Zheng He at an event in May 2016:

> Mr. Zheng He, the greatest navigator in Chinese history led a colossal fleet composed of over 200 vessels and more than 27,000 crew members and carried out seven maritime expeditions to the Western Seas. He reached four times the eastern coast of Africa, where current Tanzania, Kenya and Somalia are located. Zheng He and his fleet introduced tea, porcelain, silk and advanced technology to the visited regions. What Zheng He took away from Africa was only a giraffe. China has been one of the most powerful countries throughout most of the history, but it has never snatched a piece of colony. Aggression and invasion have never found their seats in mainstream Chinese culture. There is indeed no gene for invasion in Chinese people's blood. (China's MOFA 2016)

The ambassador insisted on narrating China-Africa ties with linguistic elements that suggest that China's history is similar to that of Africa. After all, he said, both were the cradle of very early and important civilizations, and China, like most of Africa, suffered the injustices and stigmas of colonialism. Today, a traveler on the Kenyan Nairobi-Mombasa train is greeted by a bust of Zheng He in the Mombasa terminal. The brand-new bust, funded by the Chinese government, serves as a "reminder" of the timeless friendly relations between China and Kenya.[21]

In reality, General Zheng He's encounter with Africa's East Coast is a very small episode in a rather long history of disengagement between China and the rest of the world. Emphasis on his expeditions are not about the past but about the future. Branding a historically peaceful China through the story and bust of Zheng He is meant to reinforce Chinese government arguments that, given its past conduct, China should be expected to continue its legacy of peaceful rise and friendly encounters. To be sure, as the Ming dynasty waned and the Qing dynasty (1644–1911) ascended to power, a closed-door policy was implemented, leading to the suspension of all expeditions and relations to the outside world. This part is, conveniently, left out of China-Africa official discourses by the current government. As the Qing dynasty ascended to power, China's interactions with Africa were significantly reduced. The weakness of the last emperor of the Qing dynasty had caused China's defeat in the Opium Wars, leading China to become semicolonialized after it had been an imperial power. During this time, China turned inward and most of its relations with the outside world were retracted. The neglect of Africa (and other regions outside of China's immediate vicinity) persisted until after the inception of the PRC in 1949. Yet, even in the period between the 1950s and 1990s, relations between China and Africa fluctuated significantly and frequently between close partnership and total estrangement.

Professionalization Programs in the Anticolonial Solidarity Period, 1950–1960s

China's contemporary interaction with the African continent goes back to the preindependence era when many African revolutionary leaders were receiving assistance from Chairman Mao and the PRC to fight European colonialism. The solidarity expressed by Mao's regime stemmed from his ideological stance against the US-led capitalist world, and from his vision for China as a leader of the Global South's fight against colonialism. One of the ways Mao's solidarity with Africans took shape in the late 1950s was through sending Chinese agriculture training staff (Li Anshan 2012, 2) and medical teams to train hospital staff in seven countries: Algeria, Congo Brazzaville, Guinea, Mali, Mauritania, Tanzania, and Somalia (Li Anshan 2012, 65). Mao also funded scholarships for outstanding graduate students from different African countries to study in China. Being a fervent supporter of the Bandung Conference, Mao went all-in with his support of the South-South revolutionary spirit.

   The Bandung Conference was a milestone for the encounter between African and Asian leaders and a decisive opportunity for China-Africa relations. The initiative for the conference started in 1953 with the "Colombo Powers"[22] and then extended the invitation to twenty-nine developing nations to meet in Bandung, Indonesia in 1955. Six of the twenty-nine countries invited were African nations: Egypt, Ethiopia, Ghana, Liberia, Libya, and the Sudan. Egypt was the only independent African nation that sent its state leader to the conference, Gamal Abdel Nasser. Chinese premier Zhou Enlai (1949–75) had close talks with the Egyptian delegation and signed trade agreements with the Egyptian president (Larkin 1971, 17). A few months later, Egypt became the first African country to have official diplomatic relations with Beijing. The Bandung Conference opened the door for Chinese officials to voice their views on common anticolonial struggles and shared goals of development. Following the conference, Beijing became more involved and interested in supporting revolutionary wars across the continent from Algeria to Mozambique, among others.

During the late 1950s and early 1960s, China sent medical teams, armaments, and equipment to support the Algerian national liberation fighters (Strauss 2009, 778). It also trained, as mentioned above, Zanzibar's army, which was aiming to overthrow the Arab regime before unification with Tanganyika (Li 2009; Taylor 2011, 11). The Chinese government has a track record of always being among the first governments to recognize newly independent nations in Africa. The PRC even established official diplomatic relations with Algeria four years before Algeria's independence from France in 1962. Shortly afterward, Algeria became the destination of the world's largest team of Chinese medical trainers (Li 2012, 65). Additionally, the Chinese government sent ten delegations to visit different African nations in 1959. This number increased to over fifty delegations by 1962. The PRC simultaneously invited African delegations to visit China. Between 1960 and 1965, Beijing established official diplomatic relations with fourteen African nations (Larkin 1971, 165).

However, during the late 1960s and with the start of Chinese Cultural Revolution period, relations between China and Africa retracted and several Chinese embassy representatives were recalled.[23] The atmosphere of mistrust that characterized Chinese domestic politics during the Cultural Revolution (1966–69), coupled with the Sino-Soviet conflict, had a jarring impact on China-Africa relations. Mao's rigid, ideology-driven foreign policy cost the PRC a lot of diplomatic advantages with African countries. Often, Mao traded foreign relations experts for radical party officers who were loyal to him even at the expense of meaningful diplomacy with the countries where they were posted (Bing 2017; Eisenman 2018a). As a consequence, several African nations broke off their diplomatic relations with Beijing,[24] while at the same time Africa was not high on the list of priorities for Chinese policy makers.[25] Instead, Mao's China was mostly concerned with stabilizing its borders, consolidating authority over Xinjiang and Tibet, and outmaneuvering US backing of Taiwan's independence. This setback in China's engagement with African countries was, however, bound to change in the next two decades due to events I account for in the next section.

Professionalization Programs during China's Developmental Period, 1970–1980s

During the early 1970s, the Chinese government used its foreign policy to reconstruct its position among developing countries as well as to redefine normal diplomatic conduct between China and other countries. The setback experienced during the Cultural Revolution period harmed China's image abroad and broke trust with several key allies in Africa. One of the ways the PRC implemented its repair strategy was through pouring in development aid money and increasing people-to-people exchanges and scholarships for African elites.[26] In the 1970s, Chinese medical training teams were dispatched to twenty-two African countries, which was a threefold increase from the previous period (Yu 2009). The majority of China's foreign aid to Global South states between 1970 and 1976 was directed toward African nations. As a result, China was able to restore relations with several African countries, replacing the Soviet Union as the main source of development aid. China also quickly overtook Great Britain as Tanzania's main source of foreign loans. During this period, Chinese leadership was mostly focused on its domestic development. Accordingly, the government kept a low profile with regard to international affairs. Nonetheless, cooperation with African countries amped up in the form of Beijing-sponsored infrastructure projects even during a time when internally it was facing many development challenges. Chief among the staple projects of China's interactions with Africa in the 1970s was the TAZARA Railway, which connects Dar es Salaam on Tanzania's coast with the Copper Belt region of Zambia. The single-track railway stretching over a thousand miles was started in 1970 and completed in 1975, with the largest share of the total cost (over $350 million) supported by Chinese funds and executed by teams of Chinese labor.[27]

China's proactive Africa policy in the 1970s was not only aimed at regaining trust and friendly relations for the sake of restoring China's positive image. Given the waves of independence from colonialism, African countries formed a new power bloc in the international system through organizations such as the United Nations. Beijing, cleverly, treated the G77 not as a group of underdeveloped countries but as group with potential for building social capital. At the time, Beijing needed all the votes it could get in order to replace Taiwan and make the PRC and not the ROC the official government of China in the eyes of international law. In 1971, a resolution for the admission of China to the UN was passed with seventy-six votes to thirty-five opposed, with seventeen abstentions (Taylor 2011, 16). African state leaders' support was crucial for the UN Security Council seat to be returned from the ROC to the PRC. It was also a way to return the favor and sympathy that Beijing had shown during Africa's waves of independence. Africa's solidarity with China during the UN vote is often brought up in officials' speeches as a reminder of the interdependent relations between Global South states and a testimony to the friendly relations between China and African counterparts.

After the death of Mao in 1976, Deng Xiaoping assumed the reins of governance of the PRC with an agenda of deploying massive economic reforms and rapprochement with the United States to maximize technical skills transfers and modernization of the industrial sector (Cohen 2010; Schaller 2015). Chinese policy makers had realized the potential benefits for China's economy if it were to normalize relations with advanced industrial countries in the Global North. Normalization of relations with the United States, beginning with Secretary of State Henry Kissinger's secret trip to China in 1971 followed by President Richard Nixon's official visit to China the next year all the way to the establishment of official diplomatic relations between the two nations in 1979, consumed most of Beijing's attention abroad. Consequently, China's stand for South-South Cooperation was put on hold during the years that Deng Xiaoping decided to focus on domestic development. Indeed, the ideology-driven support of the developing world was much less important to Deng Xiaoping than to his predecessor (Bing 2017; Yu 2009). During the years of Deng Xiaoping's rule, Chinese-sponsored professionalization training programs for Africans declined and the relations between China and its African counterparts experienced a setback until the early 1990s.

Professionalization Programs Post-1990s and the Steps Leading to FOCAC

Deng Xiaoping's detachment from South-South Cooperation did not last beyond the late 1980s. The protests around Tiananmen Square in June 1989 earned China much bad press and criticism from the West on the basis of human rights abuses and repression of democracy. As a consequence, several governments recalled their diplomatic missions from Beijing and pressed for sanctions against the Chinese government. These events, which tainted China's reputation abroad, led Chinese foreign policy makers to focus on cultivating strong relations with developing countries, mainly in Africa. Chinese foreign policy makers realized the value of scoring good public relations points with these countries and this marked another milestone in China's interactions with African nations. Beijing also quickly realized that most African leaders did not take part in the criticism of Beijing's handling of the protests. It goes without saying that the Chinese government welcomed this nonreaction, which coined the term "All weather friend" to describe its relations with African states (Strauss 2009,791).

Much like in the 1970s, the 1990s were also an era when China proactively worked on improving relations with Africa on two main fronts: increasing people-to-people exchanges and financing development projects. During trips by Chinese ministers and premiers, the rhetoric of South-South cooperation was revived mostly through invoking solidarity between China and African nations to counter Western hegemonism and neocolonialism. It became evident that despite a clear ebb and flow and rise and fall of Africa in China's foreign policy priorities, "the PRC continues to trumpet its past 50-odd years of involvement in Africa as positive, progressive and grounded in the eternal and principled truths of non-interference, mutual benefit, unconditionality, and special friendship and understanding towards Africa" (Strauss 2009, 778). Ultimately, at the turn of the new century with Chinese policy makers' interest in further opening up to the outside world, relations between China and African counterparts were rebooted and China initiated a new phase of strategic partnerships.

As part of this new phase of strategic partnerships, the Chinese government had its eye on investing in netting close ties not only to Africa's leaders of the time but also to the next generation of African elites. Through a mix of professionalization trainings in the CCP's party school in Beijing and education scholarship for hundreds of African students, Chinese and African party officials' relations were strengthened. The examples are far too many to summarize in this paragraph, but a few illustrations are in order. Since 2011, after the declaration of South Sudan as an independent nation, China has offered at least four thousand scholarships and short-term trainings (Kuo 2016). Many of the short-term trainings were offered to delegations of party members to attend the CCP's party school for seminars on party organizational structure, cadre management, party national-local civil servant relations, tax collection trainings, and media relations. Since 2007, China's Ningbo Polytechnic's campus (located in Zhejiang Province) has hosted more than a thousand trainees from forty-eight African countries. African elite capture by China "can translate into a willingness to work with China and view China's internal policies favorably in the future" (Nakkazi 2018). Similarly, China's ambassador to Uganda said that every year about 500 Ugandans are offered professionalization trainings in China (Xinhua, 2018). In brief, there have been close to fifty official visits and study group exchanges between the CCP and various African political parties. See table 1 for more details on which political parties visited more frequently and for how long.

Overall, between the second meeting of FOCAC in 2003 and end of the sixth FOCAC in 2015, no less than 63,000 African professionals received professionalizing trainings in China. Most of the trainings were provided in the form of multilateral short-term programs drawing participants from across the continent. By 2013, China ranked among the four largest professionalization training program providers in the world next to India, Germany, and Japan (King 2013, 49), but it has since then overtaken them all. The latest FOCAC meeting announced thousands more scholarships for Africa's top students, more training for teachers, journalists, engineers, military officers, and civil servants.

THE SCOPE OF CHINESE PROFESSIONALIZATION TRAINING PROGRAMS

For a start, a branch in China's Ministry of Commerce called the Academy for International Business Officials gives public access to aggregated data on all the training programs that Beijing sponsors for African officials.[28] Surveying this workshop database allowed me to see whether there was a correlation between the countries that receive most of the training program opportunities and the countries possessing natural resources or having other geopolitical assets of importance to China. There are over forty workshop categories ranging from diplomacy to health, sports, agriculture, infrastructure, public administration, education, and art, among other topics. The trainings appear to come in three different categories depending on who the targeted participants are. Some training courses are for ministerial cabinet level officials, others are for senior civil servants, and the last category is for unofficial officials. By the end of 2013, the Academy for International Business Officials has organized 603 training workshops (of varying durations) divided among forty-three ministerial-level workshops, receiving 14,545 officials including 483 ministerial officials and one vice premier from 152 countries and regions around the world. Over a third of the total workshops targeted African officials. In September 2018, at the Forum on China-Africa Cooperation, Chinese president Xi Jinping made pledges for training 1,000 Africans, hosting 50,000 workshops (in areas as diverse as party politics,

TABLE 1. Party-to-party exchange activities between CCP and African counterparts (sample data from 2016 to 2018)

Number	Country/Party	Activity	Date and Location
1	Patriotic Front of Zambia	Delegation led by the general secretary of the Patriotic Front, Davies Chama	January 17–21, 2016 in China
2	Rassemblement des Republicains (RDR) of Ivory Coast, Partido Democratico de Guinea Ecuatorial	Wang Jiarui, vice-president of Chinese People's Political Consultative Conference.	Visit to Ivory Coast, Equatorial Guinea, and Sierra Leone from January 17 to January 25, 2016
3	The Ethiopian People's Revolutionary Democratic Front (EPRDF)	Delegation led by Muferihat Kamil, EDRPF's head of organizations	February 23 to March 3, 2016 in China
4	Political parties of Guinea-Bissau	Study group led by Augusto Antonio Da Silva, member of the Political Bureau of the Partido Africano da Independência da Guiné e Cabo Verde	February 29 to March 9, 2016 in China
5	Workshop for African young leaders of political parties	African National Congress of South Africa, South African Communist Party, Zimbabwe African National Union–Patriotic Front, SWAPO Party of Namibia, Democratic Progressive Party of Malawi, Patriotic Front of Zambia, Lesotho Congress Party, Botswana Democratic Party	March 3 to 11, 2016 in China
6	Alliance pour la Republique of Senegal	Delegation led by Benoit Joseph George Sambou, ministerial adviser	March 24 to April 1, 2016 in China
7	Chama Cha Mapinduzi (CCM) of Tanzania	Delegation led by chairman of CCM and former president, Jakaya Mrisho Kikwete	April 17 to 23, 2016 in China

TABLE 1.—*Continued*

Number	Country/Party	Activity	Date and Location
8	SWAPO Party of Namibia	Delegation of Central Committee members led by Secretary General Nangolo Mbumba	April 8 to 16, 2016 in China
9	Rassemblement des Republicains (RDR) of Ivory Coast	Delegation led by RDR deputy secretary Doumbia Brahima	April 19 to 29, 2016 in China
10	Partido Frelimo of Mozambique	Study group led by Frelimo's Management and Financial Secretary Esperanca Laurinda Bias	April 20 to 29, 2016 in China
11	National Democratic Congress (NDC) of Ghana	Delegation led by party president Kofi Portuphy	May 8 to 13, 2016 in China
12	Parti du Peuple pour la Reconstruction et la Democratie (PPRD) of the Democratic Republic of the Congo	Study group led by Lusuna Nsenga Jean, staffer of the Secretary General's Office of the PPRD	May 9 to 19, 2016 in China
13	Chama Cha Mapinduzi of Tanzania	Study group led by party member Pindi Chana	June 20 to 29 in China
14	South African Communist Party	Study group led by national treasurer and member of the Politburo, Joyce Moloi Moropa	June 13 to 22, 2016 in China
15	New Patriotic Party of Ghana	Delegation led by deputy flag bearer, vice presidential candidate for 2016 elections, Mahamudu Bawumia	June 12 to 17, 2016 in China
16	Union pour la Republique (UNIR) of Togo	Study group led by led by Kwadjo Fiatuwo Sessenou	July 12 to 21, 2016 in China
17	Rwandan Patriotic Front (RPF)	Delegation led by Francois Ngarambe	July 6 to 11, 2016 in China
18	Ruling coalition of Senegal	Study group led by president's political adviser El Hadji Malick Sarr	August 30 to September 9, 2016 in China

TABLE 1.—*Continued*

Number	Country/Party	Activity	Date and Location
19	Militant Socialist Movement (MSM) of Mauritius	Study group led by MSM's vice president, Leela Devi Dookun-Luchoomun	November 1 to 10, 2016 in China
20	President of South Africa, the Ethiopian government, and Djibouti People's Rally for Progress	Visit by Li Yuanchao, member of the Political Bureau of the CPC Central Committee and vice president	November 15 to 24, 2016 in South Africa, Ethiopia, and Djibouti
21	Parti Nigérien pour la Démocratie et le Socialisme (PNDS)	Delegation led by the president of PNDS, Mohamed Bazoum	April 10 to 15, 2017 in China
22	Ethiopian People's Revolutionary Democratic Front (EPRDF)	Delegation headed by EPRDF member Fetlework Gebregziaber	April 19 to 29, 2017 in China
23	Forces for the Defense of Democracy in Burundi, the Cameroon People's Democratic Movement, the Rally of the Guinean People, the Rally for Mali, the Patriotic Salvation Movement of Chad, and the Union for the Republic of Togo	Young leaders training class	May 3 to 12, 2017 in China
24	Nigerien Party for Democracy and Socialism (NPDS)	Delegation led by Sani Iro, NPDS communications director and first deputy speaker of National Assembly	June 8 to 13, 2017 in China
25	Ethiopian People's Revolutionary Democratic Front (EPRDF)	Cadre study group led by minister of rural politics and the organization department, Tefera Deribew	June 9 to 19, 2017 in China
26	Gabonese Democratic Party (GDP)	Study group led by Dodo Bounguendza Eric Charles, director of Political Research Center	June 22 to July 1, 2017 in China

TABLE 1.—*Continued*

Number	Country/Party	Activity	Date and Location
27	Defense of Democracy (CNDD-FDD) of Burundi	Cadre study group led by Déo Guide Rurema, minister of Agriculture and Livestock	August 30 to September 9, 2017
28	People's Rally for Progress (PRP) of Djibouti, the People's Movement for Progress (MPP) of Burkina Faso	CPC delegation led by Guo Yezhou, vice-minister of the International Department of the CPC Central Committee	March 3 to 9, 2018 in Djibouti and Burkina Faso
29	Patriotic Salvation Movement of Chad, Egyptian government, and Tunisian government	CPC delegation led by Chen Min'er, member of the Political Bureau of the CPC Central Committee	June 24 to July 2, 2018 in Chad, Egypt, and Tunisia
30	People's Party of Seychelles and Revolutionary Party of Tanzania	CPC delegation led by Song Tao, minister of the International Department of the CPC Central Committee	July 12 to 19, 2018 in Seychelles and Tanzania
31	Chama Cha Mapinduzi (CCM) of Tanzania, the New Patriotic Party of Ghana, and the Botswana Democratic Party	CPC delegation led by Xu Lyuping, vice-minister of the International Department of the CPC Central Committee	July 14 to 24, 2018 in Tanzania, Ghana, and Botswana
32	Forces for the Defense of Democracy (FDD) of Burundi	Cadre study group headed by Evariste Ndayishimiye, secretary general of the FDD.	September 2018 in China
33	African Independence Party of Guinea and Cape Verde	Delegation headed by Domingos Simões Pereira, former prime minister of Guinea-Bissau, and president of African Independence Party of Guinea and Cape Verde.	September 2018 in China
34	SWAPO Party of Namibia	Delegation headed by Deputy Secretary General Marco Hausiku.	September 2018 in China

TABLE 1.—*Continued*

Number	Country/Party	Activity	Date and Location
35	Kenya's Jubilee Party	CCP delegation visit.	September 19 to 21, 2018 in Kenya
36	Free Egyptians Party	CCP delegation led by Wu Yuliang, deputy minister of the Organization Department of the CPC Central Committee.	September 22 to 25, 2018 in Egypt
37	People's Movement for Progress (MPP) of Burkina Faso	Delegation headed by MPP's acting president Simon Compaoré.	October 2018 in China
38	Chama Cha Mapinduzi (CCM) of Tanzania	Seminar attended by a delegation headed by Tanzania's ruling party's secretary general Bashiru Ally.	October 2018 in China
39	People's Liberation Movement of Angola (MPLA)	Senior cadre study group of the MPLA headed by Pedro de Morais Neto, member of the Political Bureau of the Central Committee of the MPLA.	October 2018 in China
40	African National Congress (ANC) of South Africa	Study group of the ANC led by Ronald Lamola, member of the ANC National Executive Committee.	November 2018 in China
41	National Congress Party of Sudan	The fifth high-level dialogue meeting between the ruling parties of China and Sudan.	November 20, 2018 in China
42	Sierra Leone People's Party (SLPP)	Cadre study group headed of SLPP's secretary-general Umaru Koroma.	November 2018 in China
43	Niamey, Niger	CPC delegation headed by Ding Yexian, executive deputy secretary of the CPC Committee of Xi Zang Autonomous Region.	December 2018, Niger

TABLE 1.—*Continued*

Number	Country/Party	Activity	Date and Location
44	Sudan People's Liberation Movement (SPLM) of South Sudan	Cadre study group led by SPLM member Jacob Aligo Lolado.	December 2018, China
45	Six Parties Delegation of Southern Africa	Party exchanges between the CCP and a Six Parties Delegation led by Humphrey Polepole.	December 2018, China
46	Rally of the Republicans (RDR) of Cote d'Ivoire	Cadre study group headed by RDR's deputy secretary general, David Soro.	December 2018, China
47	South African Communist Party (SACP)	Senior workshop for a delegation headed by SACP's first deputy secretary general, Solly Mapaila.	December 2018, China
48	Ethiopian People's Revolutionary Democratic Front (EPRDF)	Cadre study group of EPRDF led by Melese Alemu Hirboro.	December 2018, China

Source: Data collected by the author from the webpage of the Communist Party of China (CPC)'s International Department, http://www.idcpc.org.cn/english/events/index.html

sports medicine, and agriculture), awarding 50,000 government scholarships—a big increase from 30,000 in 2015—and sponsoring 2,000 student exchanges.

China's professionalization trainings target diverse countries, but Anglophone countries seem to benefit more from these programs than Francophone ones because it is easier for Chinese trainers who are more proficient in English than in other languages. It also was visible after ranking countries by numbers of short-term seminars and training programs each of them received that Ghana, Ethiopia, Tanzania, Kenya, and Mauritius ranked at the top of the list of countries targeted by these trainings. It is not possible to conclude that natural resources are the main driver here given that Ethiopia is one of the top five countries while it is a country that does not export natural resources. Likewise, it was difficult to single out one defining characteristic or pattern in the audience these trainings were targeting other than the aforementioned Anglophone vs. Francophone dynamics. Rather, the survey findings suggest an interest on the part of Chinese foreign policy to expand its circle of relations and interact with as many country representatives as possible. As explained in the manual put together by China's Ministry of Commerce, these trainings "complement China's comprehensive foreign policy needs, help train the human capital of developing countries, and drive forward friendly *relations* and trade cooperation with developing countries."[29] The manual briefly explains that the trainings contain "an advanced quality: Course content should reflect China's broad development achievements and strengths in relevant fields or disciplines, and point out that China's economic development achieved substantial success principally after the reform and opening period."

China's professionalization trainings for Africans are not limited to the political elite or to one profession. They target a wide range of groups from diplomats to entrepreneurs, teachers, and agriculture experts, to name just a few. Of the different sectors, this book is concerned with three case studies: military and defense, media staff and journalists, and professionalization trainings through Confucius Institutes.

Although the question of what China wants in/from Africa is important and helps in excavating and understanding China's motives in the continent both in terms of positive and negative implications, it is not enough. A question that China-Africa scholarship has not explored is what are the consequences of China's investments—not in natural resources—but in human resources in Africa on Africans' perceptions of China and China's image? This question is also related to the question of how China conducts its foreign policy toward the Global South. As discussed in the section on China's dual image, China is a powerful actor and there is a power asymmetry in its relations with most countries within the South-South cooperation framework. Another question that this book is concerned with is related to intangible investments in China-Africa relations and accounting for them in examining the faces and mechanisms of China's power. Whereas research tends to associate China's interest in Africa with material gains such as energy resources and infrastructure contracts, I am more interested in exploring the nonmaterial gains that Chinese investments are targeting through professionalization training programs and capacity-building projects. In the next chapter I develop a theoretical framework that allows for examining nontangible investments such as network-building and social capital investments.

CHAPTER THREE

Relationality, Social Capital, and the Future of Power

The case of Cui Chun, an examiner in the ninth century C.E., illustrates the operation of personal networks in the [Chinese] imperial bureaucracy. One day Cui's wife suggested that he buy some land to bequeath to his descendants. With a smile, he replied, "I have thirty excellent manor houses with rich fields spreading all over the empire. Why should you worry about real estate?" When his wife asked him what he meant, he answered, "You remember the year before last I served as examiner and passed thirty candidates. Are they not excellent estates?"

   —MAYFAIR YANG, *GIFTS, FAVORS, AND BANQUETS*

[Chinese] practices had been biased conspicuously toward human relationality, having invented much more nuanced terms for people of differential relationships in their language while borrowing only in recent times directly from abroad terminologies in the natural sciences.

   —QIN YAQING, *A RELATIONAL THEORY OF WORLD POLITICS*

POWER IS A CENTRAL CONCEPT across many approaches to the study of global politics. Scholars analyze hard and soft power, smart power, nuclear capabilities, and the power of international norms and international agreements, to name a few. This chapter develops an approach to power that foregrounds the "relating" part of International Relations—the mechanisms that link relationality, power, and foreign policy. The approach accounts for the power of relation-building by unpacking the mechanisms of diffusion and projection of power through social and political relations. It theorizes power in relational terms through the case of China's foreign policy in Africa in which people-to-people exchanges and social capital building are both policy goals and means to strategic ends.

China is quickly rising to the status of superpower. Some scholars already treat it as a great power.[1] Regardless of where in the process of (re)transitioning to a global power China is, a few factors stand out. China is a non-Western, nondemocratic state with a very different history and background than the traditional great powers that are often the reference point for mainstream IR theorizing. This book does not argue that traditional or mainstream IR theorizing is useless in accounting for China's power relations with developing states merely because China is a different type of state. It also does not argue that, by the mere fact of being a non-Western power, China is an automatically different case that requires totally different frameworks to analyze. Yet, at the same time, culture shapes social relations and foreign policy making in significant ways (Barnett and Finnemore 1999; Johnston 1996; Katzenstein 1996; Narlikar 2011; Weldes 1999). Thus, assuming that what applies to theorizing traditional great power politics travels and applies to the case of China (a non-Western and nondemocratic state) could be hit or miss.

Conventional approaches to theorizing power are not enough to understand a big portion of the question of how emerging powers build and project their influence. Much of China's foreign policy making and international influence is centered around the capacity to expand social networks, build strong people-to-people relations, and enlarge circles of relationships. As a result, theories of power that are limited to measuring military capabilities or economic prowess lack the breadth to account for the role of social capital in Chinese foreign policy. When looking at how China's rise is happening and how its foreign relations work, mainstream approaches to the analysis of power need to be supplemented to explain a rising non-Western, non–Global North superpower. The argument of this book is that social capital and relational networks matter in power-building and power diffusion and should be taken as complementary to rather than competing with traditional accounts of state power in global politics.

The relational framework I propose draws from Qin Yaqing's work on relationality, Foucault's understanding of the power-knowledge nexus, and a variety of research on the role of institutions as socializers, teachers, and conveyors of norms and values. Fusing these three elements allows me to make three interlinked arguments. First, networks among high-level government officials, joint military exercises, and other people-to-people exchanges are diplomatic practices that enhance relational networks and expand influence through them. These structures and events are both a practice of power and a measure of power. As illustrated in the epigraph story, examiner Cui counts his relationship to his successful mentees as his real estate. Second, network-building activities and various people-to-people exchanges are spaces that start as informal but through repetition and routinization can become institutionalized. Indeed, foreign policy making that takes seriously people-to-people relations and investments in human capital eventually will formalize these informal practices. Third, institutions are important to foreign policy conduct because they allow for the formation of epistemic communities that—as a result of intensive exchanges between diplomats within and across institutions—produce expert knowledge, values, and norms on topics related to governance, development, and security. They also serve as conveyor belts for the diffusion of the expert knowledge produced, as well as the values and norms that result from frequent exchanges and epistemic communities. In the case of Global South rising (super)powers, norms, values, and expert knowledge produced in these settings are relevant to the study of interstate relations because they are about putting forward alternative (or non-Western) models and values of governance, development, and security. The framework I develop over the course of this chapter and use throughout the book captures the power of social capital and relational networks in creating spaces for the production and diffusion of new norms, values, and models that promote China's development model as an alternative to the dominant Western-led liberal order.

Traditional IR approaches that understand power exclusively in terms of coercive mechanisms, repressive measures, and focus on war/nuclear capabilities as measures of the rise of major powers in the international system are incomplete. Such approaches to power cannot capture some vital mechanisms and aspects of emerging powers' foreign policy conduct. The risk of exclusively focusing on military and economic capital, I contend, is that it may blindside IR research on rising powers by neglecting or misunderstanding the power of networking and cultivating social capital. Power, as I show through this book, is relational. It circulates, magnifies, and retreats through relations. A relational approach to power understands actors to be as powerful as their networks make them. Actors activate, build, and project power through their relations. Relationships impact power, and the type and quality of a state's relationships with other states can strengthen or weaken it. Actors share, enlarge, and strengthen their networks and relationships by investing more social capital in them and by intensifying the overlaps with others' circles of relations. From this perspective, (China's) foreign policy making should be viewed as a dense network of relations that both produce power and are in turn produced by it. Indeed, in this theoretical lens, relations are prior to power. Relations are necessary to activate power, but power also produces and strengthens relations by multiplying the social capital through network density (or by reducing it).

A relational account of power measures it not only by material assets (such as military bases or natural resources) but also (and more importantly) by nontangible/nonmaterial assets (such as connections within networks and human capital). When theorizing power in international relations, it is vital to take into account China's investments, not just in natural resources, but more importantly in human resource development and people-to-people exchanges. China has emerged as the single largest contributor of professionalization training programs for Africa, for example. While some might see this fact as tangential to understanding power, I argue that it is actually central to a comprehensive theory of power for twenty-first-century rising (super)powers. This professionalization is both a manifestation of and a building block of power. China's emphasis on expanding networks, solidifying ties among military officers, and enhancing people-to-people social capital is central to its foreign policy and toward African states specifically, as this book demonstrates.

This chapter lays out the book's approach to power. It begins by contextualizing the utility of current understandings of power in IR, utilizing Lukes's (1974) "faces of power" in conjunction with IR research that thinks about global politics relationally. In the second section, I argue that social relations generate power and are in turn made stronger through power dynamics and that relationality (more specifically, through guanxi) is key to power status and projection. A third section applies this framework of relational productive power to people-to-people relationships and knowledge exchanges. It argues that intensifying people-to-people exchanges and human resource investments facilitate the diffusion of norms, values, and expert knowledge. People-to-people exchanges and investments in human resource development, I argue, present the opportunity to simultaneously invest in trust-building and network expansions as well as the opportunity for the production and diffusion of expert knowledge about development, security, governance, and so on. People-to-people exchanges present an opportunity for the creation of epistemic communities, which in turn socialize state leaders and other important actors to accept new norms and values. The chapter concludes by contending that this approach to power can account for these missing elements in theorizing contemporary great power politics in IR.

POWER IN INTERNATIONAL RELATIONS THEORY

As is the case for any complex concept, there are a number of different ways to discuss the idea of power in the study of IR. Here, I use the "faces of power" approach (Lukes 1974) as a starting point with which I frame the development of my argument. Steven Lukes used the term "faces of power" to describe the different aspects of power that he saw as related and interdependent. An advantage of Lukes's approach when applied to this empirical situation is that it highlights relations between actors and analyzes the concept of power relationally. Using such an approach to examine existing scholarship, then, seems fitting. Still, as I explain in this chapter, Lukes's understanding of power is a starting point, as I reinterpret the productive power dimension and focus on relationality.

The faces of power approach has been used by a significant number of scholars, most of whom focus either on the first face (the power to coerce behavior) to study instances when foreign policy decision-makers in a country seek to influence decision-making processes in another country (for example, see Baldwin 1985, 1989, 2013) or on the third face (the power to change actors' preferences and wants) to develop a Gramscian perspective on international political economy (for illustrations, see Baldwin 2013 and Gill and Law 1988, 1989). These studies do not characterize the faces of power as separable or mutually exclusive. Rather, they accept but add to each face new elements on theorizing power to improve our understanding of how power works (see Barnett and Duval 2005; Abrahamsen 2004, 2016; Leander 2005). I take a similar approach. As I discuss the different faces of power, I show both their strengths and limitations in explaining power in the context of emerging (super)powers' foreign policy conduct.

The first "face" is a coercive type of power manifested in the power of decision-making. It builds on Robert Dahl's definition of power, which is the capability of actors who possess power to prevent other actors (who are without power) from doing what the latter would prefer to do. In brief, Dahl analyzes the compulsory face of power by focusing on situations of coercion where an actor A gets an actor B to do what B would not otherwise want to do (Dahl 1957, 201). When used by scholars of global politics, this approach is applied to understanding how one state coerces another state to do things that the latter would not otherwise do. This dimension of power is too narrow because it only applies to contexts of making decisions on issues over which there is an observable conflict of interest (Lukes 2005, 19). Indeed, the first face of power fails to reveal the less visible ways in which power is exercised. What about the second one?

The second "face," agenda-setting, aims at remedying the shortcoming of Dahl's conceptualization of power in not taking into consideration the ability of actors to control the process of decision-making. Bachrach and Baratz (1962), who are interested in public policy decision-making, critique Dahl's view of power on the grounds that it only considers the power of decision-making processes in a given institution. In their view, this neglects strategies of mobilizing bias to prevent discussion of certain issues and thus to determine what issues are important to the negotiations table and which are silenced prior to agenda-setting.[2] Bachrach and Baratz specifically argue that Dahl's view of power does not take into account the fact that power is often deployed to confine the scope of decision-making to relatively "safe" issues.[3] For them, it is important that a conceptualization of power be suited to answer questions relevant to what defines safe issues, what type of agenda items are relevant for the issues and actors at stake, and, perhaps more importantly, what type of agenda items do not make the cut and why (Bachrach and Baratz 1962, 947). Scholars of global politics have asked questions about this second "face" of power, including how transnational agendas are set and how states manipulate both other states and organizations to limit options. Yet Bachrach and Baratz's analysis is limited to examining individual decisions made to preclude certain demands from becoming politically threatening. A deeper analysis of power should also concern itself with "all the complex and subtle ways" in which factors such as the sheer weight of institutions inhibit certain societal groups from participating in political decision-making (Lukes 2005, 40).

That leads to the third face of power, ideological power. This face goes beyond analyzing apparent conflicts of interest and pays attention to observable as well as concealed conflicts. Dahl's coercive notion of power and Bachrach and Baratz's power to control the agenda are shortsighted in assuming that conflict is necessary to power and that there needs to be a conflict of interest for power to be exercised. As Lukes (2005, 27) points out, this assumption fails to consider the crucial point that oftentimes a more effective face of power is to tacitly prevent such conflicts of interest from appearing in the first place. Lukes's value-added therefore lies in highlighting a type of power that does not appear to be overtly conflictual or coercive but is rather exercised through interaction.[4] Yet power in his framework is instrumental and is viewed as a capability that one actor possesses over another.

This is where my approach differs from the three faces developed in Lukes's framework. His examination is concerned with exploring the instrumental and causal relations between actors A and B. What B is coerced to do (in the case of the first face) is caused by A's influence on B and can only be examined when the relations between A and B are investigated. This conceptualization of power in Lukes's framework understands power as a capability or a possession, in that actor A is capable of changing the behavior of B whether it is through direct coercion (first face), through implicitly shaping the agenda (second face), or by tacitly shaping actor B's desires and interests to match actor A's (third face and closest to soft power). Power in this approach is about A's capacity to achieve its interest by overpowering actor B either explicitly or implicitly. Power in this approach is an object that either belongs with actor A or B.

While Lukes's approach remains focused on cause and effect, my approach sees power as a process rather than a possession and takes relational power as constitutive and productive of meanings, actors, other relations, and of power. This view of relational networks as the locus of power is compatible with Foucault's conceptualization of power as

> exercised through networks, and individuals do not simply circulate in those networks; they are in a position to both submit to and exercise this power. They are never the inert or consenting targets of power; they are always its relays. In other words, power passes through individuals. It is not applied to them . . . the individual is a relay: power passes through the individuals it has constituted. (Foucault 2003, 29–30)

Power, from a Foucauldian perspective, is not something that states, elites, or other actors *have* or possess. Rather, there are nodes/ties that connect individuals in the networks of power that they influence and are influenced by. These nodes are relations, connections that help us view power not as an instrument but as a set of relations and processes. To view power as a process means to think beyond what actor A can make actor B do with or without the consent/knowledge/consciousness of actor B. Power as a process takes actors in a power relationship as agents with a feedback loop of exchanges of favors, gifts, and debts that connects all the actors. One actor becomes powerful not in an absolute but in a relative way to other actors when its relationships with other actors are strong and multiple.

RELATIONAL POWER AND RELATIONALITY IN IR

Relational power and relationality in IR have been examined by several scholars who were interested in moving beyond the conceptualization of power in terms of instruments or as material possession by actors in IR (Agathangelou and Ling 2003; Baldwin 2013; Guzzini 2013). Relationality has, for example, been a central concept to a robust body of feminist and postcolonial IR scholarship.[5] For both postcolonial and feminist scholars who follow a relational approach, power is generally understood as a relationship of inequality—be this a gender-based inequality or unequal relations permeating imperial encounters.[6] Postcolonial scholar Sanjay Seth explains that "relational ontology" is at the heart of postcolonial theory, and highlights that relationality is important for postcolonial approaches to power, war, and security because relational ontology insists "that the modern world was formed in and through imperial encounters and thus that the colonizer and colonized each shaped the other" (Seth 2013, 7). Relationality is also significant for postcolonial works that examine actors' identities (race, class, (im) migration status, among others) as they are framed in relation to other actors' identities. Identity is "relational and all relations have a necessary character" (Laclau and Mouffe 1985, 106).

Furthermore, Randolph Persaud argues that it is not sufficient for identity scholars to work with the simple fixed binaries of we/they, us/them, and so on. Instead, identities are complex, multidimensional, and are *activated differently in different relations to other actors*. He argues that "the control of borders" along racial lines has been "critical in the production and consolidation of a US national identity that privileges whiteness" (Persaud 2002, 64–65). Therefore, identities are better examined relationally in order to capture the processes that constitute power relations. However, one limitation of some postcolonial and feminist perspectives on relational power is that they equate power with domination by the colonizer over the colonized, by one class over another, or one (super)structure over agents. Yet other critical approaches in postcolonial theory analyze the agency of the oppressed by studying the ways in which oppressed or colonized peoples can exercise agency and power over the seemingly dominant power (see Agathangelou 2017; Grovogui 2013). In much of this scholarship, power is still viewed as a possession of one actor that is used to influence other actors and form relationships of domination.

By contrast, the notion of relationality adopted in this book is one that understands power to be located and diffused in the interactions between different actors and understands power in terms of social and human capital. I expand on it in greater detail in the next section but here I give a brief overview. For Chinese IR scholar Qin Yaqing, the most significant difference between mainstream IR and a relational perspective on IR is that the former is steeped in a rule-based normative order, whereas the episteme of Relational IR appears to be grounded in relational governance (Qin 2011, 2012, 2014; Kavalski 2013).

Power is relational. The denser the network nodes/relations are, the more powerful actors are. In this approach, relational power is "similar to both hard and soft power in that it is the ability to change the attitude, motivation, or behavior of others and thus make them conform to one's will during the process of social interaction" (Hwang 1987, 947). Yet it departs from those traditional faces of power because it does not view power as "a possession" of a particular actor. Indeed, as Guzzini (2011, 564) notes, "such relational concepts of power are opposed to views that see power in terms of its resources or instruments: power exists in and through a relation." Relationality also involves a process of managing one's relational circles and manipulating them to one's advantage. Accordingly, political actors are considered more powerful when they belong to "larger relational circles, more intimate and important others in these circles, and more social prestige because of these circles" (Qin 2016, 41). Relational power, therefore, "focuses on the governing of relations among actors rather than of actors per se" (Qin 2016, 41).

If this relational power is not something actors *have* or *possess*, how do we understand actors' relation to it? Foucault (1980, 119) dismissed the idea that power should be viewed only as repressive, insisting that "if power were anything but repressive, if it never did anything but say no, do you really think one would be brought to obey it?" For him, the apparent faces of power, such as sovereign power and juridico-discursive power, focus much on interdiction, domination, war, and inflicting death while they fail to reveal the concealed operations of power.[7] Barnett and Duvall (2005, 4) build on this approach to argue in favor of conceptualizing power in a way that "detaches discussions of power from the limitations of realism" and encourages scholars to seek power's multiple forms. For them, and other social constructivists, power is produced socially and shapes actors' ability to determine their own fate.

Barnett and Duvall suggest the utility of four categories of power: compulsory, institutional, structural, and productive. Compulsory power is in many ways the direct equivalent of Lukes's first dimension and Dahl's coercive power: it concerns the direct control over another actor's actions. However, for Barnett and Duvall, "compulsory power is not limited to material resources and also includes symbolic and normative resources" (2005, 13). Institutional power is about actors' control over socially distant others. Here, the authors are concerned with "the formal and informal institutions that mediate between A and B, as A, working through the rules and procedures that define those institutions, guides, steers, and constraints the actions" (Barnett and Duvall 2005, 15). Structural power is about the mutual constitution of the capacities of actors, and as its name suggests, it's about structure. Barnett and Duvall explain that structural power "shapes the fates and conditions of existence of actors in two critical ways. One, structural positions do not generate equal social privileges; instead structures allocate differential capacities, and typically differential advantages, to different positions. . . . Two, the social structure not only constitutes actors and their capacities; it also shapes their self-understanding and subjective interests" (Barnett and Duvall 2005, 18). The fourth category of power, which is the one of interest to this section, is about the production of subjects through diffuse social relations. The key difference between productive and structural types of power is that the latter works through direct structural relations (formal or informal institutions) whereas the former entails subtler and diffuse social processes. Unfortunately, in examining productive power, the two authors do not provide an illustration or application of how to put the framework to work and use it as an analytical tool.

Understanding and Using Relational Power

This book takes Michael Barnett and Raymond Duvall's analysis of power further. It develops a theoretical framework of relational productive power for the global politics of today and tomorrow, engaging it as complex and intersubjective, with reference to and application of the making of Chinese foreign policy. It does so in three steps. First, it defines power from a social/ human capital perspective using a guanxi approach to global politics. Second, it argues that routinized practices of relational power building (via people-to-people exchanges, for example) lead to institutionalizing the practices and that doing so provides the space for norm-making and expert knowledge production. Third, drawing on scholarship on the role of institutions in norm diffusion and common sense making, it examines the mechanisms through which guanxi relations and expert knowledge production, in the context of emerging (super)powers, are spaces for the diffusion of an alternative set of values, norms, and models of development and governance, among other things.

Guanxi

Guanxi simply put means "connections" or "relations" in Mandarin Chinese. *Guanxixue* is the study of relations and connections, and the term for "International Relations" in Mandarin consequently translates as international connections/relations. Several scholars have dedicated much of their careers looking at the dynamics of guanxi in society, business culture, and politics. Anthropologist Mayfair Yang is one very prominent scholar who wrote a seminal study on "Gift, Favors, and Banquets: On the Art of Social Relationships in China." For Yang (1994, 8), the art of guanxi "places an emphasis on the binding power and emotional and ethical qualities of the personal relationships." Favors, gift, and banquets (or, as usually referred to, wining and dining) are practices that establish personal connections, bind guests to hosts with favors, and establish an emotional and ethical bond between them. Yet "what distinguishes banqueting in the art of guanxi from other kinds of banqueting is its role as a medium of not only social, but especially economic and politics exchange and its stronger binding power on the guest to repay" (Yang 1994, 139). Banqueting in Chinese culture, as Yang explains, "is not merely a tactic in the art of *guanxi*, but also an important ritual in the social sphere." Banquets "bring much social prestige to the hosts" (Yang 1994, 137).

Even though the art and examples of banqueting mentioned are often of Maoist China, guanxi continues to be relevant in China today, decades after the opening of market reforms conducted by Deng Xiaoping. Many scholars, such as sociologist Yanjie Bian, study the evolution of the concept of guanxi in Chinese society and ask whether guanxi is still relevant today. Bian (2018) looks at the hypothesis that, in moving toward a market-driven system (capitalism), merit-based rather than relational recruitment and influence will become more relevant in China. The claim is that market logic and the rationalism of institutions/legal-based systems will create fewer incentives to be socially connected to powerful links in companies, which are now private rather than state owned. This means that guanxi is not fixed or static but is resilient. Its significance goes up significantly with the combination of high market competition and high uncertainty levels. With privatization, guanxi increases rather than decreases (uncertainty) but the inclusion of more merit-based recruiting systems tends to decrease the significance of guanxi (without eliminating its relevance).

Understanding the workings of guanxi in light of China's rising power is a topic of controversy among contemporary theorists. On the one hand, sociologist Doug Guthrie (1998) argues that China's entry into the global economic market decreases the importance of guanxi. Guthrie's claim is based on research interviews he conducted with a handful of large state-owned firms in Shanghai where top officials stated that they recruited based on merit not guanxi. Guthrie views guanxi "as favoritism-laden relations" and believes that "guanxi practice and guanxi influence will be reduced to a minimum when markets and legal systems develop to maturity." Yang (1994) disagrees, advocating for taking guanxi as a cultural repertoire instead. Yang argues that Guthrie's sample was too small and limited in that he only talked to high-ranked officers in those firms and took their word at face value. Much of guanxi is conducted outside of office hours, outside of work premises. She argues that Guthrie portrays guanxi as more static than it actually is. By contrast, guanxi is a resilient and evolving practice. It takes many forms and moves between tangible to nontangible depending on the institutional context in place. Whereas guanxi in the 1960s and 1970s was more focused on tangible resources such as food products and other limited supply products, guanxi today may take different forms but will not just disappear because it is a cultural trait.

To get how guanxi works, it is important to understand that both tie-strength and multiplexity are involved in guanxi relationship-building. Tie-strength is the level of intensity of a social relationship. In guanxi, tie-strength is not just about individually powerful relationships but about "the totality of several dimensions of social interactions between ego and his/her alters: frequency of interactions, degree of intimacy, degree of emotional attachment and extent of resource exchanges" (Bian 2018, 605). Multiplexity is the "overlap of roles, exchanges, affiliations in social relationships" (Bian 2018, 605). It "operates according to the relational logic of asymmetrical exchanges." What is interesting to note about the logic of these exchanges of gifts and favors is that it shows how flexible guanxi is. It is flexible both in terms of the type of payback that can be given and the time when it's paid back. Favors don't have to be reciprocated or returned immediately or directly. There is also a lot of flexibility with the form of social capital that is generated through guanxi relations, which can be a mix of tangible and intangible sources of power and influence. Diplomatic banquets illustrate the importance of producing "friendly feeling which personalizes the social process, infuses it with a sense of obligations 'to give, to receive, and to repay'" (Kavalski 2018, 8).

Guanxi and Relationality in International Relations

The concept of guanxi is widely used in academic scholarship from a variety of fields including marketing, finance, and organizational behavior. This kind of scholarship often aims at identifying for non-Chinese business firms seeking to operate in China reliable ways of understanding the importance of guanxi in the conduct of business in China and identifying the more/most important nodes of any organizational network. Unlike in anthropology, business studies, and organizational structure research, the concept remains less used in the study of international relations and foreign policy scholarship, despite increasing attention to China's place in global politics and its relations with other states.

The concept of networking/guanxi is receiving increasing attention in IR theory, especially in literature looking at non-Western approaches. Several IR scholars have led the work of introducing relationality to IR debates (Kavalski 2018; Nordin 2016; Pan 2018; Qin 2018; Shih and Huang 2016), but the concept remains theoretically underdeveloped and empirically underused. These pioneering scholars have focused on the question of *what power is* in this perspective, and answered it by examining Confucianism, Chinese cultural traits, and so forth. While this is a useful start, the burgeoning literature has not looked at the question of *how* power works from this relational perspective. That is to say, analyses of the mechanisms of power building from a relational perspective are missing from the scholarship. In *Shaping the Future of Power*, knowledge production and norm diffusion facilitated by relational people-to-people programs are central to understanding mechanisms of power building and power projection. Developing the concept of guanxi can enrich understandings of power in global politics both theoretically and empirically. In this context, guanxi is a manifestation of the power of relations with the goal of increasing one's social capital through the medium of network-building, bonding, and *renqing* (人情), or "human feeling."[8] This is a core idea of a relational approach to power.

Relational power takes as a basic, central unit "relation" and takes the world in general and world politics in particular as composed of "dynamic relations." It "focuses on human relations and holds that relationality is the key to understanding social phenomena and meaningful human actions" (Qin 2018, 207). The logic of relationality means that an actor takes into account social relations when making judgments and decisions. Accounting for social relations means both thinking about the immediate specific others involved in a given decision and how that fits in the totality of one's relational circle. This also implies that based on this relational logic, an actor's desires, calculations, interests, and preferences are not fixed but can change, evolve, and vary across contexts (Qin 2018, 208).

In more traditional mainstream IR theories, the two logics that are most recurrently used to discuss the difference between realist and constructivist theories are the logic of consequences and the logic of appropriateness (March and Olsen 1984). The logic of consequences follows instrumentalist rationality and the logic of appropriateness follows normative rationality. In IR, structural realism and neoliberal institutionalism are typically associated with the logic of consequences because crucial to both of these theories is how actors calculate behavior to maximize individual interests. Constructivism, on the other hand, if often classified as part of the logic of appropriateness because individuals' behaviors consider social norms and values (Sending 2002). Actors act based on what is considered the right thing to do. However, the binary of these two logics handicaps any analysis that seeks to explain or understand overlapping areas between ideational and material aspects of international politics. A relational logic more successfully captures the overlap areas that neither the logic of appropriateness nor the logic of consequence captures. Relational logic allows us to analyze the ideational as material, which is an important feature of international politics in the Global South.

The logic of relationality necessitates accepting a set of crucial concepts. First, social actors are "relators" who are defined by their capacity to have relationships with others. They are agents that shape their relations and the outcomes of these relations rather than passive observers of a relational structure that dictates their actions. Second, social actors have relational circles. Actors see themselves as the center of multilayered concentric relational circles. Third, relations have context. Actors' relational webs overlap and affect one another. These relational circles "compose a multidimensional and multilayered relational complexity" (Qin 2018, 210). This complexity is what constitutes the relational context, and more overlap between different relational circles can contribute to increasing actors' influence.[9] Therefore, in this framework, relations are not a substitute for material possessions in traditional approaches. Power is not defined in terms of how many relations states/actors have (simply paralleling the way traditional approaches count tanks and missiles as power). Relations in themselves do not equal power. It is the process of reciprocation, manipulation, favors exchange, and indebtedness that amount to how power is conceptualized in this approach.

On explaining the role of agents (relators) and their interests, Qin (2018, 223) contends that "like the rational choice theory, the logic of relationality assumes that relators pursue their self-interests and seek tangible and material gains through the relational circles by asking for and exchanging favors." The difference is that the actors' interests, in the logic of relationality, "are located often in relations and their pursuit of interests tends to be through managing, manipulating, and expanding their relational circles" (2018, 223). Relational actors manipulate, grow, and manage their social capital and relational networks to maximize their gains and secure a wide variety of interests. An example of this can be seen in Chinese foreign policy's rankings of potential and current partner countries. For instance, a comprehensive strategic partnership is the highest form of diplomatic relationality (the most intimate circle), comprehensive partnership and strategic partnerships are next in rank and prestige, and then there is "partnership" (which is the least intimate). Countries that enjoy the highest rank of diplomatic relations with China are probably countries that also have the most overlap in terms of relational circles.

Thinking about the Future of Power in Global Politics

Power from a relational approach is located, activated, and expanded in social relations. Relations precede power and shape it yet at the same time the power generated by relations can in turn reinforce and expand social networks. This understanding of power is built both on previous work on relational power and my exploration of the links between guanxi relations, expert knowledge production, and norm diffusion. Rather than answering the question *what is power*, I look to show the mechanisms through which social capital, people-to-people connections, translates to power (especially within the context of foreign policy making). These mechanisms are the intricate interplay between developing and expanding influence via social capital, through the exchanges of favors, gifts, and banquets. To give a brief illustration, an important (and expanding) area of China's foreign policy with Belt and Road states revolves around people-centered diplomacy and investments in human capital programs. In these programs the Chinese government sponsors seminars, trainings, and exchanges between Chinese state officials, high-ranking military officers, media staff, and so forth, and their counterparts from Belt and Road participating states. From a relational productive power perspective, regarding the question of *what* the source of power is in the illustration above, the answer lies within the networks of personal and professional relations and exchanges of gifts and favors that make China a powerful state with a development model that other governments are attracted to and seek to mimic. In addition to answering *what power* looks like in that example, another necessary question is to examine *how* these relations between Chinese and counterpart officials translate to power dynamics. The mechanisms include knowledge production and norm diffusion as they occur during the routine exchanges and professionalization trainings.

From a relational productive power approach, power is not formed prior to relationships. It emanates from them. Power resides with the relations. It is relationships that move power and increase it. They are reinforced discursively and practiced through people-to-people diplomacy, cultural exchanges, and investments in human development programs. From this perspective, a relational approach to power prioritizes normative, nonmaterial, and cultural aspects over material or tangible elements. In this approach, being powerful does not equate to having the biggest military presence or the most money. Instead, being powerful is understood as a function of having strong social capital, expanded networks, and solid people-to-people exchanges. Power lies within the multiplicity of these relations, and securing interests is done by manipulating these relations, exchanging favors, and reciprocating behaviors. Furthermore, a necessary follow-up step is to look at social capital as a space that both allows exchanges of favors, gifts, and personal bonding among the people involved but also allows for knowledge production, exchange of ideas, and norm making.

RELATIONS, KNOWLEDGE, NETWORKS, AND INSTITUTIONS

So far, the IR scholarship that has engaged a relational approach to power and to international politics has neglected some of the mechanisms through which relations lead to power and how agents manipulate that relational power to pursue their interests. To rectify this, I both demonstrate how taking a relational approach to power is necessary to understanding current developments within the international order with the rise of China and other Global South powers, and explore the knowledge-power nexus to analyze the mechanisms of power projection in a relational approach to IR. Indeed, relational power that is generated in the context of social networks and relationships is also a space for expert knowledge production, norm making, and norm diffusing. In order to develop these mechanisms, it is necessary to revisit IR scholarship that probes how state interests are shaped and how international norms are created and diffused via international institutions.

State interests are not "out there waiting to be discovered," as Martha Finnemore says. Instead, they are "constructed through social interaction" (Finnemore 1996, 2). Finnemore also recognizes that internationally held norms and values change, and when they do, they generate coordinated shifts in state interests. She explains that "states are embedded in dense networks of transnational and international social relations that shape their perceptions of the world and their role in that world" (ibid.). One of the most interesting contributions about this is that it urges IR scholars to look at international organizations not as bits of furniture that states interact with, but as dynamic players with the power to change and shape the preferences of states. In this context, Finnemore pays attention to the importance of international organizations in teaching "good norms" to international actors. It is this teaching/socialization that gets international actors to learn to behave appropriately (according to the logic of appropriateness). The United Nations Educational, Scientific and Cultural Organization (UNESCO) for her played the teacher's role in shaping the identity, interests, and behavior of the states concerned.

Scholarship on the importance of norms and values in complementing material conceptions of power in international politics is well established. Building on research by Finnemore (1996), scholars have explored how institutions shape states' interests (Abbott and Snidal 1998; Pouliot 2016) and how international legitimacy relates to institutions (Legro 1997); they have expanded the scope of norm entrepreneurship to norm challengers and norm antipreneurs (Bloomfield 2016). However, these perspectives have looked mostly at Western-led institutions and how such institutions define and constitute states' interests (such as the case of the International Committee of the Red Cross for Finnemore), or how developing states get socialized into the international order by joining international institutions (such as the case of China's socialization via the World Trade Organization for Johnston 2008). Up to this point, the international organizations analyzed in IR scholarship on norms were for the most part institutions that more or less fit in the international liberal order (e.g., the UN, UNESCO, the International Monetary Fund, the World Trade Organization, and the Geneva Conventions). The assumption was that such Western-led institutions socialize the Global South and other states into the Western-led Westphalian liberal order. Global South states and developing states are viewed as consumers, recipients, or at best resistors/challengers of these international norms.

A decade after Finnemore's groundbreaking work, another group of scholars expanded on its scope and problematized existing norm scholarship for being Eurocentric and inadequate in capturing non-Western ideas, norms, and institutions. For example, in *Against International Norms*, Charlotte Epstein and others (2017) reflect on postcolonial perspectives to international norms. From a postcolonial perspective, socializing developing countries into accepting and mimicking international norms infantilizes them and takes away their agency (Epstein 2017). Similarly, another group of scholars explore non-Western actors not only as norm challengers but also examine Global South institutions such as BRICS and norms such as *Tianxia* (all under heaven).[10] This book contributes to enriching the existing scholarship that deals with the influence of emerging powers and their initiatives in establishing institutions that not only challenge the existing order but make norms and socialize states into accepting them as their preference over the status quo (the international liberal order). This book examines the interplay between social capital, relational networks, expert knowledge production, and norm-making in Chinese-led institutions. Indeed, since international organizations are the conveyor belts of international norms and since the Forum of China-Africa Cooperation is an institution, FOCAC can and should also be viewed as a conveyor belt of international norms. Yet it remains to be seen what/whose norms FOCAC and other China-led institutions will diffuse, and through what mechanisms these norms will be produced and spread.

Fields of Knowledge and Relations of Power

In foreign policy making, social relations and networks that are enhanced through routine people-to-people exchanges can transition from being informal relational networks to becoming formally institutionalized. Concretely, with frequency and consistency, exchanges and professionalization trainings allow for expert knowledge sharing from trainers to trainees in a more institutionalized manner. In the case of China's foreign policy, the trainings pledged by the Chinese government during the Forum on China-Africa Cooperation have become institutionalized with specific agencies and institutions in China that fund, host, and organize the trainings. These institutions do not lose their identity as relational networks when putting on a bureaucratic hat while sharing technical expertise and skills with the trainees. Instead, their function as knowledge producers solidifies the social capital and relational bonds. Formal institutions solidify the social bonds formed within networks and allow for the routine exchanges of ideas, joint discussions of problems, and joint thinking through solutions to existing problems.

How, then, is expert knowledge produced and internalized/normalized by international actors and legitimized by international institutions? Existing research on epistemic communities sheds some light on these processes by looking into epistemic communities. Simply put, an epistemic community "is a network of professionals with recognized expertise and competence in a particular domain and an authoritative claim to policy-relevant knowledge" (Haas 1992, 3). Epistemic communities help identify the self-interests of a state and can play a significant role in turning knowledge and ideas into policies. This can be done through a variety of diffusion mechanisms. One such mechanism is institutional learning where actors and agents learn and assimilate the knowledge produced and shared by experts. Institutional learning occurs "directly, through interpersonal persuasion, communication, exchange and reflection." In this process, leaders are socialized to accept the new ideas, values, and views.

In the next three chapters, I further explore socialization processes and normalization when examining the impacts of Chinese-backed professionalization trainings in private security (in chapter 4), in media and journalism (chapter 5), in cultural and education exchanges (chapter 6) and reflect back on socialization mechanisms from the perspective of a rising power in the concluding chapter. For now, it is important to note that socialization literature has been subject to substantial critiques from Global South perspectives on grounds that it is patronizing and infantilizing of the actors-to-be-socialized, which often are developing countries (Chowdhury 2017; Epstein 2012; Zarakol 2014). In China's foreign policy conduct in Africa, especially through professionalization trainings, knowledge and expertise are passed on from Chinese to African under a narrative of *relating* where Chinese trainers relate to their African counterparts through shared history, developing countries' identity, and Global South solidarity. In the context of Chinese foreign policy making, the narrative of *international relating* differs, at least in theory, from the hierarchical, Eurocentric socialization mechanisms in that it relies on consensual knowledge production facilitated by strong social capital and guanxi networks. This opens the opportunity to explore the case of China's foreign policy *relating* with Africans for its potential implications for socialization scholarship.

Knowledge/Power Nexus as a Framework for Analyzing Emerging Powers

The knowledge/power nexus refers to understanding power as being based on knowledge and viewing knowledge production as an exercise of power. For example, in the relationship between a doctor and a patient, the doctor's scientific/medical knowledge produces the patient who is only a patient in that relationship to the doctor. The patient submits willingly to the doctor's knowledge and expertise by undergoing examinations and taking prescriptions. It is not physical or economic power that defines this relationship, it is expert knowledge that dictates how the two interact. When translated to global politics, knowledge and the power of expertise is often described as "soft" and as being a stark contrast to coercive power. However, I don't think that this is necessarily the case as knowledge and expertise can be just as violent as coercive power. Yet they are packaged differently than coercive exercises of power. The invisibility of their coercion and the appearance of *softness* are what makes knowledge-power work.

Emerging powers and Global South states, such as China, acknowledge and relate in official discourses to the legacies of colonialism and histories of exploitation by foreign powers of third world countries. In this way, emerging powers are not only more cautious about the negative perceptions of coercive power, they denounce colonial practices to both distance their rising power from traditional European powers and to relate, bond, and identify with developing countries that are potential consumers of their technologies, ideas, norms, and values. Developing strong social networks and strengthening people-to-people bonds is a very crucial part of this relating.

Relational networks serve to enhance trust-building between the rising superpower and other developing states. They introduce state elites and government officials to new sets of values and norms when professionalization trainings are organized. Understanding the centrality of relationality and the processes of expert knowledge production through people-to-people exchanges and social network-building programs are key to unpacking China as a rising superpower. These relations are manifested in the case of Chinese foreign policy in steadily increasing quotas for scholarships to international students, people-to-people exchange programs under the Belt and Road Initiative, and joint workshops and professionalization training programs offered to elites, civil servants, military officers, and citizens of various developing countries. Chinese government-sponsored professionalization trainings serve different specialty areas, but they all result in producing expert knowledge whether through seminars, workshops, or joint-navy drills.

Viewed from a productive relational perspective, Chinese government-sponsored professionalization trainings and people-to-people exchanges are not some kind of neutral skills transfer activities. They build connections among high-ranking officers and, even more interestingly, they provide opportunities to align ways of thinking and reacting to real security, governance, or development issues. Taking a relational notion of power helps us make sense of Chinese investments in human development in the developing world broadly and in Africa more specifically. In my analysis, I accept and operate under the assumption that "power and knowledge directly imply one another . . . [in that] there is no power relation without the correlative constitution of a field of knowledge, nor any knowledge that does not presuppose and constitute at the same time power relations" (Foucault, cited in Digeser 1992, 986). I take people-to-people exchanges and professionalization training programs and investments in human resource development to be spaces that facilitate the constitution of a field of knowledge, on the one hand, and the widening of the relational networks, on the other.

This book empirically substantiates this relational productive power approach by examining Chinese professionalization trainings for Africans in three areas: military and security relations, for journalists, and people-to-people relations through Confucius Institutes. In the analysis, I start by looking at official discourses of Chinese foreign policy on professionalization training programs in Africa. Analyzing these discourses is central to the methodology of this study because discourse is taken as the vehicle that shapes not only the nature of China-Africa relations but also as the vehicle through which knowledge and norms are disseminated. As I explained in the introductory chapter, rhetoric and discourse are important tools of China's foreign policy making. In each of the empirical chapters, I start the analysis by looking at the *articulation* of discourses in the Forum on China-Africa Cooperation and other foreign policy documents.

Application and Analysis

Guanxi's centeredness on the power of building and nurturing personal relationships for the success of business deals is not restricted to domestic contexts. IR theory is well served by examining the role that guanxi and social capital occupies in foreign policy conduct in the context of the Global South. With a specific look at China's sponsorship of professionalization training programs for African diplomats, military officers, civilians, journalists, and the like, this study aims at analyzing Beijing's investments in human resource development programs across Africa. In doing so, I do not claim to uncover Chinese foreign policy's motivations or intentions toward African recipients as a plan to have the trainees be socialized into Chinese norms, or have their knowledge shaped in favor of China's image. Rather, I am concerned with examining the consequences of said investments and not the motivations or rationale behind these training programs.

After conducting extensive interviews at the office of the deputy for African affairs inside the Chinese Ministry of Foreign Affairs, along with dozens of other interviews with civil servants and think tank specialists, a number of issues became clear to me. First, Chinese foreign policy making is highly decentralized. There is not a single bureau in charge of crafting China's Africa strategy. Rather, the officials working at the Ministry of Foreign Affairs are one link in a long chain of command. The Ministry of Education, the Ministry of Commerce, the China Export/Import Bank, Chinese ambassadors to African countries, and officials at the Ministry of Defense are all key players when it comes to drafting China's Africa strategy. Second, investments in human development resources are an important part of the holistic approach of engagement that Chinese foreign policy follows in Africa. By holistic I mean that the Chinese government engages on almost all levels of cooperation at different paces and in diversified areas. It is multifaceted and does not focus exclusively on security cooperation or natural resource extraction. This is also reflected in the sheer diversity of topics for which the government holds professionalization trainings. I limit my analysis to a few cases that I see both as most salient to China's foreign policy in Africa and that are also present in China's foreign policy toward states other than in the African context.

As discussed in chapter 2, both discourse and practice are key to the conduct of China's foreign policy. Consequently, there is a need to treat discourse and practices not only as the medium within which Chinese-African's interactions are expressed but also as *productive* of these interactions. To illustrate briefly, in almost all Chinese official speeches about Africa, phrases such as "mutual benefit," "win-win relations," and "equal partners" are repeated over and over to become a normalized part of the discourse on China-Africa relations. They are almost always used as a heuristic association or a conventional wisdom on China-Africa relations. It matters to take discourses as sites for producing meanings and ensuing verbal and nonverbal practices.[11] The discourses stemming from China-Africa summits, Chinese strategy papers, government officials' statements, media representation, and academic exchanges and symposia on China-Africa are productive of how Sino-African relations are understood, rationalized, and practiced. Furthermore, discourses are an ongoing process of producing and reproducing as well as transforming meanings rather than just stabilizing or fixing them. Consequently, in order to examine professionalization trainings and capacity-building programs in China-Africa relations, two steps need to be taken. The first step is analyzing Chinese foreign policy official discourses on investments in human resource development as stated through the Forum of China-Africa Cooperation action plans and official speeches by the Chinese president as well as by African counterparts. The second step is examining the professionalization training practices on the ground by looking at the different mechanisms and programs put in place through workshops, scholarship programs, language classrooms at Confucius Institutes, military trainings, and so forth. Together, these steps examine professionalization trainings as asymmetrical places of interaction between expert Chinese trainers and African trainees to how creating social capital produces power and how people-to-people exchanges facilitate knowledge production and norm diffusion.

To illustrate, applying a relational productive power framework to China's military diplomacy and security practices in Africa highlights the proliferation of professionalization trainings offered by the Chinese government to bring African military officers to China for training in its party school. These trainings open up opportunities for introducing African military officials to Chinese defense strategic thinking, military facilities, and safety practices. These aspects of China's military diplomacy in Africa, for instance, do not come up if one is limited to examining the capacity of China's military base in Djibouti. In the next chapter I analyze, in depth, the nature and impact of Chinese-funded professionalization trainings for African military officers, private security staff, and peacekeepers.

CHAPTER FOUR

Guanxi in Military Diplomacy and Security Trainings

ON MARCH 3, 2018 US Congressman Bradley Byrne wrote a letter to US Secretary of Defense James Mattis warning that "reports that Djibouti plans to gift a major port to the Chinese government could negatively impact the ability of U.S. military and intelligence officials to conduct critical counterterrorism operations" (Byrne 2018). The Djiboutian port in question, Doraleh Port, was the subject of another letter of concern sent by US Senators Chris Coons and Marco Rubio to US Secretary of State Mike Pompeo and Secretary of Defense Mattis on November 7, 2018. The senators warned that much of Djibouti's debt is owed to the Export-Import Bank of China (China Exim), and that they "believe these developments provide major strategic benefits to China and risk undermining the balance of power in East Africa and around the Bab al-Mandeb strait." For the senators, "China's control of Doraleh could allow it to impede U.S. military operations in the Horn of Africa, as well as those of the U.S. allies like Italy, Japan, and France, which maintain military bases in the region" (Coons and Rubio 2018). The letters of concern show how China's newly established naval base in Djibouti and Djibouti's financial reliance on China are ringing the alarm bells for US foreign policy makers. China's expansion in Djibouti's security scene is viewed from a zero-sum perspective to be a risk that could "provide major strategic benefits to China," allow China to undercut US military power, and that this would risk upsetting "the balance of power" in the region. What these letters have in common is that they view the threat coming from China in the form of military interest (counterterrorism explicitly listed), and financial (debt trap). What the letters fail to understand is that the bulk of China's military ties to African states run through an elaborate network of military-to-military exchanges, defense forums, and trainings of African security personnel.

To this effect, the seventh Forum on China-Africa Cooperation agenda pledged "expanding defense and military personnel training," and that "China will continue to step up training for African service personnel, . . . deepen academic exchanges and cooperation among military academies and research institutes and enhance cooperation on military medical science." The meeting's announcements came shortly after China had hosted its first ever Defense and Security Forum with Africa in July 2018. During the forum, which lasted fourteen days, high-ranking officers and military attachés from over fifty African countries attended seminars, talks, and tours of Chinese military facilities. Just two months later, the seventh China-Africa meeting pledged to host more of these collaboration workshops and meetings between Chinese and African military cadres. As an implementation of FOCAC 2018 pledges, in July 2019 China's military hosted 100 army chiefs and defense ministry officers from fifty African countries in Beijing. The army chiefs were in Beijing for a week to participate in the China-Africa Defense and Security Forum.[1]

Given the importance of military-focused personnel trainings as part of China's overall diplomacy of human capital investments, this chapter takes a closer look at China's security policy in Africa from a relational approach.

The Chinese government released its first Africa white paper, an official document that outlined China's foreign policy strategy toward Africa, in tandem with the first Forum on China-Africa Cooperation that was held at the summit level in 2006.[2] The white paper was updated into a second edition in 2015 around the time that the second China-Africa summit was held in South Africa. A quick content analysis of both papers reveals that the word "security" (in the sense of stability) was mentioned five times in the first paper (2006) while the word "terrorism" was mentioned only once in passing in the same paper. Approximately a decade later, the word "security" was mentioned fifteen times in the new Africa white paper (in the context of peace and stability), whereas the word "terrorism" was mentioned five times. The focus on peace and security cooperation in China-Africa relations is indeed a recent development but one that is gaining a lot of attention very quickly.[3]

The growing interest in security is also reflected in a burgeoning body of Africa-China scholarship addressing security cooperation from different angles. Extant literature has examined the contribution of China to peacebuilding efforts and how that reflects on norm-making and norm following (Alden 2014; Alden and Large 2015), China's role in conflict resolution in South Sudan (Large 2008b, 2009, 2012), debates regarding China's adherence to the noninterference principle in Africa (Aidoo and Hess 2015; Wang 2012), debates over Beijing's response to the crisis in Libya and the principle of responsibility to protect (Garwood-Gowers 2012; Fung 2015), the controversial Chinese arms exports to sub-Saharan Africa (Benabdallah 2018; Shinn and Eisenman 2012; Lynch 2012; Hanauer and Morris 2014; Shinn 2014), the development-security nexus in China's approach to security (Benabdallah 2016; Benabdallah and Large 2018; Carrozza 2019), and Beijing's multilateral cooperation with the African Union (AU) on peace and security issues (Van Hoeymissen 2010; Benabdallah 2015).

Yet, missing from these analyses is an account of the people-centered and relationship building in China-Africa security relations. China's investments in professionalization training programs for military officers, peacekeeping forces, and private security personnel are a vital aspect of China-Africa security relations. Though China has been expanding its peace and security cooperation with African states, Chinese presence in Africa (so far) does not reach the level of the US Africa Command (AFRICOM) initiative, which, paired with drone operations, puts the US presence on the continent at about 1,500 officers and thirty-four military outposts.[4] In fact, French military operations in the Sahel and even India's advanced maritime surveillance cooperation with African island states remain on a larger scale than Chinese involvement. Still, the combination of the rapid growth of the Chinese presence and the different form it takes means that there is a need to probe the potential implications of building strong social networks and personal connections between high-ranking Chinese military officials, China's navy, and Chinese private security firms and their African counterparts. These strong people-to-people ties between Chinese and African military officials are manifested in high-level visits, technical training programs, military-to-military diplomacy, and trainings provided by Chinese private security firms in Africa.

In chapter 3, I outlined a conceptual framework that consists of three main elements: social networks, norm diffusion, and knowledge production. In this framework, power is understood not as a possession but as a process. That is to say, power is not measured by material possessions, economic prowess, or even the number of relations and social networks. Instead, power is viewed as a process of cultivating social relations and networks and engaging in social exchanges and investments in relations to expand social capital. It follows that relations and relationality shape power and powerful actors are those who manipulate their social networks. In the realm of military and defense relations within the China-Africa context, this involves intensified exchanges between high-ranking military officers, joint navy drills, and hosting multilateral defense forums. I will apply the framework to three cases of Chinese-sponsored training opportunities for African military and security personnel.

To analyze security-focused trainings, this chapter is organized in three main sections. First, it gives a general overview of China's gradually increasing involvement in Africa's security. Second, it analyzes the professionalization trainings funded by Beijing for African security and military personnel, specifically trainings for high-ranking military officers, for peacekeepers, and for private security staff. The final section applies the relational power framework and analyzes the impact of these trainings in terms of guanxi networks, knowledge production about security theories, and threat-response operating procedures. The chapter ends by probing the effectiveness of China's human capital investments in military diplomacy in Africa.

IF MIGHT MAKES RIGHT, WHAT MAKES MIGHT?

Between 2013 and 2017, China sold weapons to forty-eight countries, making it the fifth largest exporting country of major weapons (Stockholm International Peace Research Institute 2018). Only Germany, France, Russia, and the United States exported more weapons. Topping the ranking is the US with a share of 36% of the total global arms exports between 2014 and 2018. Comparatively, China's total exports came in fifth position with 5.2% of the world arm exports in the same period of time. China also is among the top five importers of arms, a list that neither the US, France, Germany, or Russia made, although Russia and France were China's top suppliers (SIPRI 2018, 6). To many analysts, this shows that China is still very much a consumer of top-tier military technology rather than a producer. Many scholars argue that China is a marginal power in terms of military influence in Africa because there are fewer Chinese troops in Africa. When counting boots on the ground or arms supplies, for example, European and US armies have a stronger presence in the continent (see, for example, Shinn 2014, 4). David Shinn looked at the joint military and naval exercises and found that China has not yet had a major joint exercise in the way the US and France have in Djibouti's Camp Lemonier (see Shinn 2014). Likewise, Holslag (2009a, 29, 32) argues that China's security engagements in Africa are "negligible" because "China has no bases in Africa as does the U.S. and France," and that China's military diplomacy in Africa "remains limited when compared with defense initiatives in other regions." While I agree that China's security practices in Africa differ qualitatively and quantitatively from those of other major players including France and the US, I find that this argument stems from taking a material and somewhat realist assessment of China's security practices. That is to say that China's military presence in Africa looks marginal only when presence is measured as material/military power. Such realist approaches offer limited analytical value for the analysis of nontangible aspects of China's military and security policy for Africa, such as creating strong networks between high-ranking military officers from China and African armies, the production of expert knowledge around understanding threats and responding to them, and the opportunities for norm diffusion during personnel professionalization trainings and joint drills. A realist approach to power misses out on these elements, which are important in themselves but can also have implications for understanding China's material and tangible military practices in Africa.

A material-power approach might argue that holding training workshops and routine exchanges between high-ranking military officers can be interpreted from a national interest maximization and utilitarian perspective. However, such an approach falls short of explaining why there is an increase in the Chinese government's investments in human capital in Africa at the same time that there is a reverse trend of decreasing financial disbursements by the Chinese government in infrastructure and other commercial ventures in Africa. By expanding the concept of power and adopting a relational productive approach, it becomes possible to account for Chinese state-funded professionalization trainings for African security/military personnel, which are a necessary element in China's foreign policy in Africa. Building strong personal networks with political elites and high-ranking military officers can also viewed as going beyond expanding the relational networks and manipulating them for material gains.

When considering China's security strategy in Africa from the limited perspective of military capabilities and arms sales, one may be compelled to conclude that China's security interests are economically driven and limited to protecting China's energy supplies and commercial interests. However, this would result in neglecting a big portion of China's foreign policy in Africa, which dedicates a lot of attention to nurturing social networks and people-to-people connections via professionalization training programs and officials' visits. The main goal of this chapter is to address this aspect of China's foreign policy in Africa with a specific look into military/security relations. In so doing, I deploy the relational productive power framework I developed in the previous chapter and examine its three essential elements: guanxi relations in informal settings, knowledge production in professionalization trainings, and norm diffusion through institutionalized networks.

Professionalization training programs that are sponsored by the Chinese government for the benefit of African military/security officials can be grouped in three categories. The first consists of bilateral training programs involving invitations for African military delegations to visit China for workshops, summits, and trainings. The second concerns training programs through multilateral platforms involving training by Chinese peacekeepers on the ground in different African countries. The third category looks into private security firms' trainings and this involves Chinese (state-owned private companies) training their African counterparts. Taking a relational productive power approach unpacks the mechanisms of defense and security knowledge production and norm diffusion enabled by the proliferation of professionalization training programs between Chinese and African armies. The processes of China's power building in Africa go beyond the scope of what material and realist approaches to power can account for. Yet, despite the limitation of this book not being a longitudinal analysis of the effects of training programs on their recipients, it does show that nonmaterial investments and expert knowledge production are central to China's influence in Africa.

China's Evolving Role in Africa's Security: A Discourse Analysis

A relational productive approach to power can help us unpack Beijing's increasing investment in security/defense forums, visits and exchanges between high-ranking officers, peacekeeping trainings, and joint navy drills with African counterparts despite shrinking financial disbursements. To be sure, not many Chinese official documents provide details on China-Africa defense and military cooperation, but going back to FOCAC documents is helpful.

China-Africa's third FOCAC meeting (held in 2006) resulted in an action plan that sketched multilateral cooperation plans for the upcoming three years. The document does not contain the words "security," "military," or "peacekeeping" —not even one time. This might lead one to believe that there would not be military cooperation. However, China's first Africa strategy paper, which was also released in 2006, states that

> China will promote high-level military exchanges between the two sides and actively carry out military-related technological exchanges and cooperation. It will continue to help train African military personnel and support defense and army building of African countries for their own security. (Ministry of Foreign Affairs 2006)

There are two noteworthy elements in this passage. The first is the emphasis on visits, trainings, and people-to-people exchanges and the second is the emphasis on Africa's ownership of its security cooperation with China. The discourse in this passage connotes China's security strategy in Africa with a commitment to encourage Africans to build defense for their own ecurity. This discourse feeds into China's broad foreign policy goals of portraying China as a foreign power that does not seek to build, shape, or influence Africans' security for them. Across Chinese official discourse on security-related cooperation, there is a dogmatic repetition of the principle of noninterference. Interfering in ongoing African conflicts is portrayed by Beijing as a practice that characterizes European imperialist motivations on the continent, unlike China's decolonialist aims. Chapter 2 addressed this in more detail, but here it helps to observe how Beijing endeavors to construct a narrative about China's security practices in Africa being centered around the noninterference principle and respect for sovereignty. This framing strives to position Beijing's policies in Africa as drastically different and distant from European colonial/imperial behavior.

Invoking the noninterference principle—even when not always adhering to it in practice—is part of a discursive move by Chinese policy makers to construct a conventional wisdom-like discourse that China is a different kind of power from the traditional European/Western powers and that it has no hegemonic or imperial motives in Africa. Training personnel and maintaining active exchange visits between military staff are framed in a rhetoric that insists on supporting African countries in building "their own security." This point is recurrent and common to discourses from FOCAC 2009 and 2012.

The Chinese Government appreciates the concept and practice of "Solving African Problems by Africans." It will continue to support the efforts of the AU, other regional organizations and countries concerned to solve regional conflicts and will intensify cooperation with African countries in peacekeeping theory research, peacekeeping training and exchanges and in supporting the building of peacekeeping capacity in Africa. (FOCAC 2009)

When it comes to conflict resolution, Chinese policy makers reiterate their support of "African solutions to African problems." To be sure, the support for those African solutions offered by the Chinese side comes in different forms: equipment donations, personnel trainings, logistical help (Chinese antipiracy patrols in the Gulf of Aden), and peacekeeping missions. Yet the rhetoric repeatedly associates China's strategy with a linguistic emphasis on nonintervention and sovereignty to create connotations about China being a peaceful rising power—one that wants to work *with* other countries rather than bully, shape, or control them. Furthermore, during the FOCAC meeting of 2015 (held in Johannesburg), the following policy commitments were announced:

1. The two sides will maintain the momentum of mutual visits by defense and military leaders, continue to deepen exchanges on technologies and expand personnel training and joint trainings and exercises.
2. The Chinese side continues to support the African Union, . . . that play a leading role in coordinating and solving issues of peace and security in Africa and further continues to support and advocate for African solutions to African challenges without interference from outside the continent.
3. The two sides will strengthen information and intelligence exchanges and experience sharing on security and will share this information timeously [in a timely manner] to support mutual efforts in the prevention and fight against terrorism, in particular its symptoms and underlying causes.
4. The African side appreciates China's counter-piracy efforts in the Gulf of Aden, the Gulf of Guinea and in waters off the coast of Somalia in accordance with the relevant resolutions of the UN Security Council. The two sides will strengthen cooperation on safeguarding the security of shipping routes in the waters concerned and peace and stabil-

ity in the region. In this regard, the two sides agree that emphasis should also be placed by the international community on addressing the root causes of piracy, namely poverty, underdevelopment and illegal fishing.

Security cooperation between China and African states is far more comprehensive and sophisticated in FOCAC 2015 than its previous predecessors. It also deepens China's rhetorical commitment to noninterference in African security affairs despite the extended scope of security/military cooperation. For example, the part about China's support of "African solutions to African problems without interference from outside the continent" sounds quite oxymoronic since it suggests that China, which is a power outside of the African continent, is proactively taking measures to make sure there is no outsider interference in African security issues. The paradox indicates that China is interested in simultaneously gaining power and trust and branding its engagement as benevolent. Beijing endeavors to construct a narrative about its security practices in Africa as being different from interventionist policies of many Western countries while reassuring African partners that China is ready to cooperate on all fronts, including security. Another highlight from the FOCAC 2015 agenda is that the connection between development, reducing poverty, creating better living conditions, and the promotion of peace and stability is clear. As explained in chapter 2, Chinese policy makers believe that poverty and underdevelopment are the root cause of conflict and that is now part of the FOCAC rhetoric on how to reduce conflict in Africa. The development-security nexus shows in China's security policy in Africa.

Examining China's official discourse on security/military cooperation with African states reveals the following important points. First, the discourse shows that Beijing officials insist on branding China as promoting African solutions to African problems rather than China imposing Chinese solutions to African problems. This suggests that Chinese policy makers are interested in showing that China's security presence in Africa is and will remain different than African countries' experiences with European and US militaries. Second, and relatedly, Chinese official discourse emphasizes—routinely—China's belief in the noninterference principle and in respecting African states' sovereignty. Emphasis on noninterference creates an association of China as a peaceful and nonaggressive kind of great power. Third, the agendas show that Chinese military diplomacy in Africa focuses heavily on providing training for peacekeepers and high-ranking army officials, as well as maintaining a momentum of official exchanges and visits between Chinese navy/army officials and African counterparts. These training categories are the basis of my analysis.

Guanxi in Military Diplomacy: Training Programs for African Army Staff

African leaders repeatedly lauded China for offering professionalization and technical trainings for African personnel during China Africa FOCAC meetings. In 2015, South Africa's president Jacob Zuma requested that Beijing provide even more of these training programs in his opening address.[5] From the supply side, the Chinese leadership has usually been responsive to these calls primarily because they pose a fairly low-risk, low-cost investments with high potential for expanding relational power. In September 2018, President Xi announced FOCAC 2018's goal of training 1,000 Africans, hosting 50,000 workshops, awarding 50,000 government scholarships—a big increase from 30,000 in 2015—and sponsoring 2,000 student exchanges. The 2015 FOCAC action plan promised professionalization trainings for 30,000 government scholarships, training no less than 1,000 media specialists, providing 40,000 professional training opportunities in China, sending thirty teams of senior agriculture experts to train African farmers, and establishing more agriculture demonstration centers.[6] Premier Li Keqiang vowed to "expand bilateral cooperation in personnel training, intelligence sharing and joint exercises and training, and assist Africa to enhance its capacity building in peacekeeping, counter-terrorism and counter-piracy" (Li 2014). Beijing's interest in "training" Africans spans many fields of specialization and in security these trainings mainly revolve around (a) official visits and joint drills, (b) trainings for peacekeepers, and (c) trainings of private security personnel.

Military Training Programs and Army Chief Visits

There are more than twenty academies and training institutes in China that host military trainings for foreign officers. Back in the 1950s, the University of National Defense of the Chinese People's Liberation Army (PLA) set up a department that specialized in foreign training. The department trained thousands of foreign officers from over 100 countries.[7] In 2004, the department was rebooted and launched as a new institute called the Defense Affairs Institute.[8] In the same year, the institute's first training course on international issues was attended by more than 970 senior army officers from more than forty nations. China's University of National Defense offers frequent training courses for African military officials, and according to a recent report, "every African army has at least one colonel or brigadier general who graduated from this university" (Thrall 2015, 56). The fact that every African army has at least one high-ranking officer who graduated from China's National Defense programs is significant in at least two main ways. First, this signals strong connections and guanxi networks between Chinese army officials and their African counterparts. Second, African army officers who participate in these trainings are familiarized with the modes of operation, military philosophy, and ways of understanding and responding to threats from the Chinese military perspective.

Beijing-sponsored military training programs for African military officers can be grouped in two categories. The first one consists of inviting military personnel from several African countries to China for training, and the second is delegations of Chinese military officers taking the trainings to African countries and hosting them in different places (Wang 2012, 78). An example of the first kind is provided by Wang Xuejun where "in May 2010, fifteen high-level officers from fifteen African countries attended a twelve-day training course in China jointly undertaken by the Academy of Military Sciences and Chinese National Defense University" (Wang 2012, 78). Another example is China's Ministry of National Defense hosting the first ever China-Africa Forum on Defense and Security Cooperation, which was mentioned earlier in this chapter. In this multilateral relation-building platform, military officers from over fifty African countries were invited to China for a two-week forum. Just the sheer number of African countries that sent defense attachés to China is a signal of the strong military-to-military relations that China's army officials enjoy with their African counterparts. However, what is most notable about the first defense forum was the two-week duration. There is little doubt that seminars and formal presentations were on the agenda of the forum, but they did not take up all the time set aside for the workshop. Instead, the allocation of two weeks created a space for a lot of focused and extended conversations and relations that would not be possible in circumstances where the meetings would be held over a short period of time. The forum is a space that allows for investments in relational capital and guanxi networks between Chinese and African militaries and also among African militaries. Spending two weeks touring Chinese military facilities, admiring China's military technology and intelligence, and discussing multilateral security and defense interest allowed plenty of time to build and nurture personal as well as professional connections between army officials. As explained by Chinese senior colonel Wu Qian: "Through these exercises, Chinese and foreign militaries build friendship and trust and improve military build-up and training" (China Military 2018a). The senior colonel emphasized the network-building benefits of these programs in his year-in-review remarks. He observed that "in the past year, we have expanded our network of friends and built a new pattern of international military cooperation that is all-dimensional, wide-ranging and multi-tiered. In the past year, we have conducted more realistic joint training exercises with foreign militaries, which made more contributions to the growth of combat capabilities of our troops" (China Military 2018a). In this way, and especially through repeated and consistent contact, a long-term effect of these military exchanges could show in terms of trust-building among Chinese and African military officials.

Additionally, some of the military training programs that take place in China are maintained on a routine basis. For instance, Angola dispatches thirty military staff every year to receive military training in China (see Holslag 2009b; Saferworld 2008; Wang 2012). The Malian defense ministry also requested that the Chinese military enhance military-to-military relations with the Malian army and support its training capacities (Ministry of National Defense 2016b). Botswana is another example of a government that sends annual delegations of military officers to China. Delegations of around eighteen Botswana Defense Force officials attend annual training courses in China (All Africa 2015).

The military training courses vary in their content depending on the rank of the targeted trainees. When delegations are more high-ranking officers, the courses are more about showcasing Chinese equipment, tactics, and strategies. For example, a delegation of high-ranking officers was in Beijing in May 2016 where they visited the PLA General Hospital and attended presentations on Chinese military's assistance to Africa in the fight against the Ebola epidemic.[9] For lower-ranking officials, the training programs include courses on Chinese Confucian values and how they shape civil-military relations. The Chinese Special Police Academy even hosts martial arts training courses for African Union–affiliated military officials to expose them to Chinese values and the Chinese concept of civil-military relations (Zhao 2015). Zhao Lei's report for the *China Daily* explains that the training consists of two parts: reading the Chinese classic *Art of War* by Sun Tzu and learning tactical trainings in the academy. An Algerian military officer who took part in the training reported to Zhao that "even though the tactics in it were thought out thousands of years ago, some of them can be applied to today's military affairs" (Zhao 2015). In the same report, a police colonel from the Sudan commented on the short course on counterkidnapping tactics, saying that the course "provided a clear picture of the strategies, greatly enhancing our knowledge base" (Zhao 2015). These training programs equip African participants with both conceptual knowledge on war strategies (as read in Sun Tzu's work) and also practical skills such as the one mentioned by the Sudanese participant. African trainees are exposed not only to Chinese material/military hardware but also to Chinese ways of thinking about war, security, strategy, and terrorism.

Yet it is important to note that there is another vital aspect of the trainings that happens outside of seminar rooms. Taking African defense attachés on tours of China to show them just how modernized, developed, and mighty China became within a relatively short period of time adds an important value to the experience. Touring Chinese megacities, military facilities, and other development highlights adds to China's image as a viable model for development and success and puts China in a place that others aspire to achieve. Additionally, African high-ranking military officers who graduated from one of China's host universities, or those who have been involved in intensive exchanges with Chinese counterparts create and expand opportunities for close relationship between their governments (or military apparatuses) and China. Professionalization training programs for African military attachés widen the network of relations and expand military-to-military guanxi between Chinese and African armies. Understanding this relational aspect is key to understanding how power relations are formed in China's foreign policy in Africa.

Military-to-military exchanges seek to invite "a variety of African specialists (party and government cadres, middle and high-ranking military officers and professional technical personnel) to visit China for opportunities to learn both professional and technical skills" (He 2009, 115). One of China's target outcomes is to increase opportunities for expanding close professional relations and military guanxi through frequent exchanges between African cadres and Chinese military officials. These connections, which offer spaces for expert knowledge production, widen China's web of relations and create opportunities for African military cadres to learn technical skills provided by their Chinese counterparts and be indebted for these trainings.

Another aspect of these military-to-military exchanges lies in routine port calls and repeated joint drills between Chinese and African navies. Navies that train together establish a shared working mode of operation, including how to react to crises. The Chinese coordination of joint naval trainings is an exercise in relational power building and network expansion. I have collected a list of all the exchanges and trainings sponsored by China for African military officials for fifteen months between 2017 and 2018 (see table 2) to show how extensive these exchanges are and their various subject matter. Indeed, beyond arms sales and military equipment deals, joint drills and military forums help to shape African military practices and increase Chinese-African webs of (military) relations (hence power). Still, defense and military training programs remain unidirectional. Chinese military staff does not go to African countries to learn technical or professional skills there, and African militaries do not host high-level defense workshops for Chinese counterparts. China's defense ministry and other relevant Chinese organs fund, plan, and lead the training programs and workshops for Africans.

Guanxi Power in Peacekeepers' Training Programs

A second type of military-related professionalization training programs that is sponsored by the Chinese government for African security forces is through United Nations peacekeeping operations (PKOs). Chinese peacekeeping missions engage in providing trainings for local security forces as well as for peacekeeping forces that are part of African Union–led missions. While participating in the United Nations Multidimensional Integrated Stabilization Mission in Mali and the United Nations Mission in South Sudan, Chinese peacekeepers were part of noncombat regiments for the most part. In Mali, China sent a force protection unit of 170 troops, an engineering unit of 155 troops, and a medical unit of seventy troops. More specifically, the engineering unit was tasked with road building and repairs and the installation of 667 prefabricated houses. The force protection unit conducted 2,710 armed patrols and security tasks, while the medical unit treated 8,120 patients.[10] Because of this wholistic approach to different aspects of economic, health, and social development, Chinese peacekeepers in Mali are not known for their combat skills as much as they are for the developmental approach they take. According to a former Malian prime minister,

Chinese peacekeepers are not only a force of peace; they are also a force of development. They understand that maintaining peace not only means weaponry and sending troops, but also means improving the livelihoods of locals. Chinese peacekeepers have won the hearts of the Malian people.[11]

Prime Minister Moussa Mara's statement indicates that Chinese peace-keepers play an important role in shaping China's image abroad and work diligently to convey the role of China in Africa as peaceful and nonaggres-sive. There are different formulations for peacekeepers' trainings; some involve short and long training courses on the ground while others are pre-deployment official PKO training. The long training courses usually involve Chinese PKO troops and security experts leading trainings while they are on missions in African countries. For an example of the short course trainings, the Chinese Ministry of National Defense invited a group of peacekeeping trainees to China for a weeklong training for the first time in June 2016 (Ministry of National Defense 2016d). The training covered twenty-three subjects including the peacekeeping legal framework, civilian protection, and logisti-cal support. In August 2016, the Chinese government offered a second train-ing program for seventeen senior officers from Angola, Djibouti, Kenya, Liberia, Namibia, Tanzania, Uganda, Zambia, and Zimbabwe.[12] The training courses are of crucial importance for a number of reasons. They are attrac-tive. They have implications for China's image being portrayed as a respon-sible power that cares about global peace and takes proactive measures to transfer technical skills to African peacekeepers. More than either, they al-low opportunities for basic network building, guanxi expansion, and knowl-edge production.

Though China came late to participation in peacekeeping missions be-cause of its skepticism about the sovereignty implications of multilateral col-lective action mechanisms, it has come around to become a vital support for peacekeeping missions in Africa and elsewhere (Alden 2014, 4). China is now the largest provider of peacekeeping troops among all the United Nations Security Council permanent members. Since 1990, when China started con-tributing to peacekeeping, its position has changed from blocking the mis-sions at the UN Security Council on grounds of the noninterference princi-ple to actively contributing personnel and funding to make them more successful. About 10 percent of the UN peacekeeping operations budget is funded by Beijing, making it second only to the US in terms of financing PKOs missions. As of 2018, Chinese peacekeepers have participated in nine out of the fifteen UN peacekeeping operations around the world and in seven out of eight UN missions in Africa.[13] While the number of Chinese peacekeepers worldwide is much smaller than that of Bangladesh (10,757), India (8,919), or Pakistan (10,656), China's big lead over the US, UK, France, and Russia in numbers of peacekeepers deployed in Africa means that China can still make a stronger case for its sincere commitment to friendly relations with African counterparts. Also, in 2015, President Xi Jinping announced in New York City while visiting the UN that China will train a standby force of 8,000 peacekeeping troops within the next three years. That pledge was also successfully met, and the 8,000 trainees passed their UN certifications by the summer of 2018.

Furthermore, despite there being structural limitations facing Chinese peacekeeping troops from interacting with local populations and other peacekeeping officers, Chinese peacekeepers often get positive feedback from local and UN authorities where they are stationed. Indeed, despite continuous threats against the safety of peacekeepers, Chinese troops are still found to be involved with local communities. Chinese peacekeeping troops are very creative in their involvement and receive a lot of praise for teaching and training locals simple and efficient ways to improve their living conditions. They often are praised (both by the UN and African governments) for playing a "significant" role in promoting peace and development in Ebola-hit areas in Liberia and Sierra Leone (Ministry of National Defense 2015b). The Sudanese government, for example, recognized the extra humanitarian efforts of Chinese peacekeepers and commended their interest in sharing their skills and expertise with Sudanese people.

It is not enough to equate Chinese peacekeepers' impressions on local populations, government elites, and the international community with soft power or good reputation. It is more important to contextualize these positive impressions in the guanxi relations and knowledge transfers—especially to local populations—that stem from the trainings provided by Chinese peacekeepers.

Expert Knowledge Production and Private Security Companies

Lastly, another security-related area with significant professionalization training programs by Chinese agencies is in the private security arena. In the previous section, I mentioned that the number of Chinese peacekeepers is increasing. In 2017, there were a total of 2,600 Chinese troops stationed across the world under UN mandates. By comparison, around the same time, Chinese private security groups were hiring no less than 3,200 employees abroad (Clover 2017). The numbers indicate that the Chinese government views private security companies (PSCs hereafter) favorably and allows their proliferation at about the same rate if not more than through UN-mandated peacekeeping missions. Private security contractors' activities are often found in areas that are high in both conflict risks and Chinese investments. Chinese security companies have proliferated to secure Chinese investments in Africa with the 2013 advent of the Belt and Road Initiative and its continuing expansion. Chinese state-owned enterprises that have high stakes in conflict prone zones hire PSCs for the protection of their staff and interests. This is a very creative way around China's noninterference principle (discussed in chapter 2) as it does not bring Chinese armies or soldiers into African countries. Chinese oil drilling companies and other big firms across Africa act as clients to Chinese PSCs, which for the most part do not even carry guns, but instead rely on local forces for armaments. Another advantage to PSCs is that they permit politicians to maneuver around sovereignty concerns in their ability to avoid international conflicts or diplomatic incidents in ways that armies and navies cannot. For example, "sea marshals working for Hua Xin Zhong An, a Beijing company, are able to use lethal force as a self-defense measure against pirates, according to their contracts, while their Chinese navy escorts can only fire warning shots unless their warship is under direct attack" (Clover 2017). Maritime security operations and piracy-fighting forces off the coast of Somalia were one of the earliest instances of Beijing experimenting with PSCs abroad. When executed successfully, they can achieve the goals of securing Chinese investments and Chinese citizens while being both efficient and keeping a low-key profile.

Many Chinese investments and high-stake financial ventures are present in regions of Africa with some of the highest conflict risk. The more China invests in infrastructure deals and energy extractions in these high-risk zones, the more it faces security challenges, and the more attractive PSCs involvement becomes. For example, when the Chinese state-owned China Bridge and Road Corporation was contracted for the construction of the standard gauge railway linking Kenya's capital Nairobi to the coast at Mombasa, it deployed private security personnel from the Chinese company De-Wei (Arduino 2018, 103). Part of DeWei Security Group's tasks in Kenya were several training sessions offered to Kenyan security agents in martial arts combat (Goh et. al 2017). From martial arts combat to strategic seminars about security, Chinese PSCs are sought to fill a security gap often caused by African armies being either underfunded, untrained, or understaffed.

For several years, criminal activities, insurgent attacks, or other forms of violence have targeted Chinese companies. In late January 2012, there was a double kidnapping incident where some twenty-nine Chinese workers were kidnapped by Sudanese rebels while another twenty-five were abducted in Egypt for ransom. The anti-Gaddafi regime change in Libya in 2011 led to rushed and poorly planned evacuations of approximately 35,000 Chinese nationals (Xinhua 2015). Additionally, in 2015 an attack on the Radisson Bleu Hotel in Bamako, Mali, led to the killing of Chinese state-owned enterprise top corporate officials (Reuters 2015). Had the Chinese army intervened to provide protection in such cases, China's adherence to the principle of noninterference (or at least the articulation thereof) would have been visibly breached, and the visibility of Chinese boots on the ground could frame Chinese security practices in Africa as "interventionist" and "aggressive." Engaging PSCs is a technical maneuver around the principle of noninterference, but in practice Chinese PSCs are government-owned and government-controlled. They are not truly private and function at the command of the CCP as much as the PLA would.

Chinese PSCs, both operating inside the country and abroad, are rather new. It was not until 2010 that the government issued a law to authorize and regulate the establishment of PSCs in China.[14] These companies are typically formed by retired military officers and work closely with the authorities. Han Fangming, the deputy director of the Foreign Affairs Committee of the Chinese People's Political Consultative Conference, has urged the establishment of a Chinese version of the US private security company Blackwater (now rebranded as Academi).[15] Han Fangming proposed that Chinese PSCs (such as Shandong Huawei Group) should model themselves after American PSC expertise abroad, and then, "when the time is right, the government might allow qualified companies" to expand internationally in order to provide armed protection for Chinese firms operating in risk zones.[16] Although Han's policy recommendation was criticized heavily by government and public opinion for the potential for a high risk of incidents on foreign soil coupled with private contractors' inexperience in African contexts, Chinese PSCs have increased their activity in Africa. For instance, the *Wall Street Journal* reported that "in Sudan, a dozen armed Chinese private security contractors have joined more than 1,000 Sudanese troops in the current rescue effort, according to Sudanese military officials."[17] In addition, PSC Genghis

Security Advisory was reported by the Xinhua News Agency to have sent 400 security personnel to guard Chinese companies abroad, including in Algeria and Libya. The report also mentioned that Genghis Security Advisory also engaged in training local forces (Xinhua News 2012). As expressed by Feng Xia to *China Daily*, it is the responsibility of host countries to ensure the safety of foreign officials and other representatives. However, when a given host country is not able to fulfill this obligation, Feng continued, then there should be collaboration between the two concerned countries to "reach an agreement to dispatch security forces to train local forces and help them build capacity" (Xu 2012). Indeed, this model is part of what's become known as private security with Chinese characteristics in which one of the characteristics is "transfers of security technologies and capabilities" via professionalization trainings (Arduino 2018, 17). Trainings of private security forces, unlike military-to-military exchanges, have to happen in the host countries because the terrains and contexts are unique.

In *Security beyond the State*, Rita Abrahamsen and Michael Williams identified that "South Africa has one of the world's most highly privatized and globalized security sectors" (2011, 98). Despite record-high numbers and South Africa having a massive private security assemblage, the introduction of Chinese business and Chinese interests created even more demand for PSCs. This led to an urgent need for training more private security personnel. In describing what the training entails, Feng Xia explained that expert teams are sent from China to learn from local security forces about the environment they will be operating in, and only after being acclimated with the terrain do they generate simulation exercises and technical trainings for the local trainees. China's first overseas joint-security company was established in 2014 in an agreement with South Africa between the Shandong Huawei Security group and Raid Tactical Pty. The joint venture includes training courses and exchange of expertise.[18] Here the questions that interest me are what is the value added of Beijing's investments in training private security staff for African states and what are the implications of these trainings for China's security policy in Africa?

Leander (2005) investigates the role played by private military companies in shaping the discourse and policy understanding of security.[19] By drawing on Lukes's faces of power (mainly the second and third faces), she finds that such companies "shape the interpretations of security through their non-negligible role in training and consulting within the armed forces and the state in matters of security both at home and abroad" (2005, 817). As explained by Feng's statement above, Chinese PSCs in Africa offer technical trainings in areas such as equipment use, fighting strategies, and other trainings. During these trainings, like trainings by formal military officers, the production and sharing of Chinese understanding of security and its transfer to African counterparts is made possible. By socializing African security forces in Chinese norms, expert knowledge, and understanding of what security is and how to counter security threats, Chinese and African militaries can communicate on the same wavelength with regard to international peace and security. Military-focused trainings are spaces for the normalization of the discourse on China's noninterference principle as well as for the dissemination of Chinese expert knowledge on private security practice. As expressed by Leander (2005, 817), "'technical' training shapes security discourses. By focusing the attention of the trainees on the use of specific types of equipment when reacting to situations of a certain kind, it is probable that such situations will be interpreted in similar ways in the future and the response will be similar." Chinese PSCs do train their African counterparts to use certain equipment as a reaction to certain situations, and African private security teams may become consumers of Chinese-manufactured equipment that's used in the training. Leander shows that private security trainees' often end up becoming big consumers of military equipment and hardware used in the trainings. This shows that offering security trainings has a commercial benefit as it serves as a marketing opportunity for states' arms industries. This is very important for China's military trainings for African armies and has important ramifications in explaining how China became a top arms exporter. Yet this is not the whole story. My framework shows the power dynamics at play in these (typically unidirectional) trainings and their implications for African military apparatuses becoming consumers not only of Chinese military hardware but of expert knowledge.

Without denying that Beijing-sponsored PSC trainings for Africans allow China the opportunity to market Chinese military equipment and hardware to African partners, it is important to note that from a market-driven analysis, low and middle-tier Chinese PSCs cost significantly less than their US or European counterparts.[20] To give an example, Karthie Lee estimates that hiring a Chinese twelve-man detachment in East Africa costs about $570 per day whereas the rates for Western companies go up to $4,000 per day for a four-man escort (Lee 2014). The point here is that there are other gains, besides the material ones, for Chinese PSC operations in Africa. Chinese PSCs are not very competitive in Europe, much less in the US. In fact, they learn a lot and mimic tactics from their European and US counterparts. In the context of Africa's security landscape, however, Chinese PSCs get to be experts, trainers, and providers of knowledge about security. These gains are more valuable than the price of escort teams.

These gains can further be explained by looking at training programs from the prism of relational productive power and expanding China's relational influence in the continent by adding a layer of human capital investment and knowledge dissemination via the staff of PSCs. In Anna Leander's account, even the on-site technical trainings, which usually include specialized courses and consulting, are designed to "explicitly shape the security understanding of those of who take the courses" (Leander 2005, 817). For Leander, it is important to highlight that trainings shape the way security is understood because this has material consequences on decisions regarding what equipment to buy and how much of it to deploy. In my argument, the focus is to problematize the knowledge transfers themselves as sites of power building. By taking power to be relational, the lack of Chinese drone bases and boots on the ground is not understood as evidence of China's marginal role in security and defense activities in Africa. Instead, relational power highlights the importance of analyzing nonmaterial investments (such as those in human resources evidenced in PSC staff, PKO, or military personnel trainings) as being just as important as investments in military and drone bases in accounting for how powerful a foreign power is. Indeed, by taking defense-related professionalization trainings as steps toward expanding China's relational network in African countries, we get a better understanding of the operations and functions of China's rising power in Africa.

How Effective Are Beijing's Investments in Security Training Programs?

From a relational perspective on power, expanding the networks of social relations and successfully manipulating networks are the main target of power. Also, processes of knowledge production and dissemination are the mechanisms through which relational power is built. It follows then that taking training opportunities and military exchanges as spaces for expert knowledge production suggests that Chinese values and discourses may be diffused to African partners.

Finnemore and Sikkink (1998, 910–13) offer a good insight into how educational programs, the dissemination of official policy, and censorship are ways by which the dominant state and secondary states can manipulate public opinion and persuade their audience to adopt new norms. Although their argument does not problematize far enough how power suffuses these educational programs, it nonetheless offers a helpful framework to unpack US influence on Japan's military education in the aftermath of World War II. The US changed the norms of military education in Japan from promoting ultranationalist to prodemocratic norms. Thus, there was interference not directly or coercively on the material capabilities of Japan's military, but rather on the mentalities of high-level officials through training and military-to-military diplomacy (Wang 2003, 107). Evidence of governmental techniques of the President Harry Truman administration vis-à-vis Japan's postwar military was that it did not run an agenda of weakening an aggressive Japanese military. Rather, it emphasized the restoration and strengthening of Japan's industrial and military strength.

Moreover, Carol Atkinson argues that "[US] military engagement activities have been designed to serve a normative persuasive function that explicitly aims to alter the political identity of the engaged states" (Atkinson 2006, 509). Indeed, in *Military Soft Power*, Atkinson primarily argues that military power does not have to only be viewed from the lens of hard/material power (Atkinson 2014, 11). Instead, she makes the case that military educational exchanges, trainings, and high-ranking official visits all play an important, albeit nonmaterial, role in projecting power and influence. Military exchanges are spaces for military officers from different countries to build social and professional networks: "The friendships and professional contacts between foreign officers studying in the United States and their U.S. counterparts certainly help to improve the ability of the U.S. military to work with allied nations as well as potential coalition partners" (Atkinson 2014, 4). Professional and personal networks promote the development of (in this case) US-centric norms, namely democratic values. What Atkinson observes in her book is not limited to or exceptional about the US military but is a process of socialization that is bound to happen in any similar training and educational exchange programs.

In fact, Atkinson and other scholars have observed similar socialization processes in training programs hosted by armies from the Soviet Union during the Cold War. The processes of socialization happen through different mechanisms, among which is transmission of cultural understandings and language. As Hannah Pitkin pointed out and Atkinson (2014, 20) recalls, "learning one's language is an intensely social activity. It is a process not only of learning words and grammar, but how to use this knowledge appropriately with one's community." I have mentioned above several examples of African navy and army officials, from Nigeria and South Africa, for example, who are trained in Mandarin language courses. Through these opportunities, similar patterns of socialization and norm diffusion mechanisms can be expected to suffuse China-Africa military-to-military diplomacy. In the same way that findings show that US or Soviet Union–sponsored military training programs facilitate a great deal of norm diffusion and expertise sharing, China-Africa military trainings and military-to-military diplomacy could be expected to, over time, influence how African military leaders view China's contribution to the continent's security matters. Yet here my approach differs slightly from that of Atkinson. That is to say, I agree with Atkinson's problematization of views on military power as necessarily coercive and repressive. Her studies show that even the seemingly most coercive power/security apparatus (the military) has a soft, constructivist aspect to it that material/realist approaches to power are not able to account for. Yet in my analysis I go one step further in that I problematize the mechanisms of the socialization that occurs during unidirectional training programs between Chinese trainers and African trainees. Applying my relational productive power lenses to the processes of socialization that Atkinson speaks about shows that socialization occurs through the production and dissemination of Chinese expert knowledge on peacekeeping, private security, and other security-related skills to their African counterparts.

Keeping in mind that the contexts are different, one could draw lessons by analogy from past studies on the effectiveness of military training programs to understand the case of China-Africa security cooperation. For example, Yale Richmond draws on a study by a former KGB general, Oleg Kalugin, who spent a year as an exchange student at Columbia University in 1958–59. Kalugin noted the importance of such programs in undermining the ideational basis of the Soviet communist system. In an interview he granted Richmond in 1997, Kalugin observed that "exchanges were a Trojan Horse in the Soviet Union. They played a tremendous role in the erosion of the Soviet system. They opened up a closed society" (Richmond 2005, 352). There is no doubt that bringing African high-ranking officials to China for training is also an opportunity to show them how far China has come with development, and to trigger their curiosity to learn more about China's know-how. Along similar lines, Atkinson argues that the influence of these education exchange programs is subtler (2006, 2) and that these programs are an effective conveyor of ideas and norms. She draws on Arthur Miller's

(2006) extensive interviews of participants in several US government-funded person-to-person contact programs in Georgia, Ukraine, Bosnia-Herzegovina, and Kazakhstan. One of Miller's most interesting findings is that while foreign aid funding does not promote democratic values and behaviors per se, one military educational exchange program, the International Military Education and Training Program, produced significantly more pro-Western attitudes and increased transnational communication (Atkinson 2006, 510). The gist of the finding is that military-to-military exchange programs are efficient because they target somewhat highly ranked officials who probably have a say in decision-making. Making an impact on these officials opens a door to making an impact on policy making.

Training programs provide opportunities for military-to-military socialization and transfer of expert knowledge including the case of the Chinese military and its African counterparts. Although I have not had the chance to test the actual outcomes of these trainings, I still examined different Chinese military-to-military diplomacy practices in Africa and I found them consistent with practices analyzed in the literature examining the US context. Indeed, many of Atkinson's findings go beyond the context of US military diplomacy to analyze the scope condition of the trainings. For instance, Atkinson (2006, 510) speaks in general when she argues that "while states primarily rely on their militaries to provide 'hard power,' military organizations might also exert a socializing or normative influence across borders as they frequently interact with each other, for example, by attending training and education programs together." Such a statement does not only apply to the case of US military diplomacy but could reasonably be expected to apply in other cases, including Chinese military diplomacy in Africa.

CONCLUSION

There are three platforms for security/military human resource development investments. Chinese investments in human resource development in the security sector through training for (1) high-ranking military officials, (2) peacekeeping troops, (3) and PSC agents are platforms and spaces for China's relational network to expand in Africa by sharing its expertise on security. When the groundwork of diplomatic and professional relations is developed, over time one can expect security partnerships to solidify and trust-building mechanisms to become stronger between high-ranking military officials from China and African states. At some level, relational power can even help us understand the more material manifestations of power in China's security practices in Africa. To be sure, with building trust and enlarging networks with African military cadres, it is easier to move the collaboration to an even higher level of security presence. With this type of relational power, China's launch of its first ever overseas naval base in 2017 is not a surprise. China's base in Djibouti does not create a powerful presence for China in the Horn of Africa but represents the effects of an already strong relational diplomacy between high-ranking officials from Djibouti and China. The base is just one example of the culmination of strong bilateral relations and one can expect to see more of these things happen in China-Africa relations.

Peace and security are now part and parcel of Sino-African cooperation, evidence of which can be found in the FOCAC action plans. Despite the fact that early editions of FOCAC were reticent toward military and security diplomacy, the more China's trade and business interests grew in Africa, the more its military engagement in the continent became unavoidable. The question was then to figure out a way to fulfill China's military objectives in Africa without coming off as a belligerent, interfering power. Therefore, even though clinging to the noninterference principle in practice lessened, clinging to it in rhetoric increased. Over the last decade, China's engagement in Africa's peace and security grew to become more substantive and wider in scope. Under Hu Jintao, China vowed to "deepen cooperation with the AU and African countries in peace and security in Africa, provide financial support for the AU peace-keeping missions in Africa and the development of the African Standby Force, and train more officials in peace and security affairs and peace-keepers for the AU" (China Times 2012). During Xi Jinping's presidency, China's foreign policy developed a more confident voice and its presence in military Africa grew even stronger. Emphasizing professionalization trainings for high-ranking military officials as well as holding academic symposia cohosted by Chinese and African think tanks became a hallmark of China-Africa security relations.

Several Chinese-sponsored programs are designed to promote the exchange of party officials between China and African states, others comprise high-ranking military official trainings in China, the training of peacekeeping troops, and even more recently private security taskforce trainings. This chapter examined a sample of these professionalization training programs. The trainings consist of seminars on theories of security, modules on peacekeeping, civil/military relations, and skill sessions in combat, martial arts, and other fighting aspects. These professionalization trainings not only provide socializing opportunities between high-ranking military officials but also allow for knowledge production and norm diffusion of Chinese ways of thinking and reacting to security threats. In my analysis, I take each one of these three practices as spaces and venues for Chinese expert knowledge to be produced and transferred to African counterparts. In all of these trainings, African personnel are the trainees and the Chinese are the experts. There is no reciprocation of African ways of viewing or responding to threats, or technical know-how to be transferred to Chinese counterparts. This goes to show the official discourse is mostly performative in that it aims at creating an image of China that is an equal, friendly, and nonaggressive partner of African states.

To be clear, this chapter is not arguing that China-Africa security strategies are necessarily unique or unprecedented in the larger picture of big powers' foreign policy conduct. The US Army provides regular trainings to African militaries through the Africa Command and its counterterrorism missions. British and French soldiers have also provided extensive trainings for African troops. China is not at all a pathbreaker in this regard. Rather, what's innovative here is the amalgamation of all kinds of people-to-people interactions and human capital investments that all together formulate the backbone of China's Africa policy and set this policy as different from its Western powers' competitors.

Finally, it is also important to note that China's military and private security forces are eager to learn from their US and European counterparts. As mentioned earlier in this chapter, China is a top importer of weapons (with France and Russia being its top suppliers), demonstrating its positionality as both a supplier of large weapons (with its top clients being developing countries: Pakistan and Bangladesh) and a consumer of foreign-made weapons. China's PSCs also benefit a great deal from Western expertise. Blackwater's founder, Erik Prince, was recruited to run China's security firm Global Frontier Systems, which trains China's elite PSCs teams. Chinese PSCs have also collaborated with British and German PSCs in Southern Africa on numerous occasions when they failed to get the results aimed for. Chinese peacekeepers also seek training abroad—often in Europe. Chinese troops deployed to Mali under the UN's Multidimensional Integrated Stabilization Mission in Mali underwent EU-run training to learn about the history and context of the conflict. Yet, despite these examples, in Africa, China exports weapons, provides trainings for military officers, and shares combat lessons with security agents. In Africa, China has the opportunity to be a supplier rather than a consumer of security practices and military technology.

CHAPTER FIVE

Guanxi in Public Diplomacy and Trainings for Journalists

IN SEPTEMBER 2018, Azad Essa was informed that his weekly column for South Africa's Independent Media Conglomerate (the second largest media company in the country) was canceled following an article he published on Uyghur detention camps in Xingjian. In an 2018 article for *Foreign Policy*, Essa revealed that two of Independent Media's shareholders are the China International Television Corporation and the China-Africa Development Fund. He argued that media investments are what gives Chinese actors censorship and silencing capabilities in a South African media outlet. Silencing negative media coverage is only one example of many techniques that are part of a Chinese state-led multibillion-dollar public relations campaign to, in the words of Xi Jinping, "tell China's story well and properly disseminate China's voice" (Xi cited in Bandurski 2017). Until the story of Essa's canceled column broke, China's media strategy in Africa did not get much attention beyond references to *China Daily*'s "Africa Weekly" edition or China's monopoly of digital TV sets in African markets.

Despite recent growing attention to China's telecommunication infrastructure investments in Africa, one important aspect that remains underanalyzed and undertheorized is China's investments in media-centered professionalization programs. Both through FOCAC and the Belt and Road Initiative platforms, the Chinese government is increasing scholarship allocations for journalists from the Global South to visit China for workshops and trainings. Analyzing China's intangible investments such as providing trainings for thousands of journalists annually is a central piece to understanding China's power building in Africa (and beyond). One of the main returns of investments of the training workshops is that they facilitate promoting strong guanxi with African journalists who are responsible for reporting the China-Africa story. This is especially valuable for China's national interest as Chinese foreign policy makers spare no effort to brand China's rise as peaceful and nonthreatening. Chinese government officials are strongly skeptical of Western-dominated news outlets in African countries. China's approach to countering Western-media-led negative branding of China-Africa is knowledge production and network building with African media experts.

In brief, this chapter argues that Chinese investments in telecommunication equipment in Africa and diffusing Chinese TV channels to African televisions are not the end goal of China's media diplomacy. Instead, they are investments that complement the hallmark of China's media diplomacy in Africa, building social capital. Material investments in telecommunication, I argue, serve the objective of multiplying the layers of relationality and connectivity between China and Africa. In fact, China's investments in Africa's media landscape are less than a decade old and the first cooperation policies can be traced to the third Forum on China-Africa Cooperation held in 2006. In the last five to ten years of Chinese foreign policy toward Africa, Chinese government officials have taken serious measures to provide media content in Africa and diffuse a positive narrative on China-Africa relations.

Chinese foreign policy officials insist that without China providing alternative media narratives, Western media will continue to monopolize the content of Africa's media landscape and portray China in ways that will harm China's reputational objectives.[1] One of the Chinese government's pressing (and ongoing) priorities is to counterbalance the Western media's portrayal of China as a hawkish, self-interested power extracting African resources, engaging in predatory investments, and setting up debt traps for Africa.[2] Yet Chinese official rhetoric interestingly brands its involvement in narrative-making and knowledge-producing as an ethical obligation by Chinese and Africans to limit colonial legacies and block the lingering imperial presence in the African media landscape. Chinese official discourse draws on parallels between China's and Africa's colonial experiences. It parallels the general trend examined in chapter 4 on producing and diffusing conventional wisdom about equal relations, shared histories, and common aspirations for future development between Chinese and African counterparts. Like the previous chapter, this chapter finds that China's rhetorical commitments to equal partnerships with Africans does not get beyond the rhetorical aspect. On the ground, Chinese journalists and media trainers act as the experts with models, values, and knowledge to pass on to African counterparts.

Broadly speaking, there are two approaches followed by the Chinese government in order to "tell China's story well." One approach is direct/material, and it consists in launching Chinese state-owned media branches and material media infrastructure in Africa. Examples of this approach include the Chinese government opening a branch of its national television, China Central Television (CCTV), in Kenya in 2012; launching a weekly African edition of the newspaper *China Daily*; opening offices for the Xinhua News Agency and China Radio International; supplying radio transmitters to local radio stations; and assisting African media's switch from analog to digital broadcasting. Yet perhaps the most visible of all of these is the giant media hub that the Chinese government built in Nairobi with CCTV headquarters being the largest foreign media station on the continent.[3] The second approach is people-centered investments and human resource development investments targeting African media staff and journalists. Examples of this approach include African journalists and media experts being invited to participate in trainings and workshops sponsored by the Chinese state. The two approaches, material and people-centered, are not mutually exclusive. One informs the other: the ideational is material and the material makes the ideational feasible. Yet, since the majority of scholarship on this topic has focused almost exclusively on the material aspect, I refer to the separate categories without buying into their mutual exclusivity.

At every FOCAC gathering, the Chinese government offers increasing numbers of scholarships and professionalization trainings for African journalists. Opportunities to attend trainings are also extended to high-level government officials who work in ministries of communication or in some public relations capacity. Over the years, the accumulation of guanxi between Chinese and African journalists has had a far more lasting impact than the Chinese state-owned media running an Africa channel from Nairobi. This approach is long term, and its returns are, even if less tangible, still very valuable since they increase China's relational power by enlarging the media and journalism networks and public diplomacy guanxi with African counterparts.

Most of the scholarship examining China's media strategy in Africa looks almost exclusively to the direct approach to analyze the content and reporting strategies of the China Global Television Network (CGTN), China Radio International, Xinhua, and *China Daily*'s "Africa Weekly" edition, or to examine China's investments in buying shares of African media outlets.[4] Little attention is paid to the indirect approach of human capital investment programs and network expansions via trainings for African journalists in China and programs that enable African media experts to obtain higher education degrees from Chinese universities. I argue that this is a mistake: looking at media-related professionalization trainings as network expansion (guanxi), knowledge production, and norm diffusion shows their efficacy, compared to the relative unpopularity of direct, material means of intervention. As with the case of military attachés, training workshops and seminars for journalists build new and intensify existing webs of friendly relations and guanxi connections. They are spaces for knowledge production aiming to correct what is perceived as Westernized and biased negative views of China's influence in Africa. Human capital investments in media diplomacy and journalism not only expand guanxi relations between Chinese and Africa media experts, the seminar components of these training promote Chinese values, history, and norms about reporting.

To show this, the chapter is structured as follows. It begins by examining the articulation of official discourse around "telling China's story well" and its context in China-Africa media relations. This section draws on FOCAC action plan texts to evaluate the centrality and growing importance of media-related human capital investments. Analysis of the discourse shows an explicit rejection by Chinese foreign policy makers of Western news media portrayals of China's conduct in Africa, and a firm stance to counter negative Western portrayals of China-Africa. The chapter continues by providing a brief background of China's direct, material media and public diplomacy in Africa. In this section, I suggest some potential reasons why this material/direct approach is far from being successful in building a positive image of China in Africa. The third section turns to the ideational/indirect approach. I outline briefly, based on extant scholarship and my own fieldwork observations, the different types of capacity-building programs that China offers for African journalist professionals and academics. Using a relational productive power framework, I show how these trainings are spaces to socialize African journalists in Chinese norms and values of journalism (such as reporting with a positive rather than critical spin on stories involving the central government). The chapter concludes by demonstrating that guanxi and relational power are advantageous compared to the limited and limiting concept of soft power which is typically deployed to analyze overlapping areas between ideational and material investments.

TELLING CHINA'S STORY WELL: DISCOURSE ANALYSIS

To compete against the Western narratives I discussed above, the Chinese government is seeking platforms to introduce Chinese culture, history, and narratives in African media outlets. Cultural influence and a news broadcasting footprint are critical achievements for any emerging power, including China. Yet it was not until the third Forum on China-Africa Cooperation (FOCAC III) in 2006 that media cooperation was listed for the first time as an agenda item in China's foreign policy in Africa. The summit action plan announced that the following policy points:

1. Support multi-level exchanges and cooperation in various forms between their press authorities and exchange more visits between media groups.
2. The Chinese side will continue to host workshops for African correspondents and invite heads of press authorities and media groups as well as correspondents from Africa to China to exchange views.
3. The two sides agreed to expand cooperation in radio and television broadcasting. China will focus on helping African countries train radio and television staff.

Exchange trips and workshops for African journalists to visit China have been part of China-Africa media relations for a long time. Still, even beyond FOCAC III, training journalists was strictly unidirectional with African journalists participating in workshops organized by Chinese universities and professional institutions. The lack of reciprocity is indicative of the power dynamics that permeate media-focused trainings in China-Africa relations. Inherently, African journalists are in China to learn, to be impressed, and to receive capacity-building expertise from their Chinese experts. Chinese journalists do not get socialized in African journalism values, receive training in African institutions, or get to tour African cities in any systematic way. FOCAC 4 and 5 were not distinctly different.

At the 2015 edition of FOCAC—the Johannesburg Summit—Chinese and African partners discussed the need to improve China-Africa media relations by increasing professionalization training programs. The action plan notes that both sides agreed to the following points:

1. Continue to implement the China-Africa Press Exchange Centre program, continue to hold training and capacity building seminars for

African countries' news officials and reporters, promote more exchanges and mutual visits between Chinese and African journalists
and press professionals, train 1,000 African media professionals each
year and support exchanges of reporters by more media organizations.

2. The Chinese side will actively provide technology support and personnel training for the digitalization of radio and TV services and
industrial development in Africa.

3. The Forum on China-Africa Media Cooperation serves as an important platform for China-Africa media cooperation and cultural
exchanges. The two sides agree to institutionalize the Forum as an
official sub-forum of FOCAC.

FOCAC 2015 increased the number of training opportunities for media
experts from 2012. The agenda shows similarity with previous FOCAC events
in that there is no reciprocation in the setup of media and communications
trainings. The Chinese side offers trainings, technological support, and
maintenance workshops, whereas African participants are invited to dis-
cover China, learn about it, and learn about Chinese journalism. There are
no systematic structures for level-field exchanges about media narrative and
journalism models.

During the 2018 edition of FOCAC, cooperation on media mimicked language from the previous action plans and continued with similar programs,
emphasizing exchanges and trainings. The proposed agenda pledged that
"the two sides will establish a China-Africa media cooperation network,"
that China will "continue the China-Africa Press Exchange Center program," and that it also "continue to hold training and capacity building
seminars for African countries' media officials and journalists, promote
more exchanges and mutual visits between Chinese and African media personnel."[5] Overall a common thread to all action plans analyzed in this chapter is that Chinese officials reiterate a discourse of mutual learning and coproduction of knowledge while at the same time the Chinese side
unidirectionally trains African journalists and media experts in Chinese institutions. The routinized articulation of China's media activities in Africa
to linguistic elements such as "non-interference," "friendships," and "equality" is a very important step for Chinese foreign policy making for shaping a
common-sense story about China as Africa's equal partner.

Telling China's Story Well: From Discourse to Policies

China has promised to up its efforts in human resource training for Africa. Invitations have been extended to a variety of African specialists to visit China for opportunities to learn both professional and technical skills as well as get an up close and personal feel for China's development experience.

(HE 2007, 28)

FOCAC agendas have explicitly expressed Chinese foreign policy's intentions to establish media outlets in Africa in order to access the "discursive field" and have a voice on how to portray China-African relations. The Chinese government started investing heavily ($6.6 billion) in a public relations campaign abroad to focus efforts on building a positive image of China in the Global South and "telling China's story well." Chinese foreign policy makers are concerned about the (mis)representation and portrayal of China's foreign policies in Western media and the negative image that Western media outlets in Africa create about China. The goal behind such investments, as expressed in FOCAC action plans, is for Beijing to counterbalance the overwhelming influence of Western media outlets in the African continent.[6] Some of the main tools for this public diplomacy include cultural exchanges and media representation. This West-East competition for a discursive field has been explicitly stressed by several academics and professionals from China:

> There is a battle for mindshare being waged in the field of international news nowadays. The USA (CNN-CNBC, VOA and several channels on pay TV bouquets), the UK (the BBC), France (France 24 and TV5 Monde Afrique, CFI, RFI, Canal+, AFP), Canada, Germany (Deutsche Welle TV and Radio) and Russia (Russia Today) are broadcasting heavily in Africa in a race for audience share, along with Al Jazeera. (Zhang 2014, 3)

Similarly, Minister Cai Fuchao explained that "by means of filing more reports on China and Africa, we hope to promote mutual understanding, and balance some of the biased opinions about us in the West" (*Beijing Review* 2012). Beijing invests billions of dollars in this "balancing" campaign through a combination of establishing news media branches across African countries and increasing exchange opportunities for journalists and students of journalism.

Telling China's Story via Material Media Investments: Launching CGTN-Africa

China Central Television (CCTV) was established in 1958 but was not made available outside mainland China until 1992 through the CCTV-4 channel. In 2000, CCTV-9 became China's international news reporting channel broadcasting in English but that was not enough to cater to African audiences in a way that reflected their booming relations with China in the aftermath of the first FOCAC in 2000. In 2009, Beijing announced plans to launch a TV broadcasting station in East Africa and established a training initiative to urge Chinese institutions to host African journalists for short- and long term visits. A few years later, the first CCTV-Africa office was launched in January 2012 with programs in English, Chinese, and Swahili and made Nairobi the hub of Chinese media operations in Africa.[7] The Chinese state-owned station consists of a team of no less than 200 employees from China as well as Kenya and from across the continent.[8] However, until recently and despite the reasonable financial resources deployed, CCTV Africa (which was renamed China Global Television Network, or CGTN, in 2017) broadcasts no more than three hours of originally produced content per day, an increase from the original agreement of one hour per day.[9]

The presence of CGTN Africa and the Xinhua News Agency allows Chinese media to counter and compete with the Western media presence in Africa. As stated by two expert analysts, "China's media expansion can be seen as an attempt to manage overseas and African perceptions of China's role in Africa. Rather than simply refuting Western media reports, China's state-led media can now produce their own content for African consumption and let Africans decide for themselves" (Hanauer and Morris 2014, 74). Chinese officials are increasingly vocal about their disagreement with Western news agencies' tendency to "contain" China and portray its conduct in Africa in an alarming overtone. Clearly, there is a strong focus on persuading African audiences that there is more to China-Africa relations than what transpires in Western media's discourse. However, despite aggressive financial investments and strong motivations, CGTN Africa suffers major challenges among African audiences. The TV station performs weakly when it comes to audience ratings, and it does not seem to be effectively competing against the BBC or CNN as a viable alternative.[10] Due to these low ratings, CGTN Africa and *China Daily* are limited in their ability to increase Beijing's image-building or power building. In many ways, CGTN Africa as well as *China Daily* are known among African audiences to be heavily controlled and censored by the Chinese government, they are seen by many as tools of Chinese propaganda, and they are not taken as reliable sources for independent information.

CGTN Africa receives particularly scathing criticism from African netizens and general critics when there are scandals involving Chinese illegal activity somewhere in Africa and the news station remains silent about such incidents. For example, in 2016, a scandal emerged in Nairobi around Chinese restaurant owners who refused service to local or African patrons after 5:00 p.m. (as an alleged safety measure). CGTN Africa, which is located in Nairobi, chose not to cover the story. There was probably not a way it could have been reported with a positive narrative, and portraying the Chinese diaspora in Kenya in a negative light was probably not in the best interest of "telling China's story well." All the other major news media outlets covered the story but CGTN Africa, and this contributed to discrediting the station as an independent and reliable source. Likewise, in 2014 Kenyan authorities arrested a group of seventy-seven hackers, most of whom were Chinese (some from Taiwan). After the hackers stood trial in Nairobi, a group of Taiwanese hackers were acquitted and deported. At the airport, Kenyan authorities refused to put the Taiwanese hackers on flights to Taiwan, making the argument that Taiwan is part of China and thereby forced the group—using violence—to board planes to China. The Taiwanese diaspora in Nairobi denounced the abduction, arguing that Chinese authorities interfered in Kenya's decision-making in order to isolate Taiwan and scare Taiwanese nationals. CGTN Africa again chose not to cover the deportation although it did cover the original arrest in 2014, yet all major international news media outlets covered this incident. CGTN Africa is based in Nairobi and has the language skills and cultural expertise to report on that particular incident, but it chose not to do so.

CGTN-Africa's reluctance to cover sensitive issues like the ones stated above (among many others) has given it a reputation for being too soft on topics that are critical of China and not serious enough competitor to CNN, BBC, Al Jazeera, and others. Yet there is still value to CGTN despite its not being as successful as imagined. Although it is not very successful in covering news independently or in attracting a large enough audience, I argue that it is best to make sense of CGTN-Africa from a relational lens. China's direct media strategy—including launching CGTN Africa, *China Daily*'s "Africa Weekly" edition, and other outlets—is best seen as adding layers of network nodes and expanding guanxi relations. Because CGTN Africa has, so far, not been effective in producing knowledge that's useful to the Chinese national goal of "telling China's story well," Chinese policy makers are supplementing the direct media strategy with investments in forming African journalists. The Chinese government sponsors training programs for African journalists in hopes of getting them to see China-Africa relations from a positive perspective following the highly curated professionalization training programs they participate in.

Telling China's Story via Human Capital Investments: Training Journalists

According to the World Press Freedom Index, China ranks 176 out of 180 countries. Given the central government's restrictions and strict censorship practices, journalism studies in China is not typically known to be a destination for high-quality journalism training. On the contrary, because of the authoritarian grip of the ruling party over news media outlets, the high levels of internet censorship, and government surveillance of both public and private media outlets, Chinese universities do not compete in international communication and journalism studies and do not attract much prestige. Yet this is changing rapidly with the introduction of scholarships and trainings for journalists from different developing countries—namely African—to China. Indeed, professionalization training programs for African journalists and students of journalism sponsored by China are evolving rapidly. They include long-term training programs, short-term training programs, as well as annual workshops/summits and frequent visits for high-level staff of state-owned media outlets in China and African countries. It should be noted that most African countries outrank China in the World Press Freedom Index and several of them are highly ranked, such as twenty-three for Ghana, twenty-six for Namibia, twenty-eight for South Africa, fifty for Senegal, while others score a little less highly: ninety-six for Kenya and 136 for Algeria.[11]

Short-Term Training Programs for Reporters and Journalists

Short-term professionalization training programs for journalists are typically held over a period of ten to fourteen days where the participants start in Beijing but take guided tours to other big cities and some rural towns. The workshops are usually held in small groups organized and funded in collaboration between the Ministry of Education and at a Beijing-based institute or university. The selection of the participants is usually handled at the level of the Chinese embassies in respective countries. When visiting delegations arrive to China, their visit schedules follow a similar pattern to the party-to-party exchange visits or military staff delegations. They are a mix of seminars, skills training workshops, a cultural tour, guided trips to several cities across China, and visits to relevant facilities and media corporate headquarters (as discussed below). The short-term workshops aim at introducing the invited reporters to experience China, travel to its ultramodern cities, and see the less developed rural areas. Taking reporters through contrasting areas of China both highlight China's developmental success story and the resemblances between rural towns in African countries and in China. Tours taking place in Beijing typically include major cultural edifices and sightseeing sites such as the Forbidden City, the Great Wall, and the National Stadium (also known as the Bird's Nest).

Taking journalists through guided tours across China feeds into several people-to-people and relational power objectives. For one, African journalists can see with their own eyes that China is still a developing country given the underdevelopment that exists in several rural provinces. This solidifies the narrative of China as a peaceful, nonimperial developing country with similar aspirations and development goals as African countries. Yet, at the same time, showing the contrast between the ultradeveloped Beijing and the underdeveloped cities shows the success story of China's development model and creates, in the imaginary of visitors, concrete images of the results of the model. Taking African journalists on cultural sightseeing tours across China aims to show them the "real" China so that they can tell the China story well in their narratives of China-Africa relations.

Another component of the short training programs is to visit the headquarters of StarTimes, which is China's media giant, located in Beijing. The visit usually involves touring the facility and taking a look at the highly advanced equipment used in the production room. Clearly, besides the cultural component of these trips, there is a commercial one where Chinese-made technology and communications hardware is advertised to the participants. From talking to a CGTN-Africa news anchor from Kenya about the training workshop she participated in, I learned that sometimes there is a tech support seminar as part of the training schedule. The seminar shows the participants how to use highly advanced technology, so that African technicians get familiarized with the equipment and learn how to troubleshoot and service it. The news anchor expressed how highly impressed she was with the technological hardware. Yet she said that the training was irrelevant to almost all the participants because their companies could not afford that equipment. The best part of the trip for her was to see China and experience traveling to China.[12] Yet, for African news outlets that can afford the equipment, they are softly incentivized to purchase Chinese-made technology since they already have trained staff for equipment maintenance and operations.

Viewing short-term programs (both the content seminars and tech-support sessions) from the relational power and guanxi network expansion lens explains China's increasing pledges to sponsor more trainings for African journalists every year. Establishing personal guanxi connections between African reporters and their Chinese counterparts and showing (through the short trips) the similar experiences of development that China and several African countries are going through also reinforces this bond of relations. In other words, China is building its network of power through human capital investments and guanxi-strengthening practices with African journalists.

Long-Term Training Programs for Journalists and Reporters

The long-term professionalization training programs for journalists are less about technical support and quick crash courses on China's culture and history. Instead, they are more academic and usually target journalists as well as communications students who are interested in getting a higher education degree. Participants are typically enrolled in a master's degree program hosted at a Chinese university with full expenses paid by the Chinese government. Unlike in the case of short training programs, the Chinese Ministry of Foreign Affairs is involved in the selection process of the participants in coordination with Chinese embassies across African capital cities. Several participants I spoke to in Beijing explained to me that the selection process in their home countries is highly competitive and that most of the time having good "connections" to government officials increases the chances of being accepted into the training programs.[13] Having strong connections with government officials and their potential influence on being selected for the scholarship suggests that Chinese-sponsored scholarships further strengthening guanxi relations between government officials in African countries and China's Ministry of Foreign Affairs.

The participants' award packages cover tuition fees, round-trip airfare, a housing allowance, health insurance, and modest stipends. This meticulous attention to detail and care for the participants by Chinese host institutions are a reflection of the hospitality of Chinese institutions and often leads to expressions of gratitude and appreciation by African participants.[14] In an interview with the administrative assistant of Communication University of China about the training program, she explained how there was mounting criticism and grievances by local Chinese students toward these training scholarships given to African journalists at their expense. Some Chinese students complain that their admission chances are diminishing because of increased admissions of African trainees. The administrative assistant also mentioned that not all the participants perform well in class and this for her raises a bigger concern in terms of profitability and return on investment for her institution. Because many of the scholarships are disbursed to relatives or close friends of African government officials instead of following a merit-based system, the competency level of many of the participants is not up to par. Yet that does not seem to result in decreasing the numbers of these professionalization trainings by the Chinese state in part because the ultimate purpose of these trainings is to create spaces for (pro-China) expert knowledge production and diffusion of positive narratives of China-Africa relations. Additionally, since the participating journalists usually work for their respective governments or have close connections to the government, creating good impressions by generously sponsoring their visits while in China is very important for the creation of strong guanxi relations. The workshops succeed where launching CGTN-Africa TV fails, which is that they create strong relations and expand guanxi relations between Chinese and African communications and press experts.

Increasing the numbers and frequency of routinized training programs makes room for processes of knowledge production and norm diffusion in addition to the professional and commercial opportunities and personal connections that expand because of such exchanges. Ultimately, these interactions aim at fulfilling Xi Jinping's objective of "telling China's story well" in quotidian reports on China-Africa when African journalists go back to their daily jobs.[15] Therefore, this shows that instead of relying only on Chinese media stations and newspapers to counter Western media's narrative, Beijing is investing innovatively in training journalists from African countries to counterbalance negative reporting of Western media by giving a positive spin to China-Africa stories. As a consequence, trainees are expected to be more knowledgeable and informed in their reporting on China-Africa given their firsthand experience of China, the hospitality shown to them during their stays, and the extensive traveling they experience with the trainings.

RELATIONAL POWER, KNOWLEDGE PRODUCTION, AND NETWORK-BUILDING IN MEDIA TRAININGS

Documents I obtained from Communication University of China's Africa Communication Research Center show that, as of 2015, sixty-four journalist-participants (with different levels of journalism experience) have been selected from twenty-four African countries to receive either a master's or doctoral degree in communication and journalism in Beijing. Out of the sixty-four admitted participants, fifty have graduated. Some of the recent graduates have decided to pursue more education in Beijing (at their own expense or on scholarships negotiated with their home governments) while the majority returned to their previous jobs in Africa. I had long interviews with twelve African participants in China-sponsored professionalization trainings, among whom nine were journalists, asking questions about their impressions of the training they received in China and their perceptions of China's role in African development. The impressions expressed by the nine journalists confirm positive perceptions of the role that their China-sponsored training plays in their views of China and China-Africa relations. For the most part, recent graduates have expressed two common impressions about their experience in China. The first is a skeptical view of Western media, charging that outlets like CNN and BBC tend to be arrogant and patronizing when reporting on China-Africa events because of fear that traditional powers such as France and England are losing influence in Africa. The second concern was with regard to African leaders' responsibility in asserting their negotiation skills with China instead of letting Beijing take the lead. In another question, I asked the journalists about professional ethics and the level of bias that training in China may have created in their coverage of China's interests in the continent. The participants confirmed that their experience studying in Chinese institutions has allowed them to learn a lot about Chinese culture and values, which they came to appreciate far more after their stay. Eight of the nine journalists surveyed did not agree that studying in China with the education paid for by the Chinese government means they are expected to make their reports on China-Africa necessarily in favor of China. They expressed that criticism will be reported where criticism is due but that the alarmist tone of certain Western media is not ethical or fair either.

Through a combination of analyzing Chinese foreign policy discourse on human capital investments and a series of interviews conducted with African journalists, I find that China's public diplomacy power in Africa is sustained not through the establishment of massive headquarters for CGTN-Africa and other state-owned media outlets but through investments in professionalization training programs. Although such programs are unidirectional and African participants are clearly on the receiving end as learners and consumers of knowledge, several participants focus on the hospitality and generosity of the Chinese host institutions and view China-Africa relations as a partnership based on respect and among equals. This shows two things. First, the discourse that China-Africa relations are based on equal relations and mutual benefits is shaping up as a dominant discourse and conventional wisdom due to Chinese investments in people-centered initiatives. Second, the tours around China offered for visiting journalists from Africa, the overall golden "treatment" by Chinese host institutions, and the content of the trainings are all part of the process of investing in African journalists to "tell China's story well." Indeed, the firsthand experience that African journalists have when traveling to China for vocational trainings leave impressive impacts on them both at the personal and professional levels—on journalists who are in charge of voicing and portraying China to their respective audience upon their return home. This answers the question posed at the beginning of the chapter on the mechanisms through which attractiveness works in the context of China's foreign policy and in Africa more specifically.

Alternative Explanations

The argument I propose in this chapter is that China's infrastructure investments in Africa's media landscape, from radio programs to TV channels, from TV sets to digital technology equipment, serves the purpose of making its relational power projection stronger. I mean by this that China's massive CGTN headquarters in Nairobi, when approached from a relational power lens, is not the symbol of China's failure to catch up to the soft power of BBC and CNN. Rather, it is a hub that serves to connect African journalists to their Chinese counterparts, to recruit from among them journalists to go on professionalization trainings in China, and to cultivate the next generation of African journalists who are familiar with China. The alternative explanations about China's media investments are explanations that go straight for an evaluation of China's hardware, equipment quality, and the reputation of Chinese channels/newspapers in Africa. I argue that the focus on the materiality of China-Africa relations in general, and in the media for this chapter, already means that the analysis is off track.

The majority of scholarship on China's media strategy in Africa is analyzed from the prism of soft power. Soft power was originally defined by Joseph Nye as "one country gets other countries to want what it wants . . . in contrast with the hard or command power of ordering others to do what it wants" (Nye 1990, 166). Establishing other actors' preferences through soft power is usually "associated with intangible assets such as an attractive personality, culture, political values and institutions, and policies that are seen as legitimate or having moral authority" (Nye 2004, 6). Nye's work on soft power is widely used in foreign policy contexts in China. Wang Hongyin's (1993) oft-cited work essentially argues that culture is the main source of a state's soft power. This is, however, different from Nye's earlier conceptualization of soft power. Indeed, Nye (2004, 11) saw soft power as being located in "culture (in places where it is attractive to others), its political values (when it lives up to them at home and abroad), and its foreign policies (when they are seen as legitimate and having moral authority)." In his assessment, "the factors of technology, education, and economic growth are becoming more significant in international power, while geography, population, and raw materials are becoming somewhat less important" (Nye 2004, 154). The appeal of soft power, therefore, is a result of the aesthetic dynamics of attractiveness. Although Nye introduces the concept of attractiveness as the core mechanism of soft power, he dedicates little attention to explaining how this mechanism works exactly.

Janice Bially Mattern understands reality as being not merely socially constructed but socio*linguistically* constituted, anchoring her position in studies that analyze linguistic argumentation and persuasion as rhetorical strategies. She argues that realities "are intersubjectively constructed matrices of beliefs through which a population signifies things, people, and ideas" (Mattern 2005, 596). Mattern's sociolinguistic-based attractiveness points our attention to China's interest in having a space to cast its own China-Africa narrative by highlighting the role of sociolinguistic constructions in persuading and attracting African audiences. In fact, Beijing repeatedly insists that its foreign policy must actively participate in the construction of representations in the media (both visually as well as linguistically).

That the role of language and rhetoric is central to increase the attractiveness of China's policies to African audiences is not in doubt. A good number of the recurrent themes or examples in China's discourse demonstrate the linguistic investment in the audience, including Beijing's rhetoric of mutual benefits, equal partners, shared history, common future aspirations, and similar struggles against Western hegemony. As expressed by China's ambassador to Kenya, Liu Guangyuan:

> In this era of fast development of information and globalization, media play a crucial role in the transformation of international relations and foreign policies. Unfortunately, in today's setting, dominant information mainly flows from the few developed countries to the developing countries. Stories and information from developing countries are often edged out. This reality creates a serious gap that affects how developing countries view themselves and the rest of the world. (Liu 2013)

Creating a bond with developing countries whose voices and media narratives are marginalized by developed countries' media corporations is certainly a work of language-based attractiveness.

Rhetorical attractiveness is present in Chinese media's rhetoric, especially when invoking the historical ties that China has had with many revolutionary movements since the colonial struggle era. The affective underpinnings of Chinese rhetoric on China's relations with the developing world can also be seen in discourses highlighting how China sees a fully equal partner in African states and that positive attitude leaves ample room for the audience to identify with China. In China's narrative about International Monetary Fund (IMF) structural adjustment programs in Africa or World Bank aid platforms, there is heavy criticism of these institutions' negligence of African voices and African agency. Chinese officials often criticize the IMF for being arrogant and imposing on Africans a set of solutions that don't work for their contexts. However attractive and interesting this rhetoric is, it remains true that when we return to the context of China's presence in African media landscape, CGTN Africa is not a popular channel for Kenyans to get international news from and the rhetoric in its reporting can hardly explain its attractiveness to ordinary citizens.

CONCLUSION

By analyzing Chinese official discourse on media diplomacy, it becomes apparent that China's interest in expanding its footprint in Africa's media landscape is at once a reaction to Western media's domination in Africa and couched in a rhetoric of anticolonialism and anti-imperialism, calling on Chinese and African counterparts to collaborate and change the narrative. What is missing from this perspective is that China is not readily open to African media outlets to broadcast the "African narratives" into China. The discursive analysis also revealed little to no China-Africa reciprocity when it comes to exchanges among news reporters. African reporters and journalists are invited to become acquainted with China's journalistic views and values but not the other way around even though several African nations rank much higher than China in the World Press Freedom Index. The discourse reproduces the vocabulary of an equal partnership, shared history, and common development goals while at the same time silencing possibilities for reciprocity and concrete measures in equal partnerships. Additionally, the repetition of such vocabulary produces a conventional wisdom about China-Africa media relations.

In order to implement the policy goal of "telling China's story better," the Chinese state-sponsored media campaign in Africa consists of two broad strategies: direct material investments in media infrastructure and human capital investments. The direct approach, launching CGTN-Africa (among other Chinese state-owned media outlets) proved insufficient in yielding the results desired to "tell China's story better" since the audience ratings were very low. Therefore, I viewed China's technical support for African state-owned media and other material investments from the perspective of relational power. Even though CGTN-Africa on its own does not seem to be a successful strategy, it should be contextualized as one more layer of relations that link Chinese to African counterparts. It is one more important connection in the web of relations that render China's presence stronger and more expansive. Additionally, China's media campaign in Africa also consists of massive human capital investments aimed at providing professional training programs for African journalists and hosting annual media summits and workshops for private and public media specialists. These routinized training programs and summits expand guanxi relations between Chinese media experts and their African counterparts and create affective bonds between visiting African journalists and their (curated) experiences of China. Professionalization trainings are also places where regimes of truth and socialization into China's history, the Taiwan question, China's development success story, and conventional wisdom vocabulary about China-Africa relations are produced. A combination of primary and secondary data strongly suggests that these trainings promote positive perceptions of China in the eyes of African trainees.

Whereas I am not able to ascertain from this study to what extent exactly this produced expert knowledge is creating African "subjectivities" or is efficient in altering the reporting strategies of trained journalists, I am nevertheless showing that in order to best understand China's power building in Africa, Chinese investments in human resource development programs need to be placed at the center of the analysis.Relatedly, as I mention in other parts of the book, providing professionalization trainings for journalists is not exclusive to China's foreign policy. Other countries provide similar opportunities and many journalists from across Africa participate in the training opportunities in China as well as in the other countries that offer such trainings. There is a lot that could be illuminated by conducting a comparative study between the vocational trainings provided by China and those provided by the US, for example, to ascertain what's particular about Chinese-sponsored trainings for journalists.

Additionally, in the book I mentioned how incorporating in the media trainings lessons on Chinese history endeavors to shape their knowledge about certain security issues that matter for the Chinese central government, such as the question of Taiwan and the Tiananmen Square events. One might claim that my analysis is representing African journalists as passive recipients of Chinese knowledge. Yet, as I mention in different parts of the book and I repeat here, there is a mix of reactions from African participants in these training programs. Some reactions, especially in media and journalism, are very critical of the content (usually propaganda-related reporting techniques) of these trainings. Many African countries, such as Kenya, have a very democratic media system and the Chinese model, which usually draws a line at any content that criticizes the government, seems to be of little applicability to their contexts. Critical voices on China-Africa relations in African media outlets abound and not all of them meet the same fate that Essa's canceled column did. Cartoonists such as Zapiro in South Africa, Kenya's Michael Soi, or Bright Tetteh Ackweth from Ghana routinely expose a very critical interpretation of the power dynamics of China-Africa relations. One of Ackweth's exhibits featured a critically acclaimed set of cartoons depicting galamsey (a Ghanaian term for illegal small-scale gold mining) with China's president taking over the continent's gold and mining resources while three West African presidents are distracted with a dispute over a plate of jollof rice. Another politically charged exhibit can be found in Michael Soi's *China Loves Africa* collection, which consists of an assortment of seventy-four bold paintings, cartoons, and drawings that offer a far from flattering depiction of China-Africa relations. One of Soi's canvas paintings depicts the African Union being chaired by a Chinese chairman while delegates from Kenya, South Africa, and other African states are taking a nap (Dahir 2018). These are a few examples of many critical voices that embody a strong and independent sense of agency in the context of "telling China's story well."

CHAPTER SIX

Guanxi in Cultural Diplomacy and Confucius Institutes

IN THE LAST COUPLE OF YEARS, several US-based universities—including the University of Chicago, Pennsylvania State University, the University of Michigan, the University of Rhode Island, Texas A&M, and North Carolina State University—have terminated their agreements with Chinese-government-funded centers of language and culture (known as Confucius Institutes). The reasons varied but the trend to renegotiate or at least question universities' agreements with Confucius Institutes culminated in a 2017 report by the National Association of Scholars calling on universities to close over one hundred existing US-based institutes. The report charged that Confucius Institutes were giving agency to a foreign government to interfere in course offerings, instructor hiring, and funding at US institutions of higher education. The 183-page document warned that "universities have made improper concessions that jeopardize academic freedom and institutional autonomy" (Redden 2017). Two universities in the state of Florida announced they were closing their Chinese-run cultural centers following Senator Marco Rubio sounding the alarm bells on these institutes as a tool for Beijing to expand its political influence abroad (Reuters 2018). The trend of suspicion toward and abandonment of Confucius Institutes extended beyond the US to universities in Canada (such as McMaster and Sherbrooke), the University of Lyon in France, the University of Stockholm in Sweden, and Stuttgart Media University and the University of Hohenheim in Germany.

At the same time that the trend of shutting down Confucius Institute is growing in North America and Europe, African countries are witnessing the reverse with more Chinese cultural institutes and classrooms opening each year. At a conference on Confucius Institutes in Africa, China's ambassador to South Africa, Tian Xuejun, noted that Confucius Institutes are "more than a place for African people to know Chinese language and culture," they are "the cultural business card of China and should try to make the 'Brand of China.'" The ambassador explained that the institutes aim to "promote Chinese culture so as to present a comprehensive, dynamic and vivid picture of China to the whole world, at the same time, showcase the image of the Chinese nation and people as open, peace-loving and hardworking" (Ministry of Foreign Affairs 2012). Confucius Institutes promote positive images of China by investing in language and cultural education programs for young students in over five hundred locations worldwide. With this many locations, Confucius Institutes are prime examples of relational network expansion and guanxi power.

As stated by Ambassador Tian, "by striking a balance between the East and the West, the traditional and the modern, we will be able to give birth to more 'messengers of friendship' who know China, enjoy Chinese culture and are willing to carry forward China-Africa friendship" (Ministry of Foreign Affairs 2012). The idea of "giving birth to more messengers of friendship" is an indication that Confucius Institutes are viewed by Chinese government officials as spaces for the production of an enhanced and embellished narrative of China itself and China-Africa relations by extension. Confucius Institutes are dynamic spaces where, on the one hand, networks and relations are weaved between Chinese authorities, Confucius Institutes in Africa, their partner universities in China, and Chinese firms in Africa. On the other hand, Chinese expert knowledge promoting a positive "China Brand" is manufactured and advertised as conventional wisdom.

In line with the themes explored in this book, Chinese government investments in human capital extend to investments in advertising Chinese culture and language to university and high school students in Africa. This chapter examines the role that trainings in Confucius Institutes (CIs) play in cultural influence, expert knowledge production, and people-to-people diplomacy in China-Africa relations.[1] It investigates the mechanisms of relational productive power through the professionalization training programs that specifically target teaching Chinese language and business culture to university students across Africa. As mentioned in the introductory chapter, existing literature on the rise of China as well as other emerging economies has mostly examined the trade leverage, natural resource investments, and infrastructure construction projects as the comparative advantage of rising powers. However, the impact of less tangible investments and nonmaterial power dynamics, such as the influence of guanxi networks or expert knowledge production and norm diffusion via human capital investments, is as important to consider. This chapter examines CIs as mechanisms for enabling productive relational power and allowing spaces for knowledge production and norm diffusion about Chinese culture and China-Africa relations. The argument presented here is that by understanding the relational productive aspect of Confucius Institutes and other cultural exchanges between China and African counterparts, scholars can explain how investments in human resource development and professionalization training programs build influence and diffuse positive narratives about China.

Branding China and Guanxi via Confucius Institutes

Confucius Institutes are funded by the Chinese government and run by Hanban, a public institution that is supervised by China's Ministry of Education. Hanban ultimately decides which universities will establish partnerships to open Confucius Institutes. Once an agreement is reached between Hanban and a partner institution, funding is made available for teachers and material while the partners assist with logistics and local facilities (Hartig 2016). The first Confucius Institute opened in 2004 (relatively late compared with similar Western initiatives) in South Korea for the purpose of teaching Chinese culture and Mandarin. By the tenth anniversary in 2014, CIs growth boomed from one to 440 institutes across 120 countries. In addition to the Institutes that are affiliated with universities, Hanban designed Confucius classrooms, which are for high school and middle school students. At the beginning of 2019, there were about 648 of these classrooms and the numbers are constantly increasing.[2]

Confucius Institutes are sometimes compared to the Alliance Française, Goethe Institute, British Council, and other language and culture-learning organizations. These institutes represent their governments in foreign countries and serve as diplomatic tools to promote culture, tourism, and language learning. However similar the broad goals of these institutes are, CIs differ structurally from their French, German, or British counterparts, marking a distinct Chinese approach to culture and knowledge dissemination. Even more, Africa-based CIs are distinct even among CIs in Europe or North America in that they differ in funding structure, function, and agreement terms.[3]

To shed light on these institutes and their impact, I begin by analyzing Chinese government discourse on cultural human resource development programs in Africa. The discourse analysis reveals a continuity in Chinese articulation of a rhetoric of friendship, a harmonious world, equal partners, and mutual benefit relations. Yet at the same time the official texts do not mention anywhere that Africans have professional skills to pass on to their Chinese counterparts.[4] The lack of reciprocity in establishing professional-ization training programs led by Africans instead of targeting them reveals a perception of Africans-as-consumers of Chinese knowledge and not experts. If the rhetoric of equal partnership held true, the exchanges would go both ways. Then I take a close look at Addis Ababa University's Confucius Institute and examine it as a network hub and a space for expert knowledge produc-tion and diffusion. In this section, I draw on fieldwork interviews and sec-ondary data to gauge the perceptions of African students of Confucius Insti-tutes. Next, I address some of the alternative explanations as they exist in relevant literature and shows their limitations. Some of the scholarly works on cultural diplomacy argues that the institutes are a gesture of solidarity and a symbol of China's good will of transferring technical skills to Africans. Others posit that the establishment of Confucius Institutes should be taken as a sign of global demand for Chinese language and Chinese culture, while some scholars view CIs as mechanisms of imperialism.

The chapter concludes by reiterating that, much like the previous chap-ters examined, knowledge production in professionalization training pro-grams and nonmaterial investments are as important to the story of China's influence in Africa if not more important than natural resource investments. They are not just about extraction; they "give birth to more messengers of friendship," produce and nurture guanxi networks between Chinese and Af-rican education experts, and diffuse positive narratives and images about China's development and its impact on Africa and China-Africa relations.

Hanban, which is a key element in China's soft power promotion and public diplomacy overseas, has hundreds of sub-branches all over the world.[5] It functions in a dense network structure where the central branch functions as the hub and "network weaver" of a complex set of five layers of intercon-nected relations. The first layer is the central hub in Beijing where the head-quarters of CI initiative is located and to which all the CIs in the world are linked. The second layer links the CI in the host university to a partner school in China. The third layer links the CI in the host institution to other Confucius Institutes in the same region. The fourth layer links a prominent Chinese university with multiple foreign institutes (they can be in different countries, like sister branch campuses). The fifth layer links all the institutes in host countries that have a common Chinese partner.

The complex set of network layers described above shows an important fact about studying the influence of China's CIs. Merely mapping where Confucius Institutes are located, geocoding them, and counting how many of them there are per country/region is insufficient to capture the extent to which guanxi power multiplies through them. Once more, focusing on counting the material existence of institutes and classrooms fails to capture a very complex set of invisible infrastructures. Indeed, what is really interesting about CIs is the (inter) linking and multidimensional features of these institutes. Hanban makes use of its connections in different countries (through CIs) to achieve business and political objectives. Hanban sponsors activities to create and maintain lively interactions between the different partners, alum networks, and the hub branch in Beijing. Events and interactions among students, faculty, and administrators magnify the network nodes from a simple linear relationship between customer (students or universities) and provider (Hanban) to network synergy. For example, Addis Ababa University's CI not only works in close relation with the Hanban in Beijing but is also connected to Shenyang Normal University (as its host institution in China) and to all the CIs that are also affiliated with Shenyang Normal University. The Institute also has close networking ties with Chinese firms established in Ethiopia, including the IT giants Huawei, ZTE, and other companies operating from Bishofu's special economic zone. Oftentimes, the CI director told me, outstanding students get internships or entry-level jobs at one of the Chinese firms, jobs that are arranged by the CI staff.[6]

Beijing's Discourse on Cultural Professionalization Training Programs

Chinese official policy discourse highlights mutual learning and the coproduction of knowledge as distinct characteristics of Beijing's approach to professionalization trainings for African recipients. China's Africa policy, which was released in 2006, puts a premium on a two-way learning discourse that is characterized as horizontal, among equals, and not hierarchical or hegemonic. Again, as explained in previous chapters, the emphasis on horizontal instead of hierarchical relations in China's official discourse is best understood as a rhetorical move by which Chinese officials distance China's behavior in Africa from that of European powers. In Africa's colonial histories, the African was (expected to be) the obedient servant of the European master. Chinese discourse articulates and connotes China's activities in Africa as a two-way learning exchange and coproduction of knowledge. For instance, China's policy paper from 2006 insists that both parties aim at further "learning from each other and seeking common development. China and Africa will learn from and draw upon each other's experiences in governance and development, strengthen exchange and cooperation in education, science, culture and health" (Ministry of Foreign Affairs 2006). The emphasis on "common development" and mutual learning sounds promising. Still, it is necessary to contrast it with what policies are implemented on the ground. Looking more closely makes it clear that claims of two-way learning and coproduction of knowledge are not reflected in the majority of China's Africa policies. In fact, Chinese students rarely if ever go to African universities for trainings or degrees.[7] African teachers are also rarely—if ever—invited to share their experiences by teaching in Chinese institutions.[8] Even the most prominent universities in China that have centers for African studies rarely have African professors for content classes—as opposed to foreign language classes.[9] In the meantime, Chinese government-sponsored scholarships and short-term trainings for African students and teachers have been growing in numbers and China is now the largest provider of cultural/educational training programs for African countries.

Trying to figure out precisely how many people participate in or are affected by China's educational and cultural professionalization programs is a challenge. China's human capital investment programs for Africa are not grouped in one policy paper or in one section of China's Africa policy paper with details for the different types of trainings. They are not managed by one agency within the Chinese government. Some of the programs are listed on FOCAC agendas under education cooperation, others under economic cooperation, people-to-people exchange, or cultural and social development, while others are announced bilaterally. Some of these independent programs include the China-Africa Joint Research and Exchange Program, which was launched on March 30, 2010 to promote exchanges between scholars, think tanks, and intellectuals. In addition, the think tank initiative 10+10 Partnership Plan, which is funded by the Chinese Ministry of Foreign Affairs, is another policy platform that promotes academic exchanges. Likewise, the Chinese government recently launched the Yenching Academy initiative, which is a residential fellowship for outstanding graduate students from all over the world to study in China for a year.[10] Founded in 2014, the

Yenching Academy program is relatively new and is broadly modeled to be China's version of the Rhodes Scholarship at Oxford University. For Yenching Academy's first cohort, four students from three African countries were selected to participate. Although the number is very low compared to representation from other countries (e.g., twenty-six from the US),[11] the overall number of African countries represented in this highly competitive, elite program totaled eleven across three cohorts.[12] The Yenching Academy is part of the cultural/educational human capital investment programs that are not mentioned in FOCAC meetings. Yenching and similar programs make it challenging to track all the cultural programs and accurately estimate the level of attention and funding dedicated to each.

Chinese official discourse stresses China's dedication to promoting mutual understanding via people-to-people exchanges and scholarship opportunities. Chinese premier Li Keqiang insisted during his visit to Addis Ababa in May 2014 that cultural diplomacy is central to his vision of flourishing Sino-African relations. He expressed that both China and its African partners

> need to work together on cultural and people-to-people exchanges. Mutual affinity grows when the hearts and minds of our people meet. We will step up cultural interactions with African countries, making such brand programs as the China-Africa Cultural Cooperation Partnership Program and the China-Africa People-to-People Friendship Action a success, setting up still more Chinese cultural centers and Confucius Institutes in Africa, and helping China-Africa friendship strike deeper roots in people's hearts and minds. China will work through cooperation programs in science, technology and education as well as enhanced vocational training and other means to help African countries improve the caliber of their human resources.[13]

Education, culture, people-to-people exchanges, and professionalization trainings are identified as important aspects of Chinese foreign policy conduct in Africa as China endeavors to build and expand relational networks between Chinese academics and African teachers and students. The communiqué referenced above explains that the rationale behind the think-tank cooperation is "to create new theoretical thinking on Sino-Africa relations and contribute to uplifting the discourse power of developing countries in international affairs" (Li 2014). Chinese foreign policy gives importance to the power of words and the power of articulating/branding China's activities in Africa from a Chinese perspective. This echoes Xi Jinping's call for Chinese media to find ways to "tell China's story well"—as opposed to reproducing Western media narratives, which tend to be alarmist representations of China-Africa relations. In tandem with Chinese government-funded professionalization seminars for African journalists, Beijing seeks to gain a more discursive field through organizing workshops, academic seminars, and publishing think-tank reports to "create new theoretical thinking about Sino-Africa relations."

Culture and Language-Centered Human Capital Investment in FOCAC

The action plan of the third Forum on China-Africa Cooperation in 2006 announced the following policy points that pertain to cultural/educational vocational training programs:

1. To strengthen exchanges between the Chinese and African civilizations and enhance bilateral cultural interactions will enrich the new type of China-Africa strategic partnership and will also set an example for dialogue and exchanges among different civilizations and thus advance the building of a harmonious world.
2. The two sides resolved to actively implement the bilateral government exchange programs and support and promote cultural exchanges. The African side expressed appreciation of China's decision to set up the African Cultural Visitors Program to enhance cultural exchanges between the two sides.
3. Help African countries set up a hundred rural schools in the next three years;
4. Increase the number of Chinese government scholarships to African students from the current 2,000 per year to 4,000 per year by 2009;
5. Provide annual training for a number of educational officials as well as heads and leading teachers of universities, primary, secondary and vocational schools in Africa.

In terms of cultural exchanges, the action plan mentions Cultural Visitors Programs without (yet) addressing the Confucius Institutes. The language used to refer to building a harmonious world through cultural exchanges implies that the exchanges are reciprocal. Yet as shown in the agenda items on education exchanges, the Chinese side *trains, helps, provides*, whereas African counterparts are willing recipients and trainees.

Another interesting point to note here is how these policy projects sound much like educational aid from other countries, including former Soviet Union trainings for socialist African countries and German and British bursaries for African elite students during the Cold War. Yet, today, China is the largest contributor of such scholarships and professionalization training programs for Africans, and Western countries' contributions lag significantly in comparison.[14]

The following Forum on China-Africa Cooperation in 2009 (FOCAC IV) states that "the two sides stressed that better education holds the key to social stability and economic development, and the two sides will build on the existing achievements to further enhance their cooperation."[15] Consequently, as a continuation of progress achieved from the previous agenda items, the Chinese government committed to these policy points:

1. Continue to promote the development of Confucius Institutes, increase the number of scholarships offered to Chinese language teachers to help them study in China, and double efforts to raise capacity of local African teachers to teach the Chinese language.
2. Help African countries build 50 China-Africa friendship schools in the next three years.
3. Admit 200 middle and high level African administrative personnel to MPA programs (Master of Public Administration) in China in the next three years.
4. Continue to raise the number of Chinese governmental scholarships and increase the number of scholarships offered to Africa to 5,500 by 2012.
5. Intensify efforts to train teachers for primary, secondary, and vocational schools in Africa, and help African countries train 1,500 school headmasters and teachers over the next three years.
6. The Chinese Government will continue to provide training for people from different sectors in Africa as the need arises. The Chinese Government undertakes to train a total of 20,000 people in various sectors for African countries in the next three years.

The numbers of exchange scholarships and training programs indicate that Beijing's investment in people-to-people relations programs has steadily increased over the intervening three years. The cultural exchange programs also include building China-Africa friendship schools and mention for the first time in FOCAC agenda plans launching more Confucius Institutes across Africa. The trend in these cultural exchange programs kept evolving in the next FOCAC meeting, which took place in Beijing in 2012. The action plan continued along the same lines from previous meetings and the two sides pledged to

1. Maintain the momentum of high-level inter-governmental mutual visits and dialogue in the cultural field and continue to follow through on the implementation plan of the China-Africa bilateral government cultural agreements.

2. Propose to implement a "China-Africa Cultural Cooperation Partnership Program" and promote the building of long-term paired cooperation between 100 Chinese cultural institutions and 100 African cultural institutions.

3. Continue to implement the program of China-Africa mutual visits between cultural personnel and strengthen exchanges and cooperation between the administrative personnel and professionals of the cultural and art communities.

4. Speed up the building of Chinese cultural centers in Africa and African cultural centers in China to put China-Africa cultural exchanges and cooperation on a regular basis and promote their sustainable development.

Chinese president Hu Jintao promised at the 2012 meeting of FOCAC "to train 30,000 Africans, offer 18,000 scholarships, and build cultural and vocational skills training facilities by 2015."[16] When compared to FOCAC 2009, FOCAC 2012 pledges represent a significant increase from 5,500 scholarships and promises to train 20,000 Africans. Investments between China-Africa did not expand and deepen exclusively in trade and natural resources. Indeed, as Kenneth King, a long-time expert on education aid, writes: "Under the category of human resource development, there is a continued commitment to the massive, short-term training of what the FOCAC calls 'African professionals in various sectors,' with numbers reaching . . . 30,000 in the triennium ending in 2015" (King 2013, 158). The pledges made in 2015 cement the observation shared by King (2013) as the two sides agreed to

1. Maintain the momentum of high-level inter-governmental mutual visits and dialogue in the cultural field and will continue to follow

through on the implementation plan of the China-Africa bilateral government cultural agreements.
2. Implement "the Program of China-Africa Mutual Visits between Cultural Personnel" and "China-Africa Cultural Partnership Program."
3. To advocate for the establishment of cultural centers in China and Africa. The Chinese side will help build 5 cultural centers for Africa, and to establish more permanent platforms for cultural exchanges and cultural cooperation.
4. Strengthen human resources training in the cultural field. The Chinese side will establish ten major "Culture Training Bases for Africa" and execute the "One Thousand People Program" for culture training in Africa.

The sixth edition of FOCAC probably has the most elaborate section on cultural human resource development programs yet, but when it comes to actual policies there is little reciprocation as there is no equivalent of Confucius Institutes established in Chinese universities to promote "African Brands" like CIs do for the "China Brand." In FOCAC 2018, China continued its pledges to provide exchange opportunities and scholarships for young Africans. The action plan announced that China will continue to invite "2,000 young Africans to visit China for exchanges to promote mutual visits of young people" and invite "200 African scholars to visit China."[17] Overall, a common thread to all action plans analyzed here is that Chinese officials maintain a discursive façade of mutual learning and coproduction of knowledge while at the same time the Chinese side trains Africans and admits Africans to Chinese universities.

Various ministries and institutions in China coordinate the different types of cultural and educational training programs. They are not all under one department inside the Ministry of Foreign Affairs. Some programs are managed under science and technology cooperation agencies, some by thinks tanks, and others are coordinated in cooperation between the Ministry of Education and the Ministry of Commerce. With the introduction of Belt and Road Initiative programs, more culture-focused scholarships and exchanges are to be managed by these different agencies. Decentralization makes it challenging for researchers to develop an exact idea of how much Beijing is spending on its public diplomacy programs in Africa and who exactly their constituencies are. It also makes it difficult to have access to information pertaining to the content of these seminars and training courses. Yet

there are overall six categories of Chinese government-funded human resource development programs for Africans. They include "high-level educational exchanges, exchanges of students, cooperative education programs,
professional seminars and workshops in China, Chinese teachers' active involvement in teaching in African countries, African studies and the training
of professionals in China" (King 2013, 37).

Cooperative Educational Programs

Cooperative educational programs are partnerships (mostly) between African and Chinese universities. They are largely financially supported by the
Chinese Ministry of Education and were established in the mid to late 1980s.
Back then, they served as platforms for both student and teacher government exchange programs. Since the first FOCAC meeting in 2000, these programs have picked up momentum and became included in the triennial
meeting's action plans. Under the auspices of FOCAC's African Human
Resource Development Fund, forty-five African professionals attended
short-term training programs in China. This does not include the military-
to-military high-level official trainings. By 2003 there were twenty-nine
higher education institutions in twenty-three African countries that had
established partnership programs with nineteen Chinese universities (King
2013, 38). Of course, some of these partnerships are more prestigious and
older than others. For instance, the partnership between Nanjing Agricultural University and Kenya's Egerton University is over a decade old, as is
Zhejiang Normal University's cooperation with Yaoundé I and II universities
in Cameroon. Where Confucius Institutes are located generally correlates
with the existence of expanded economic and political relations. Adding
one more layer of connections—the cultural and language teaching layer—
through opening the institutes and organizing cultural activities enlarges
the web of bilateral relations.

Additionally, as part of FOCAC's promise to train Africans, the Ethio-
China Polytechnic College (ECPC) has been offering short- and long-term
trainings for administrative staff and other professionals. The Polytechnic
College received no less than four hundred staff from China in the early
2000s and then it launched an African Vocational Educational Studies in
2003 in partnership with Tianjin University of Technology and Education
(TUTE).[18] The Polytechnic cost $15 million and was not only built with Chi-
nese funds but also staffed with eleven Chinese heads of departments pro-

vided by TUTE. The goal of the college, which opened in 2009, was to train sixty staff for master's degrees through the China Scholarship Council (King 2013, 42). However, Kenneth King finds that, despite impressive numbers, the quality of training in the Chinese-ran ECPC does not outperform German capacity-building programs in Ethiopia, which are considerably smaller in size and more efficient.[19] On top of that, South Korean and Italian training initiatives caught up with the Chinese one and also proved to be better perceived if much smaller in scale.

What is particular about the Chinese initiative, however, is the level of density in the webs of its relationships and connections with African counterparts. Confucius Institutes are integrated on many fronts into China's activities and policies in the host country including in education partnerships. For example, shortly after its opening and no later than early 2010, the ECPC launched a Confucius Institute. Unlike usual procedures where African institutions apply to host a CI, in this particular case the institute was proposed by the Chinese side, which picked TUTE as the African partner institution instead of letting the host institution pick its partner, as is the norm. In addition to opening a Confucius Institute at the ECPC, the action plan of FOCAC IV in Egypt (2009) announced the launch of a 20+20 partnership program for twenty Chinese universities to be create some form of partnership or exchange program with twenty African partner institutions. The ECPC was selected to be part of the 20+20 initiative and was paired with TUTE for yet another layer of partnership now involving a Chinese university, a joint polytechnical college, and a Confucius Institute (FOCAC IV action plan).

Capacity-building programs from Germany, South Korea, and Italy that I mentioned above do not have as much overlapping relationality and network density. In this sense, they are rather flat and unidimensional. By contrast, the Chinese-backed ECPC is an example of the complex density of the web of relations interconnecting these partnerships. ECPC and TUTE enjoy at least three different types of partnerships: the initial (Technical Vocational Education and Training (TVET) project, the Confucius Institute, and the 20+20 platform.

Chinese Teachers and Researchers in Africa

Sending Chinese teachers to Africa has been an ongoing assistance policy since the 1950s. At least five hundred teachers were dispatched between the early 1950s and the early 2000s (Li 2012). Originally, the Chinese teachers sent to African schools were a part of promoting Cold War ideologies. The number of Chinese teachers was very limited compared to European or American teachers dispatched across Africa in the same time period. However, the number of Chinese teachers in Africa has increased significantly between 2000 and 2018, especially with the creation of Confucius classrooms and Confucius Institutes. Indeed, there were more Chinese language teachers and researchers in Africa in 2013 alone than there were total between 1950 and 2000.

Similarly, Mandarin is becoming one of the most popular languages for African students to learn. Very recently, Uganda announced that thirty-five secondary schools will begin teaching Mandarin starting in the fall of 2019, adding to a rising trend of several African governments choosing Mandarin as a mandatory foreign language in their schools. The willingness and readiness of African leaders to elevate the teaching and learning of Chinese language to such a high status—in countries like Nigeria and Mozambique, military officials have mandatory Chinese language classes—is a manifestation of relational productive power in China-Africa relations. African government leaders who are invited to tour China and are given special economic deals are also encouraged to open up their societies to learning the Chinese language.

Confucius Institutes' Role in Relational Power Building

There are more Confucius Institutes in Europe and the Americas—with 173 and 161, respectively—than there are in Africa, which has fifty-two institutes as of 2018 (Brown 2018). However, the numbers are not totally static due to recent shutdowns of CIs in the US and Europe and the growing embrace of the institutes in Africa. There are fewer Confucius Institutes across Africa than in the US and Europe in part due to financial and structural differences between the CIs that China opens in Africa and the ones in developed countries. For example, CIs in Canada are funded on a ratio of 1:1 between the Canadian and Chinese side, which makes them equitably cofunded. In most CIs established in Africa, Beijing provides most of the funding (if not all of it). For this reason, some scholars argue that CIs and professionalization training programs should be viewed as "aid projects" because there is an asymmetrical relationship between the funding country and the recipients. Regardless of whether CIs in Africa are taken as foreign aid projects or not, they are symptomatic of a hierarchical relationship with China doing the training and Africans being on the receiving end.

This funding disparity has impacts and ramifications beyond the apparent asymmetric influence of Chinese funders on decision-making processes. Indeed, as I mentioned above, despite Confucius Institutes having fewer branches in African countries, CIs are expanding in Africa while they are contracting (often involuntarily) in Europe and North America. The level of autonomy and leverage that European and North American universities have on their CIs is not expected to be replicable in the cases of Confucius Institutes in Africa, given the funding hierarchy. This affects hiring and curriculum decisions. For example, a professor from Botswana University explained that avoiding addressing politically sensitive material in Chinese classes is a compromise that his university is comfortable making given the benefits of partnership with Hanban.[20] In other words, Hanban and other Chinese authorities have the ability to censor and silence some parts of China's history (especially related to historical events such as the Tiananmen Square events of 1989, the question of Taiwan's independence, or more recently Xinjiang's internment camps) for African students and academics. Chinese teachers at CIs in Africa, for example, normalize the Chinese party line that Taiwan is part of China through their teaching of China's history and current affairs without host universities resisting such narratives. This structural power gives CIs in Africa a unique leverage they do not enjoy in other contexts where host universities have a say on hiring processes, admissions, curricula, and events hosted by the institute. Chinese foreign policy uses Confucius Institutes as a space for expert knowledge production that normalizes certain narratives, silences others, and shapes the perceptions of African students of China's history and current politics in positive ways. This is parallel to the case of the South African newspaper column that was cancelled after a reporter published an article on a topic sensitive to the Chinese government. Given these aims and the political complexities, it is very hard to argue that Confucius Institutes in Africa are the equivalent of Goethe Institutes, the Alliance Française, or the British Council.

More differences come to mind when thinking about Confucius Institutes in Africa and how they compare to the Alliance Française or the British Council. Confucius Institutes are always hosted inside universities and not independent like their French or German counterparts, which are established outside the university and independently of other institutions. In the case of CIs, once officials from a potential host university get in touch with the Chinese embassy to request collaboration, they are invited to visit the headquarters in Beijing to start talks about which Chinese university to partner with and decide on the terms of agreement. In the case of many CIs established in Africa, Hanban is in charge of funding the construction (or remodeling in some cases) of the facility that will host the Confucius Institute. More often than not, these are inside the campus of the host university but the building itself is either renovated or constructed from scratch with Chinese funding. Besides renovation or construction costs, the Institute is also staffed and equipped through Hanban funding and resources. The African host university provides the necessary space and logistical support of enrolling students and advertising the program and the Chinese side absorbs most of the expenses.[21]

The Confucius Institute I visited in Ethiopia is hosted inside the Addis Ababa University in the building of the foreign languages department. However, despite the university (and the building) being somewhat old, the CI offices definitely stand out compared to other language units. The Institute's activities are well advertised with big banners outside and inside the building. The Institute is located in a renovated wing. It is well equipped compared to the other language units and is staffed with native speakers of Chinese. Once inside the Institute, one can see many bulletin boards with pictures of successful students who earned a trip to China, of important Chinese political leaders who visited the Institute, and of cultural events the Institute hosts for the university and the local community.

In contrast with this, the Institute of Alliance Française in Addis Ababa is located in the Piazza area of the capital city and is hosted in a fenced old, house-like premise. It is far away from the campus area. The Institute of Alliance Française can be difficult to find for someone who is new to the city. It holds events open to the public, hosts photography exhibits, and has Amharic language classes and various art-related activities for the members. It does not, however, advertise opportunities for local students to visit France for exchange studies nor does it have language immersion programs like the CI does.

In this regard, the Confucius Institute can be viewed as being firmly integrated in the university and local community and having wider webs of connections to students, business firms, and so forth than its French counterpart. This kind of guanxi capital that is weaved between Confucius Institutes and different segments of society increases locals' positive perceptions of China and inspires many students to join the Institute for all the opportunities it makes available. With this, I think that the Confucius Institute in Addis Ababa distinguishes China's cultural diplomacy brand from that of Western counterparts in its deep integration in the local community along with its focus on investing in networks of relations that put China in the center. From what perceptions I gathered, the Alliance Française is viewed as an elitist venue in Addis where only people of a certain social class spend some leisurely time on the weekend or after work hours. By contrast, the Confucius Institute at the University of Addis Ababa is frequented by students, faculty, and community members (including traders and business owners interested in going to China for business). It works in close connection with the local community, with Chinese companies established in Ethiopia, and has more potential for closer network relations between traders, students, faculty, translators, and largely everyone interested in learning about China.

Intangible and nonmaterial aspects of power are as important as material aspects when examining China's exercise of influence in Africa. Much as Chinese-sponsored journalist seminars and training workshops for military officers diffuse Chinese expert knowledge, the Chinese desire to influence the "hearts and minds" of Africans extends to cultural exchanges. Weaving a strong network of relations between the Chinese trainers and the African trainees is indeed part of Confucius Institutes' structure and mission. CIs are about cultivating and maintaining relationships by viewing culture as a process and including the use of networks and digital communication accordingly (Zaharna 2014, 13). Yet, similar to the professionalization training programs discussed in earlier chapters, these relations are unidirectional with no reciprocation of Chinese military officers or primary schools learning African languages. The attractiveness of CIs lies not in an inherent appeal of the Chinese language or culture but in the relational dynamic created through the network communication approach. This relational dynamic has the advantage of connecting the trainees and language students in a web of relations with fellow CI students from other countries and with Chinese students in the partner universities in China. The power of the network and personal guanxi connection is as an essential part of Chinese foreign policy conduct in Africa more generally, and of cultural diplomacy specifically.

Network synergy consists of three interrelated relational processes: internal relationship-building, external coalition-building, and incorporating diversity. An example of internal relationship-building in CIs consists of the different cultural activities that CIs organize, such as celebrating Chinese New Year with concerts and other cultural events that encourage students to

128 SHAPING THE FUTURE OF POWER

engage with each other regardless of their language proficiency. Each CI is tasked with organizing a certain number of events that are open to the community at large and inclusive of all who want to participate. This is how external relationship building boosts the extent of the network's reach, its resources, and legitimacy through network bridges with the local community. It is also a way of making the CIs visible in the local communities and of advertising the classes to potential students. Celebrating traditional Chinese festivals are also an opportunity to communicate an image of Chinese culture in its most festive and positive occasions. Hanban headquarters dedicate a budget for CIs to spend on these cultural events and require reports from the institutes detailing the planned activity, which needs to be approved. The online portal of Hanban is another way to keep the institutes in interaction with each other through social media platforms and it encourages a diversity of ideas for cultural activities and feedback on students' experiences in the different institutes. Diversity and innovation are also encouraged through holding an annual conference for CIs in Beijing to facilitate face-to-face interpersonal communication and the exchange of ideas.

Confucius Institutes and Knowledge Production

A study conducted by a Zhejiang Normal University professor surveyed African students who have studied at Confucius Institutes in Cameroon and South Africa about their experience and perception of China. The questions in the survey pertained to how the students viewed China before and after being exposed to Chinese classes at their respective CIs. The survey also asked students about their job prospects and where they were going to be hired upon completion of their degrees. The majority of the students surveyed answered that they had opportunities to work in a translation capacity for Chinese businesses in their respective cities. Another group of students had government jobs lined up for them, while some were hoping to be hired by Hanban to teach Chinese language for high school students in their respective countries. When asked about their perceptions, the majority of students had acquired a much more positive image of China after their training at their Confucius Institutes than they had before. Students also expressed their sense of gratitude toward Chinese staff for teaching them Mandarin and giving them the opportunity to access well-paying jobs. Another question asked whether the students feel connected to China and whether they would establish business relations with Chinese companies in China in the future. Here, too, the majority of students responded positively. One of the shortcomings of this study is that surveys were administered by Chinese staff or Chinese researchers, which may have indirectly influenced the participants' reporting positive experiences with Chinese-funded language classes.

Despite its limitations, this study confirms impressions I got from students I have spoken to in Addis Ababa and Nairobi as well as from students of media and journalism whom I met on a research trip to China where they were receiving degrees at Chinese universities. Being exposed to Chinese language and culture while studying in China allows African students and trainees to have a better grasp of China's culture and history and to appreciate it in more substantial ways. The students who received scholarships from the Chinese government to study in China said their predeparture perceptions of China were completely different (stereotypical and incorrect most of the time) from what they learned while in China.[22]

Students I talked to at the Confucius Institutes in Addis Ababa and Nairobi were confident that studying Mandarin Chinese and learning about Chinese business culture would open up better job prospects with Chinese business firms established in their countries or local firms seeking to open offices in China. The Confucius Institute in Addis Ababa plays a role in connecting its most successful students with Chinese companies that are hiring locally. In addition to sending the best students to China on an exploratory trip, CIs promise jobs upon completion of their university degree. As one of the students explained during an interview, "Our formation here gives us concrete results and good jobs."[23] When I asked another student how he decided to study Mandarin of all other languages offered in the same building he said it was the "best way to get a good job with a good salary." Another Ethiopian student said although her Chinese teachers are tough and that classes are harder than many other languages, she is optimistic that the reward of getting a good job will be worth it. In a similar vein, the Sino Africa Centre of Excellence, or SACE, a Chinese consultancy based in Nairobi, taps into the connectivity of Confucius Institutes to find potential hires.[24] SACE started a small-scale experiment called the Sino Africa Technical Vocational Education and Training project in Nairobi. The project offers practical trainings for specific skills that Chinese companies demand, and the Confucius Institute staff play a role in recommending students to be recruited for trainings. Nairobi's CI not only socializes college graduates into Chinese business culture and equips them with language skills but also connects them to SACE, which supplies them the technical skills that they need for jobs at Chinese firms. From interviewing SACE's chief executive officer, Adedana Ashebir, I learned that this model really works for SACE because on-site training is more cost effective than flying trainees to China. Without training, the Chinese companies would not be able to justify hiring local labor as their university degrees are not practical enough. Additionally, from the perspective of Chinese companies, the trainings contribute to promoting an image of China as a source of high-quality services and technology transfers.[25]

Furthermore, even though this book does not test the impact of investments in human resource development on their recipients or their returns for Chinese authorities, other research supports this argument. To illustrate, Jorge Nijal examined Chinese-sponsored education programs for Mozambique and their influence on the political and economic relations between the two countries. Nijal (2012, 14) observes that "in the long run former students (trained) in China may be of help for the government of China. . . . In the perspective of Beijing, if part of this group is placed in high-ranking positions within the government (including diplomats in China) it will be beneficial for the Chinese side." Right now, Mozambique staffs its embassy in Beijing with two former students of Chinese studies who were recipients of Confucius Institute scholarships to China. This suggests that African trainees are assets for promoting future relations between Beijing and different African capitals, especially if Mozambique is one example among many. Nijal's study finds that another major line of employment for students who have acquired Chinese language skills or have studied in China is Mozambique's national Center of Investment Promotion. Again, staffing the center with employees who are knowledgeable about Chinese business culture and language suggests interest in increasing investments from Chinese patrons (Nijal 2012, 14). Nijal's study reveals the networks and relations that permeate Sino-Mozambican education exchanges. Nonetheless, Nijal's study demonstrates China's foreign policy interest in creating a strong network of professional and guanxi relationships and shows how the potential benefits for Beijing expand its relational power in Africa through human capital investments. The findings improve understanding of what sort of relations are built as a result of China's investments in human resource development.

Based on these studies and my own interactions with students, taking a relational power approach to examining Confucius Institutes provides a better understanding of China's power projection in African countries. As mentioned previously, not all Confucius Institutes in Africa focus exclusively on language and cultural teaching. Kenya, for instance, has an agriculture Confucius Institute, located in the fertile Rift Valley area. This Institute functions much like the other CIs except it is geared for exchanges that are specific to Chinese ways of farming and cultivating land. Yet, like other CIs, it seeks to groom outstanding students to take on jobs at Chinese firms operating in Africa. Training students in Chinese business culture is also a way for China to promote its norms and ways of doing things. China pushes for a Chinese alternative to West-centric norms and institutions whenever possible, and Confucius Institutes provide the space for that. In addition, CIs also present the best image of China to students in universities overseas. CIs indeed create and maintain close relations between Chinese companies and businesses and a potential labor force in the cities where they are located and make it a point to help their students find leading jobs with Chinese companies. Cultivating a close network of personal and professional relationships is a strategy that attracts African students who seek successful professional careers. This strategy explains China-Africa power dynamics more accurately than theories that only account for China's financial prowess or military capabilities as an indication of power.

Alternative Explanations

In this section I explore alternative explanations to Beijing's culture-related investments in human resource development in Africa. I find that the majority of scholarship on China's cultural diplomacy in Africa fall on either end of a binary between selfless solidarity among Global South states and outright neocolonial programs making Mandarin into an African language. Neither of these extremes necessarily capture all the nuances of China's cultural diplomacy and African agency in the China-Africa encounter. The two extreme narratives (selfless and neocolonial) also reflect a clash between, on the one hand, a sense of anxiety about China's rise among established powers (like the US) and a strong commitment by Chinese policy makers to sell a brand of a nonthreatening rising China, on the other. Several Chinese scholars take at face value Confucius Institutes and other Chinese investments in human capital as evidence that China is sincere in its friendship with African countries by sharing knowledge and skills. Meanwhile US foreign policy makers increasingly take a zero-sum game approach, canceling US Department of Defense funding for Chinese-language programs at universities that host Confucius Institutes.[26] In this section I explore these two alternative explanations of China's cultural diplomacy and show how they can explain a small portion but not the whole picture.

Some scholars view China's investments in capacity-building programs as a symbol of solidarity and good will on the part of Chinese government to offset criticisms of neocolonial exploitation. For instance, Li Anshan wrote a book on *The Politics of Human Resource Development* (2013) where he examines in detail the history of China's vocational training programs for Africans in the 1950s and how they have evolved over time. Li views these programs as evidence of China's solidarity and commitment to improving the quality of life in its strategic African partners. He argues that cultural and educational capacity-building programs are a constant in China's relations to African countries since their revolutionary movements when several African elites were trained in Chinese universities. To him, regardless of how challenging the economy was for China back in the 1950s, it still stood by its vision to help African friends train the labor force and elite class it needed for its postindependence governance. From this perspective, emphasizing the routinized capacity-building programs is also used as a way to defend Beijing from accusations that it is interested in extracting Africa's natural resources without giving anything back.

Whereas there is little doubt that Beijing has kept its promises to African state leaders asking for transfers of technology and scholarships for African students, this perspective is limited. It takes for granted rather than problematizes the consequences of Chinese knowledge and expertise transfers, which are suffused with knowledge production and norm diffusion. Moreover, although this argument makes sense in a historical context, the South-South solidarity argument has little purchase in examining today's Chinese-funded professionalization trainings for Africans. To a certain degree, the African continent has largely been a safe place for Chinese foreign policy experimenting. If anything, Africans are not the only learners in this relationship and China benefits from providing trainings to Africans because it learns from these experiences what works and what does not.

On the other hand, some critics have viewed Confucius Institutes' diplomacy as a neocolonial practice of China's potential quest for global hegemony. The goal of projecting Chinese culture internationally and investing significant amounts of resources in making Chinese language and culture visible abroad are met with skepticism by some scholars. Rya Butterfield (2014, 13), for instance, posits that Confucius Institutes are not only about reviving Chinese traditions and bringing more positive image to audiences abroad. He also sees them as part of China's governance strategy. Cull et. al (2003, 73) observe that "the earliest surviving texts on governance in China pay great attention to the need for rulers to control and formalize language to secure their authority." There is no such mention of governance on the Hanban official website or documents, yet for scholars like Butterfield there is a subtle governance agenda behind the rapid expansion of Confucius Institutes.

Allegations of "cultural imperialism" and "conquest of the mind" are made about CIs' operations in Africa especially because of the internal asymmetrical structures of the partnerships between African institutions and the Chinese government-backed Hanban. African institutions have very little bargaining power or agency (compared to European or Asian institutions) when it comes to decisions on funding, hiring teachers, and material to be used in classroom. All of this is decided by the Chinese government through Hanban offices or via the Ministry of Education, and most of the time the African side simply provides logistical support and little to no decision-making contributions. As such, Confucius Institutes can be seen as part of China's statecraft, as a mechanism of Chinese foreign policy making rather than independent cultural missionaries. Yet, at the same time, silencing African agency with regard to CIs is problematic. From interactions with Ethiopian students who take language courses at CIs, Chinese language courses are a welcome addition to their university. From this perspective criticizing Mandarin Chinese for being a hegemonic tool of China's influence does not make any sense in a context where English, French, and Portuguese are in fact colonial languages.

Confucius Institutes in Africa are neither agents of Global South solidarity nor symbols of China's neocolonial policies in Africa. They are part of the intricate network of relations and social fabric that are shaping the future of power with China's continuing rise.

CONCLUSION

China is by no means a frontrunner in cultural diplomacy via language teaching and education training programs. Germany, the United Kingdom, and Japan all take human capital investments seriously and dedicate significant funding efforts to a great number of short-term trainings. The former Soviet Union also used to provide education training programs for African socialist countries. A lot has changed, however. Since the end of the Cold War, Russia's interest in these programs has declined. Since the financial crisis of 2008, the United Kingdom and other European countries have scaled back funds for these programs. The governments of "Korea, Japan, Germany, and also India continue to believe that the direct exposure of students and trainees to their own development experience is vital" (King 2014, 161). Yet China has now become the largest provider of professionalization training programs for Africans and has filled in the void left by the United Kingdom and other European countries that cut back on providing these.

A decade after the first Confucius Institute was launched, the numbers of Confucius Institutes opening up in Africa and elsewhere are on the rise. The Confucius Institutes are not only spaces for language and culture learning but also for networks of connections between Chinese firms and African skilled labor to expand and multiply. Confucius Institutes in Africa perform a bridging function of connecting Chinese businesses in China with opportunities and needs in the host countries. They also promote Chinese business culture by grooming outstanding students for jobs (or training) at Chinese firms. Students who attend Confucius Institutes are equipped with the necessary knowledge about Chinese business culture to earn them jobs in Chinese firms operating in Africa. Many African students who attend Confucius Institutes and end up getting jobs in political, business, or diplomatic sectors present positive relations prospects with China, which suggests that these investments have positive returns for the interests of the Chinese government.

Despite the setbacks for CIs in Europe and North America, their numbers are increasing in African universities. These institutes expose African students not only to Chinese culture and language but also to Chinese studies and Chinese business culture classes. Increasingly so, CIs are expanding to include trainings in technical skills such as the case of the Confucius Institute of agriculture and farming in Kenya. Despite differences in how each CI is negotiated and established, all the institutes share a main goal of portraying the strengths and appeal of China's culture and traditions. Another similarity is that many times the Institutes (in their teaching curricula) diffuse and normalize the Chinese regime's party line and its official stance on sensitive topics like China's human rights record, Taiwan, minority rights, and the Hong Kong separatist movement. What distinguishes African-based CIs from the rest is that the African side does not have much leverage to resist Chinese authorities' grip on curriculum design and other decisions. "CIs work to unstick such adverse signs, figures and objects from China and in their stead, 'stick' more affirmative (and thus benign) ones such as Chinese characters, Confucius, and tea" (Schmidt 2014, 356). The adverse signs referenced here include communism, environmental pollution, the Tiananmen Square events, poor minority rights records, and authoritarian governance. These often evoke negative associations in the imaginaries of foreigners. Confucius Institutes' silence these events or repackage and normalize them in versions more in line with Hanban and Chinese government rhetoric. "Correcting" the image of China abroad is done both through the production of expert knowledge and regimes of truth that are shared with the audience enrolled in these courses. Indeed, an effective way to view CIs in Africa is to take them to be investments in human resource development. As such, they are spaces for expert knowledge production and diffusion. Part of the reason why Confucius Institutes become so attractive to African students is the combination of learning about China in a fun interactive way as well as being able to find good jobs both at the level of local governments and Chinese businesses upon completion of language programs.

Yet the challenge and limitation of this chapter lies in distinguishing Confucius Institutes' many missions, from business strategy to cultural diplomacy, from foreign aid to investment projects, across a wide variety of sectors and governmental agencies. Often, there is a great deal of overlap between these different categories. The overlap is made more complicated with the layers of networks built around these initiatives. The large Ethio-China Polytechnic College in Addis Ababa, which was built, staffed, and equipped by China, is a good example. The college fits at least two types of cooperation programs. It was built to fulfill FOCAC's commitment to opening China-Africa friendship schools, and then later it added a Confucius Institute inside the establishment. When the CI was added, the school became a site of cultural diplomacy, and later it was established as one of the schools on the 20+20 China-Africa education exchange platform. It is clear that the college cannot be considered solely as a bilateral education exchange, as foreign aid, or as cultural diplomacy since it is all of these at once. Other similar projects that cross several categories include building a new Science University in Malawi, building universities in Liberia, funding the development of a clinical master's degree in nursing in the Democratic Republic of the Congo under the auspices of contributing to the AU's New Partnership for Africa's Development education and training program (Jensen 2015, 164). Understanding what type of projects these are or why they are sponsored by the Chinese government is challenging at best.

Confucius Institutes play an important role in expanding relational productive power in China-Africa encounters through networks and connections weaved between the Hanban's administration, African students, Chinese business firms, and universities across China. They connect institutions throughout the mainland with their host universities in Africa. They also cultivate and maintain strong connections with Chinese businesses conducting business in Africa for the purpose of enabling outstanding students to be hired by Chinese companies.

CHAPTER SEVEN
Relational Power beyond China-Africa

CHINA'S RISE TO POWER has become one of the most discussed questions in both International Relations theory (IRT) and foreign policy circles. IR scholars have, for many decades, been interested in the concept of power and have studied it from multiple angles. Analyzing different ways of conceptualizing power and dominance in international affairs has been central to contemporary IR schools. Although power has been a core concept of IRT for a long time, the faces and mechanisms of power as it relates to Chinese foreign policy making have reinvigorated and changed the contours of that debate. With the rise of China and other reemerging or newly emerging powers across the global political arena comes a new visibility for different kinds of encounters between states, particularly between China and other Global South states. These encounters have been present all along, but they are made more visible to IR scholars now because of the increasing influence and impact of rising powers in the international system. This book has demonstrated that these foreign policy encounters have distinctive features that require new theoretical frameworks for their analysis—frameworks developed to study Western "great power politics" and the power diffusion mechanisms just do not provide enough explanatory leverage.

I began *Shaping the Future of Power* by probing the type of power mechanisms that build, diffuse, and project China's power in Africa. The crux of what this book has shown is that it is necessary to consider the processes of knowledge production, social capital formation, and skills transfers in Chinese foreign policy toward African states to fully understand China's power-building mechanisms. By examining China's investments in human resource development programs for Africa, the book examined a vital yet undertheorized aspect of China's foreign policy making. The theoretical framework developed in chapter 3 accounted for these investments as mechanisms for network-building and spaces for constructing and normalizing certain representations and practices of China-Africa relations. This framework and its application in the case study chapters have shown how power and hegemonic formations permeate Global South encounters. This chapter (1) summarizes the book's main argument and findings, (2) develops the implications of the argument and their transformative potential for IRT, (3) explores the implications of the book's argument and theoretical framework on material (realist) conceptualizations of power, (4) expands the scope of the framework to assess its potential applications to cases beyond China-Africa relations, and (5) looks forward to potential future implications for the analysis of global politics.

Social Capital, Knowledge Production, and Norm Diffusion

In the context of Chinese foreign policy toward Africa, this book has illuminated several dynamics. It has shown the ways that processes of knowledge production and skills transfers are particularly vital to power building. These processes wield so much influence because they create solid people-to-people relations and build networks of guanxi. Sponsoring capacity-building programs for African government officials, journalists, military officers, and other professionals creates routinized opportunities for exchanges and contributes to enlarging Beijing's network of people-to-people relations. Being powerful in the sense of guanxi means having expanded networks of relations that are expected to facilitate the conduct of trade, business, and diplomatic exchanges. Relationships in and of themselves do not equal power but the manipulations of relationships—including nurturing and expanding them—are the key. Therefore, in making sense of China's increasing investments in human capital, it is necessary to think about the social capital and network-building value of these foreign policy tools.

Additionally, this book delved into Chinese government-funded professionalization training programs and found that, through repetition and institutionalization, routine exchange programs and workshops and seminars for African officials become spaces for diffusing norms, normalizing discourse, and marketing Chinese models as an alternative to West-centric norms. The book pursued how relational power (or guanxi) and the power-knowledge nexus work through investments in skill transfers programs and people-centered diplomacy. To do this, it deployed the two-pronged methodology of examining discourse and policies. Investing in seminars and workshops for thousands of Africans provides a space to reinforce the articulations of Chinese officials' discourse and turn them into conventional wisdom brandings of China-Africa relations. As chapter 4 on military diplomacy and guanxi shows, during the extensive and routinized workshops held by high-ranking Chinese military officers for their African counterparts, strengthening guanxi is not the only outcome. Indeed, shaping the discourse on issues of security, threats, techniques of how to respond to them, and equipment used to respond to them are ways that endeavor to socialize African trainees to become knowledgeable about Chinese standards for responding to security threats.

In a nutshell, without neglecting the importance of economic statecraft such as investments in infrastructure projects and natural resource extraction, it is crucial to explore the processes of knowledge production and dissemination of China's foreign policy toward Africa, especially as manifested in human capital investments. The three cases analyzed in the book show that the target audience is wide, including elite government officials, high-ranking military personnel, peacekeepers, journalists, teachers, and university students. The cases demonstrate that professionalization training programs and exchanges are very important both in fostering bonds of trust and cooperation between military officials in China and their African counterparts *and* in incentivizing Africans to adopt Chinese governance practices and strategies. In fact, even when the content of the professionalization trainings is not useful, the all-expense paid trips to China generate an awe effect through witnessing and admiring China's development success. Touring China's big cities, military facilities, and ultramodern infrastructure projects with delegations of African government officials, journalists, and students results in an amalgam of affective, guanxi, and soft power bonds between African civil servants and their Chinese counterparts.

When all-expense-paid trips are offered to journalists and media staff from across Africa, the personal guanxi bonds that are developed aim to get African journalists to see China in a positive light. Chinese officials' stated goal is to diffuse a positive narrative about China's activities in Africa to effectively counter Western (typically) critical takes on China's debt trap and other neocolonial policies. Training programs for journalists also have a content component that teaches African journalists about sensitive political and historical topics about China's history (from Taiwan to Xinjiang and other issues), as well as Chinese journalism values and practices (such as refraining from criticizing the government and framing things positively).

Likewise, in chapter 6, "Guanxi in Cultural Diplomacy and Confucius Institutes," human capital investment programs combine trainings for students attending the cultural institute, teachers being trained to teach Mandarin, and Chinese volunteers who teach Mandarin in African middle and high school classes. Each of these empirical cases show both how investments in human resource development expand China's relational power and guanxi and how they result in very concrete policy gains. Those policy gains include branding China as a country whose successful development story is attractive to African elites, showing off China's stability and security record to military officers, and making its language and business culture attractive to young people aspiring to get decent-paying jobs in Chinese firms operating in Africa. Material conceptualizations of power fall short of accounting for the impact of China's influence in Africa or the mechanisms of attraction to China's model.

Contributions to Thinking about Global Politics

This book offers an innovative contribution to the old question of power/social relations and knowledge production in IR. Although political scientists have long acknowledged the essential role of knowledge production in power building (going back all the way to Confucius's teachings that by investing in shaping minds one can conquer nations), concerns about mechanisms of norm-making and diffusion and their impacts on foreign policy making in the Global South have been marginalized. Through examining China's foreign policy conduct toward African states, this study refines IR scholarship on China's rising power and the intersection of social relations and foreign policy making both theoretically and empirically.

Empirically speaking, the case of China's interactions with African states has not attracted much attention in IR scholarship largely because China does not (yet) appear to be a great power in Africa if we understand great power politics in terms of material and military dimensions of power. Until very recently, China did not have any military bases in Africa and did not project much military influence, which can be viewed as the main reason why many IR scholars thought China to be a marginal power in Africa, at best. This book showed the errors in "conventional wisdom" or recurrent representation of China's capabilities, not by correcting for the estimates of Chinese material capability, bases, and military power projection capacity in Africa, but by expanding the concept of power to include relational and productive dimensions. *Shaping the Future of Power* offers a new empirical study that is important in itself and for the theoretical innovation it allows.

Theoretically, this book's starting point was the framework of the faces of power (Lukes 2005; Barnett and Duvall 2005) where it identified the fourth face (power as productive) to be most promising for analyzing Chinese foreign policy conduct. It built on extant scholarship and developed an innovative theoretical framework to make sense of how great powers project their influence and how countries are socialized into new norms. The framework—relational productive power—has three essential elements: social relations (guanxi), knowledge production, and norm diffusion. Relational productive power helps us understand the ways in which Chinese foreign policy maneuvers and navigates its social/diplomatic networks in order to both advance its interests and couch them in a friendly, peaceful rising power narrative. With China's continuing rise as a regional and global power, more scholarly attention should be devoted to analyzing China's rise using innovative perspectives. By accounting for both the role of investments in knowledge production and norm diffusion and the role of building and expanding social relations, the framework adds to scholarship on post-Western perspectives and non-Western actors concerning China and its foreign policy conduct in Africa.

Can a Relational Productive Approach Apply to Material Dimensions of Power?

Analyzing China-Africa relations should shift away from focusing on the material manifestations of power dynamics in China's Africa policy (such as natural resource extractions and financial investments). It is important to start looking at less visible and less material types of investment (in social relations, network expansion, and human capital). By expanding the concept of power and its mechanisms to include investments other than the usual (material) targets, we can account for a big portion of China-Africa power dynamics. By putting social relations and guanxi networks at the center of the analysis, I was able to explain trends such as the decline in loans and grants pledged by China for Africans in 2018, which was accompanied with an increase in its disbursements of human capital investment programs. Here the story is not about financial capital (or the lack thereof), it is about the (re)allocation of the capital from industrial and natural resource sectors to human resource development programs.

However, it is important to point out that the difference between these two types of power dynamics is not as clear-cut as a binary of material/non-material might suggest. In fact, the flow between them is more fluid than one might think. For example, my relational power framework can be used to explain material power dynamics in China-Africa relations. Take, for example, China's naval base in Djibouti. On the ninetieth birthday of China's People's Liberation Army, in October 2017, the deputy commander of the People's Liberation Army Navy, Tian Zhong, and Chinese ambassador to Djibouti Fu Huaqiang officially launched China's first foreign base ever and Djibouti's fourth foreign base.[1] The base has the capacity to host up to 10,000 People's Liberation Army soldiers, which is two and a half times the capacity of Camp Lemonnier, the US base in Djibouti. Unsurprisingly, the Chinese official discourse around the launching of the base stresses that it will strictly be used for medical evacuations, natural disaster relief, and in defensive ways that would require the protection of Chinese nationals and assets in Djibouti. The base was the product of a long process of negotiation between Djibouti's president Ismaïl Omar Guelleh and the Chinese government, was concealed by Chinese official rhetoric, and was long described as a refueling station.

Distancing the base from being a military outpost for China serves several purposes for China, namely projecting an image of China as a peaceful rising power. In addition to keeping a narrative about the base not being meant for war or offensive purposes, the base plays a cultural role that aims at fostering relations and communications between Djibouti's population and China's (military) culture. To illustrate this role, there is a joint program with Djibouti's Ministry of Education to bring Djiboutian primary school students to visit the Chinese naval base. At each visit, up to one hundred kids are exposed to the innovative facilities of the base, they get to see China's military strength, but also build a personal connection to the base, playing in it for half a day and putting a human face to it. According to China's military website, the visits aim to "help Djibouti primary school students know more about Chinese culture and the Chinese military, promote communications between local people and the Chinese troops stationed in the support base, so as to carry forward the friendship between the two peoples."[2]

China's military base, in the example above, serves a relational purpose that works in tandem with its material purpose. It is used to bring primary school children on school field trips to China's military base to show them China's military capabilities and leave impressionable memories after showing them around the premises and giving them parting souvenirs. China's military base plays a role of investing in social relations with kids who are still in primary school, and this cultural feature of the military base is unique to China. One of the direct benefits of such cultural programs includes not thinking of China's military base as a suspicious, unknown, or even hawkish naval base. Bringing children and adult civilians to the base to use its fitness facilities, tour it, and take pictures with its military equipment and staff makes it feel accessible to the ordinary Djiboutian citizen. It gives it a human feel. The US base, and US Africa Command, engage in soft power diplomacy too but usually these are humanitarian actions such as donating equipment to Cameroonian schools or performing medical surgeries (which the Chinese side does as well).[3] Nurturing relations in the way that China does, by investing in future generations' perceptions of China, is very powerful and cannot really be captured using a traditional material understanding of power. Therefore, even the material naval base of China in Africa can be more fully accounted for by paying attention to its relational and social capital dimension.

Moreover, it is also interesting to note that as the military base deal was in the negotiation phase, Chinese diplomats insisted on a narrative of how profitable to local people the base will be by bringing economic, security, and social mobility opportunities for the Djiboutian people. China's base was marketed as a support facility for the People's Liberation Army in its antipiracy escorts (citing thirty escort trips in the last decade), United Nations peacekeeping operations deployments (especially for missions in South Sudan and Somalia), and providing evacuation plans for Chinese nationals working in the region when needed. This narrative stands as a stark contrast from the counterterrorism justifications of the US and French bases in Djibouti. While negotiating the base, the Chinese side sought to organize a network of social capital connecting the base to China's adjacent multipurpose port and to a pledge to construct a smart city in Djibouti. Blending economic deals with the military base project is another illustration of China's foreign policy shifting away from the traditional separation between military/defense and economic/social diplomacy. Right now, "most of Djibouti's fourteen major infrastructure projects, which have been valued at a total of $14.4 billion, are being funded by Chinese banks" (Chaziza 2018, 153), something that's completely lacking from US-Djibouti relations, which are mostly about countering terrorism. The Chinese approach banks on social networks and also strengthens them through projects that connect its military base to a multipurpose port that employs up to 60 percent local staff. In this way the military base is not viewed as fulfilling China's geostrategic national interests only (even when it does), but is contributing to the local economy in significant ways.

What Does Relational Productive Power Mean for China's Impact on the International Order?

Chinese foreign policy makers are interested in promoting a Chinese model of development (which, as I explained in chapter 2, is known as the Beijing Consensus) and disseminating Chinese cultural practices, language, and technical skills to rival European and American alternatives. As Andrew Lui (2010, 27) argues, "China seeks to solidify its position as a central node in a network of states that is inclined towards a particular non-Western view of human rights, governance and sovereignty." More so than just challenging some international norms that Beijing finds unsatisfying, Lui continues to explain that "Chinese foreign policy is attempting to expand the size of this network and to strengthen existing relations by appealing to new members." From this perspective, China's activities with African states can be seen as endeavors to challenge the existing order and create new niches of influence for Chinese diplomacy. They are policies in and for Africa, but they are part of a larger context of how China plans on facing the global political arena in the twenty-first century.

What does Chinese activity in Africa reveal about Beijing's larger foreign policy goals and its impact on the international order? Is China trying to write a new global order, reinterpret parts of the existing one, or is it strengthening the current order by creating new initiatives that are compatible and congruent with existing rules? The empirical cases examined in this book are not instances of Chinese investments that are exclusive to China's conduct in Africa. Confucius Institutes are established in all corners of the world, agriculture demonstration centers are being opened in Latin American countries, and as I mention in chapter 2, the professionalization training programs and workshops target officers, civil servants, and journalists from over a hundred countries. Therefore, the findings of this book suggest trends in Chinese foreign policy making that are broader than the case of China-Africa relations. In fact, a focus on investing in human resource development programs is even evident in China's most recent global initiative called the "New Silk Road," which is also known as the Belt and Road Initiative (BRI).

The Belt and Road Initiative was announced by Xi Jinping in 2013 with the goal of reviving the old Silk Road paths of trade, communication, energy, and customs collaboration and connectivity.[4] The New Silk Road is designed to link China to Central Asia, Africa, and Southern Europe, and position China at the center of the development projects of the regions around it (Godehardt 2016, 20). As it stands, it consists of two major corridors: an overland Eurasian network that economically links China with Asian, Middle Eastern, Gulf Cooperation Council, and European countries, and a maritime corridor connecting Chinese port cities to the Indian Ocean and expanding to the South Pacific and the Mediterranean. The initiative is massive in its outreach, creating a regional and global network of connectivity through circulation of goods, communication technology, power grids, cultural exchanges, and railway construction encompassing over seventy countries (and growing) (Zhang 2015, 123). This mix of material and ideational investments in modern China's grand strategy is another indication of Chinese foreign policy giving as much importance to natural as to human resource investments. But the BRI neither lends evidence that the Chinese government is becoming more socialized in the liberal order by adopting its norms of governance, development, and human rights, nor that it is interested in completely redoing the international system. Rather, the BRI is a good exemplar of Beijing's moves to claim its own brand of development, governance norms, and values, and the way to diffuse these is through its investments in professionalization trainings and cultural exchanges.[5]

Beyond Africa: China's Human Capital Investments via BRI

At the opening ceremony of the Belt and Road Forum held in Beijing in 2017, President Xi Jinping announced that "in the coming five years, we will offer 2,500 short-term research visits to China for young foreign scientists, train 5,000 foreign scientists, engineers and managers, and set up fifty joint laboratories."[6] This pledge adds to the dozen programs already in place for teachers' trainings, Mandarin language classes, and other exchange forums between China and Central Asian countries along the Belt and Road. Indeed, although BRI is primarily about connecting China to Central Asia and Eastern Europe by building massive infrastructure projects, facilitating integrated markets, and promoting trade, a major component of the initiative is Chinese government-funded skills transfer programs such as teacher training programs and seminars for public officials from countries along the BRI, among other people-to-people diplomacy programs.

Human capital investments in the form of capacity-building programs, Mandarin language trainings for future teachers, seminars for journalists, defense forums, and other workshops for government officials have become a signature of China's foreign policy in the Global South. These trainings are funded by the Chinese government and backed by several educational institutions in China. They are unidirectional where participants come from a variety of countries across the Global South and the trainers are from China. When teams of Chinese experts need expertise or technical trainings, they typically use their connections in Western countries (Germany, the United Kingdom, Australia, and the United States, among others) to obtain the expertise needed.

To be sure, socialization through cultural diplomacy is not new to foreign policy making in general and not new to China's foreign policy. Chinese foreign policy practices that go back all the way to imperial China lend evidence of hegemony via cultural diplomacy.[7] Looking at China's position in the pre-Westphalian world order, one can observe how the tributary system acted as "an indispensable social milieu within which Imperial China tried to socialize others" (Zhang and Buzan 2012, 17). China's practices of socialization, then, were mainly driven by "assertion, coercion or coaxing [the other], into accepting basic institutional practices favored by Imperial China in managing its relations with others" (Zhang and Buzan 2012, 19). China's self-sense of superior identity in the pre-Westphalian order did not result in China conquering territory to impose its bureaucratic system and norms on others. Instead, institutionalized cultural practices such as kowtow and tribute-giving were required of foreigners to perform as they addressed China's emperor for protection or trade access. In contemporary Chinese foreign policy, the element of cultural diplomacy and people-to-people exchange is ever more present and central to the CCP's rising power. The connectivity and network approach of the BRI has to do with people-to-people networks as much as power grids and infrastructure connectivity.

How Does Africans Agency Fit in International Relations Scholarship?

In 2016, journalist Lily Kuo wrote an article entitled "China's Model of Economic Development Is Becoming More Popular in Africa Than America's" where she finds compelling evidence that the Chinese model is a better "fit" for Africa. She explains that "China's state-led economic reforms and prioritization of stability over an active civil society has been appealing for countries like Ethiopia and Rwanda, which have followed a similar model" (Kuo 2016). The impression of China's model being more fit for African experiences is based on recently released survey data by Afrobarometer.[8] The surveys were distributed to 56,000 participants randomly chosen from across thirty-six African countries. The results show that 24 percent of survey respondents picked China as the best development model for their countries. The report released by Afrobarometer also showed that about two-thirds of the people surveyed reported that they find China's presence in the continent to be "very" or "somewhat" positive. The report states that "despite considerable criticism in the media of China's interests and operations in Africa, Africans view China's emergence as an addition to the economic playing field" (Kuo 2016). Although the surveys do not include questions on the reasons behind Africans' positive impressions of China and their attraction to China's development model, this book has shown that human capital investments, paid-for trips to China, cultural activities, and other social capital-building activities play a significant role.

Even though the scope of this book did not focus on examining the ways in which African state leaders and foreign policy makers leverage and negotiate their preferences with their Chinese counterparts, another line of future research that's inspired from this book's findings is about examining how African states are navigating the changing dynamics of the international system. Although this book examined mostly Chinese foreign policy conduct toward African states, it also took into account the perceptions of African elites and professionals of the professionalization training programs and skills transfers sponsored by Beijing. One of this book's limitations, which I discuss in chapter 2, "Network-Building in China-Africa Relations: Past and Present," is that it assumes power relations between China and African states to be asymmetrical and does not examine ways in which African actors (public and private) exercise power in their relations with China. Given the unidirectional dynamics of the professionalization trainings and the lack of African counterparts to China's Confucius Institutes, this book assumed hierarchical power dynamics in the China-Africa relations. Still, there is also no doubt that there exists an important degree of variance in state capacity among the different African states, which means a variance in African states' capacity to shape and challenge the CCP. This book did not account for these variances given that it examined multilateral (not bilateral) relations between China and African states. Therefore, future research can build on this study to examine in more depth the Africa rising narrative and how much this framework applies to African agency.

Moreover, as explained in earlier chapters, this book has not yet accounted for the direct impacts of Chinese government-backed professionalization trainings of African elites. It has not conducted a systematic or longitudinal analysis to ascertain to what extent CCP-funded human capital investments are resulting in socializing African states to adopt Chinese models of governance, development, and values of journalism and human rights. This book gave many anecdotes and examples of how these mechanisms work. To illustrate, when South Sudanese politician Anthony Kpandu led a delegation of party members to China for professionalization trainings on governance by officers from Beijing's Central Party School, he stated that they "have learned quite a lot from the CCP." Upon returning from one of several training trips he took, Kpandu wrote a report recommending that his party, the Sudan People's Liberation Movement, acquire surveillance drones that he saw being used during his trip to China (Ang 2018). Similarly, commenting on scholarships provided by the Chinese government to hundreds of South Sudanese students at the University of Bahr el Ghazel, the school's vice chancellor observed that "in 10 years' time, one of [these students] will be the leader of South Sudan" (Kuo 2017). From these examples (and others), there is evidence that these approaches are successful from the Chinese government's perspective given the continuous increase in their number and scope. At the very least, more exposure to China, its development and industrialization model, and creating opportunities for networking between high-ranking government officials in China and African countries are outcomes of the trainings whether targeted or unintended. Future research could look into the impacts of these professionalization training programs to assess— over time—the extent to which, say, journalists or party members who receive trainings in China become more favorable toward China and China's politics in their respective countries.

Overall, a common thread to many of these areas of future research revolve around closer examinations of the position and role of Africa in the global order. Are African states diversifying their dependencies from traditional powers in the North and West to rising power in the East and South? Such questions fall within an agenda of decentralizing theories of IR to include post-Western IR approaches, actors, and perspectives. They open up a conversation about the differences between the conduct of hegemons and great powers in the context of the Global South, which is substantially different from the traditional, colonial trajectories of European powers. In this sense, the realist expectation that all great powers are expected to act alike once they reach a certain threshold of material capabilities is a limiting way of analyzing global politics today.

Ultimately, since international relations and foreign policy making are at the very base relational, political science must pay attention to relationality and relational productive power. To suggest that there is a link between foreign policy making, socialization, relational power, and social capital in foreign policy making might seem clear at first because much of diplomacy is about relations between states, state elites, and peoples. Yet there are complex mechanisms that translate relations into guanxi and even more complex mechanisms that guarantee that guanxi translates to achieving successful policy goals. *Shaping the Future of Power* was not only about how relationality matters in foreign policy making and IRT, it was also about showing how social capital, knowledge production, and norm diffusion are essential mechanisms of international *relating*.

Notes

Chapter 1

1. World Bank data, http://povertydata.worldbank.org/poverty/country/ CHN

2. Sun 2016; Ang 2018; Hawkins 2018; Prasso 2019; Zeng 2015.

3. Sun 2016.

4. See Table 1 for a more extensive list of party-to-party delegation visits scheduled between 2016 and 2018.

5. China's trade volume with Africa is larger than that of emerging economies such as India and Brazil, and that of traditional actors such as European countries, which have in the past been very influential on Africa economies. In 2003, only 6 percent of sub-Saharan African exports (natural resources primarily but also some agriculture crops and finished products) went to China whereas 37 percent were destined to Europe. A decade later, the volume jumped to 27 percent for China and declined to 23 percent for Europe. For more on China-Africa trade volumes, see China-Africa Research Initiative trade database: http://www.sais-cari. org/data-china-africa-trade/

6. The eight platforms are "industrial promotion initiative, an infrastructure connectivity initiative, a trade facilitation initiative, a green development initiative, a capacity building initiative, a health care initiative, a people-to-people exchange initiative and a peace and security initiative in close collaboration with African countries in the next three years and beyond, to support African countries in achieving independent and sustainable development at a faster pace" (FOCAC 2018).

7. For more discussion of the relational turn in IR, see, among others, Anderson and Neumann 2012; Guzzini 2000, 2011; Jackson and Nexon 1998. I expand on this in more detail in chapter 3.

8. Interview in Beijing, May 2014.

9. My interviewees included academics from Peking University, Renmin University, Communication University of China, and Zhejiang Normal University in Jinhua. These interviews were conducted in English.

10. Some interviewees (especially with interviewees from North African countries) switched frequently between Arabic and French.

11. Interview in Addis Ababa with a Nigerian diplomat in February 2015. The diplomat also mentioned how much he appreciated that, during these trips, the Chinese side typically gives a monetary allowance or spending money to the participants. Receiving an honorarium meant, to him, that his time was valued and appreciated.

Chapter 2

1. Development Reimagined 2017.

2. Initially these principles were formulated in the context of India-China relations in 1954 in a visit between Indian prime minister Jawaharlal Nehru and Zhou Enlai. China has adopted these principles as guidelines for its relations not just with India but with other countries as well. By the same token, India's foreign policy making also draws on these principles. For more on this, see Li Anshan 2012; Daniel Large 2008; Julia Strauss 2009; Ian Taylor 2006.

3. Article 54 of the PRC's first plenary session of the Chinese People's Political Consultative Conference (1950, 19-20). These principles and goals remain standing till today.

4. Phone interview with a Chinese Institute of Contemporary International Relations scholar and expert in Chinese foreign relations—Beijing, summer 2014.

5. For more on China's ancient belief that the Chinese emperor was the Son of Heaven and that all else was under heaven (Tien Xia), see Fairbank (1974). For analyses on how this sense of cultural superiority informed China's conduct with other countries (through practices such as the tribute system), see Kelly (2012). For a critical analysis on how pre-Westphalian China used to behave internationally and how that still informs (if only partly) its contemporary foreign policy conduct, see Godehart (2016).

6. South-South Cooperation is a vague concept but in 2012 UN Secretary General Ban Ki Moon provided the following definition: "a process whereby two or more developing countries pursue their individual and/or shared national capacity development objectives through exchanges of knowledge, skills, resources and technical know-how, and through regional and interregional collective actions, including partnerships involving Governments, regional organizations, civil society, academia and the private sector, for their individual and/or mutual benefit within and across regions. South-South cooperation is not a substitute for, but rather a complement to, North-South cooperation" (2012, 7).

7. Brazil, Russia, India, China, and South Africa are grouped together as middle-income economies that are driving much of the global economy.

8. This list is includes Indonesia, Mexico, Nigeria, and Ethiopia.

9. For more on China's dual identity and its implications for its foreign policy, see Wu (2001)

10. This is a recurrent description of China by Chinese officials. One example was Xi Jinping's speech at the 19th National Congress of the Communist Party of

China, where Xi Jinping said that China's international status as the world's largest developing country has not changed (Xinhua 2018).

11. Scholars of Chinese foreign policy do not disagree that China's identity is at once a great power and a developing country. However, the disagreement in the literature is around whether China is displaying status-quo behavior more or revisionist behavior more. By taking measures such as the Asian Infrastructure and Investment Bank, and the Belt and Road Initiative, and the Beijing Consensus as exemplary of China's revisionist intentions toward the international order, obscures the fact that China is increasingly becoming a solid support for UN Peacekeeping Operations, the International Monetary Fund, and other West-dominated initiatives. Qin (2014, 285) argues that "continuity through change is a realistic description of China's present international strategy." For him, there is no questioning that there is a mix of status-quo and revisionist practices but he argues that ultimately there is more continuity than change.

12. Such initiatives include but are not limited to the Belt and Road, the Asian Infrastructure and Investment Bank, and the China Africa Fund. For more on this, see Benabdallah 2019; Hagström and Nordin 2019.

13. The concept of noninterference (不干涉原则 Bù gānshè yuánzé) in Chinese foreign policy is referred to as encompassing both noninterference and nonintervention in some cases. The delineation between the two in Chinese foreign policy literature is ambiguous; in some official documents the concept of noninterference is used interchangeably with nonintervention (不干预 Bù gānyù).

14. Chinese Ministry of Foreign Affairs, China's Initiation of the Five Principles of Peaceful Co-Existence.

15. Calls to boycott the Beijing Olympics (calling them the Genocide Games) is a good example of this pressure from the international community.

16. More substantially, in 2007 a Chinese-ran oil field (in Defra) was attacked by a Darfur-based opposition group, the Justice and Equality Movement. The spokesperson for the rebel group declared that it had targeted Chinese interests in the region on purpose because of Chinese support for the Sudanese government. The rebel forces declared that all foreign companies that stayed in South Sudan beyond the evacuation deadline given to them would be considered guilty of assisting the Sudanese government in purchasing weapons used to violate the rights of South Sudanese families. See, for more details, Shinn (2009, 90).

17. Foreign Minister Wang Yi giving an interview to Al Jazeera on January 9, 2014.

18. The International Criminal Court, it should be noted, despite its resolute condemnation of Gaddafi's use of force, had no qualms about exempting NATO's allies from investigations of their 2011 campaign in Libya (Ba 2017, 56).

19. This was just one example among many. For more on China's aid and its potential impact on voting behavior and electoral campaigning, see Dreher et al. (2019). The study finds that the birth regions of presidents receive up to three times the aid flows from China in the years when they are in office than otherwise. Other relevant literature includes Alden (2007), Brautigam (2009, 2015), and Corkin (2008a, 2008b).

20. Taylor further documents Zhou Enlai's 1965 tour of Tanzania, where he said, "My colleagues and I do not find ourselves in a strange land. Relations between our countries dated back to nine hundred years ago. Some five hundred years ago, the Chinese navigator Cheng Ho (also spelled Zheng He) reached East African coasts" (New China News Agency, June 5, 1965).

21. Stopping the clock, so to speak, with the statue of Zheng He can be misleading on many levels. The country of Kenya as we know it today was not even a country at the time of the admiral's voyages. Yet the dedication plaque celebrating endless peaceful relations between "China and Kenya" is an example of how history (and cultural edifices) is used to manipulate the present and future.

22. The prime ministers of Burma, Ceylon, India, Indonesia, and Pakistan met in Colombo, Sri Lanka in April 1953 to organize what would become the first Asian-Africa conference in Bandung, Indonesia.

23. The peak of the cultural revolution (in terms of Chinese foreign policy making) was in 1967 with the "Boxer Diplomacy" when the Red Guards started explicitly interfering with the operations of the Ministry of Foreign Affairs, going as far as occupying it at some point.

24. China suffered a major setback in its relations with African nations. The governments of Kenya and Tunisia, for example, were particularly aggravated by Mao's abuse of power against intellectuals and artists and broke off their relations with Beijing. Ghana was undergoing a regime change in 1966, ousting Kwame Nkrumah (who was in China during the coup) and expelling all Chinese in Ghana.

25. The Sino-Soviet conflict had a role to play in the deteriorating relations. As explained by Yu (2009, 10), "During the 1960s and the 1970s, China's ruling Communist Party repeatedly rejected requests by African states and political parties to establish relations, based upon the latter's stand toward the former Soviet Union."

26. According to Le Pere and Shelton (2007, 56), from the mid-1950s to the mid-1970s, China gave about $2.5 billion in aid to thirty-six African countries.

27. For more details on the TAZARA construction, see Georgy Yu's "The Tanzanian-Zambian Railway: A Case Study in Chinese Economic Aid to Africa," in *Soviet and Chinese Aid to African Nations*, ed. Warren Weinstein and Thomas H. Henriksen (New York: Praeger, 1980), 117–144, and Jamie Monson's *African's Freedom Railway: How a Chinese Development Project Changed Lives and Livelihoods in Tanzania* (Bloomington: Indiana University Press, 2009).

28. http://china-aibo.cn/. The webpage is in Mandarin Chinese.

29. Emphasis on the word "relations" added.

Chapter 3

1. Scholars take various positions in debates on China's power status, with characterizations ranging from partial power, status-quo power, regional power, superpower, and revisionist power. For more on this, see Johnston 2003; Shambaugh 2013; Nathan and Scobell 2012; Pu 2019.

2. Bachrach and Baratz (1962) argue that besides asking the question "who rules?," as sociologists do, or "does anyone have power?", we should be looking at what agenda items are left out of the discussion.

3. This is what Bachrach and Baratz (1962, 952) call "non-decision making," which refers to the "extent to which and the manner in which the status quo-oriented persons and groups influence those community values and those political institutions."

4. Foucault (1982, 790) argues that "freedom may well appear as the condition for the exercise of power (at the same time its precondition), since freedom must exist for power to be exerted, and also its permanent support, since without the possibility of recalcitrance, power would be equivalent to a physical determination."

5. It is beyond the scope of this section to do a thorough survey of the rich postcolonial and feminist perspectives on relational power. For more details, see Agathangelou and Ling 2004; Allen 1998; Enloe 1989; McEwan 2001; and Piedalue and Rishi 2017.

6. For more on a Foucauldian feminist appraisal of relational power, see Cooper 1994.

7. The juridico-discursive perspective on power is principally understood from the perspective of repression as reflected in interdiction, law, censure, constraint, and law. Foucault critiques this form of power on the grounds that it assumes power to be a substance, a possession instead of a relation. For more on this, see Lemke 2001, 32.

8. The concept of renqing is about "human feeling." Yang explains that these come from Confucian thoughts. Renqing sentiments and feelings are the source of "proper conduct of social relationships and social events and affairs that made possible and preserved the whole social order" (1994, 67).

9. An example of overlapping circles of relations include China as a developing country, as a member of the Association of Southeast Asian Nations (ASEAN) 10+3, a permanent member of the UN Security Council, a founding member of BRICS (Brazil, Russia, India, China, and South Africa), the Asian Infrastructure and Investment Bank, and a sizeable IMF lender.

10. Acharya 2014; Suzuki 2014; Thies and Nieman 2017; Abdenur and Gama 2015; and Zhang and Buzan 2012.

11. Epstein (2008, 9) argues that what becomes experienced as "common sense" is produced within historical contexts in which some meanings are sealed and others are left out. She takes the discourse on banning whaling as productive of the meaning of whales as well as regulating the practices regarding whales. This discourse led to the creation of many NGOs that carried out the new anti-whaling discourse and turned it into a practice of protecting whales. For more illustrative works that show how meanings are produced through discourse that become enshrined in practices, see, for example, Doty 1993; Abrahamsen 2004; Mattern 2005; Hansen 2006; and Larsen 2013.

Chapter 4

1. More details on the Forum are discussed in Deutsche Welle 2019.

2. For the full text, see China's MOFA 2006.

3. One of the reasons why cooperation on peace and security is off to a later start compared to other fields of cooperation such as agribusiness and trade is due to Beijing's adherence to the principle of noninterference. Evidently, security cooperation (especially if understood as military presence on African countries' soil) seems to be a direct violation of that principle. However, as discussed in subsequent parts of the chapter, pressures from international institutions, local African governments, as well as Chinese nationals and business owners, have all weighed in on the shift from a strict interpretation of noninterference to a more lenient "selective engagement."

4. The US Africa Command, or AFRICOM, was initiated in 2007 and announced at the same time that the Chinese premier was touring Africa. It has an effective force of 1,500 officers and its headquarters are in Stuttgart, Germany.

5. Zuma's closing remarks during FOCAC 2015b.

6. Section 4.3.6 of the action plan of FOCAC 2015c. Section 4.3.2 announces that the "Chinese side will offer 2000-degree education opportunities in China and 30,000 government scholarships to African countries." Section 3.1.11 explains in more detail the trainings in agribusiness and agriculture. Section 5.2.1 expands on the seminars sponsored for African journalists (radio and TV) to be exposed to Chinese theories and practices in journalism.

7. Major General Zhu Chengdu cited in Xinhua News 2004. http://www.china.org.cn/english/2004/Aug/103238.htm

8. "Military Institute Set Up for Training Foreign Officers," Xinhua News, August 7, 2004

9. Chinese Ministry of Defense, http://eng.mod.gov.cn/DefenseNews/2016–05/12/content_4657092.htm

10. White Paper on China's National Defense released in July 2019. For the full text in English, see http://www.xinhuanet.com/english/2019–07/24/c_138253389.htm

11. Interview with Xinhua on June 4, 2016, http://eng.mod.gov.cn/Opinion/2016–06/06/content_4670851.htm

12. "China Growing Its Peacekeeping Presence," Defense Web article, http://www.defenceweb.co.za/index.php?option=com_content&view=article&id=44855:china-growing-its-peacekeeping-presence&catid=56:diplomacy-a-peace&Itemid=111

13. The seven missions are in Darfur, the Democratic Republic of the Congo, Liberia, Mali, and South Sudan, as well as small contingents to Cote D'Ivoire and Western Sahara (Thrall 2015, 54).

14. Chinese Central Government, http://www.gov.cn/zwgk/2009–10/19/content_1443395.htm

15. 政协外事委副主任韩方明：探讨建立中国黑水公司, http://cppcc.people.com.cn/GB/35377/17010201.html. The title of this report translates as "Deputy

Director of the CPPCC Han Fangming Urges the Establishment of China's Version of Blackwater."

16. Erickson and Collins 2012.

17. See Spegele, Wonacott, and Bariyq 2012.

18. Shandong Huawei Security Group, December 21, 2014, http://www.hwbaoan.com/sysen/News_View.asp?NewsID=425#.V1tV4Vcdf-Y

19. PMCs are different from PSCs in the following way. The former tends to deploy military techniques and use counterterrorism trainings when approaching security while the latter happens at a much more civilian level (sometimes not even involving weapons). Many scholars use the two interchangeably because many companies offer trainings and service in both at the same time.

20. China's top-tier PSCs are comparable in cost to their US or European counterparts (Arduino 2018).

Chapter 5

1. Deng (2012) reported in the *China Daily* that in order "to make the rest of the world aware of China's role in Africa, the Chinese mass media have to break the monopoly of their Western competitors in Africa and spread the facts, as well as the views, of the Chinese government and think tanks across the world."

2. See Benabdallah (2015) for a study on how the *Economist* magazine represents China-Africa relations through a "China Threat" lens and how the Chinese government is countering such representations.

3. On December 31, 2016, CCTV was renamed China's Global Television Network (CGTN). I use the two names interchangeably.

4. Ronning (2014) looks at public diplomacy as a mechanism of soft power; Zhang (2015) proposes constructive journalism as a way for Chinese media to portray African stories positively, yet not naively; Wekesa (2014) examines FOCAC agenda plans to trace China's interest in establishing CGTN headquarters in Africa; Wasserman and Madrid-Morales (2018) survey students' attitudes toward CGTN in Kenya and South Africa.

5. Forum on China-Africa Cooperation Beijing Action Plan (2019–21), https://www.focac.org/eng/zywx_1/zywj/t1594297.htm

6. African and Chinese media are asked to present a positive relationship between China and Africa, or, as stated by Liu Guangyuan (2013), Chinese ambassador in Kenya, to "tell the real story of China and Africa." The Chinese government estimates that China-Africa relations are thus to be (re)defined by cooperative media outlets that report on the positive side of China-Africa relations rather than the challenges and negative aspects.

7. http://english.cntv.cn/program/africalive/20120111/117620.shtml

8. Information obtained from interviews conducted in March 2015 with reporters for CGTN Africa.

9. According to http://CGTN.cntv.cn/lm/CGTNafrica/, *Air Time for Africa Live* runs for one hour late at night on weekdays, for half an hour on Saturday, and one evening hour on Mondays and Sundays.

10. See Wasserman and Madrid-Morales (2018) for a study on perceptions of CGTN in Africa.

11. See the 2018 World Press Freedom Index, https://rsf.org/en/ranking

12. Interview on March 2015 in Addis Ababa, Ethiopia.

13. Information obtained in June 2014 in Beijing from interacting with several African journalists who were attending CUC for their master's or PhD degrees.

14. Again, China is not a pioneer in these all-expense-paid exchange programs. The main difference, though, is that the Chinese-sponsored scholarships are disbursed to African government officials and their "connections." Unlike other scholarships, which are given on a merit basis, the trainings I examine are mechanisms of reinforcing government-to-government relations between China and African counterparts. The good care for African participants is reported to African government officials who are going to associate China's policy in Africa with these positive caring aspects.

15. As explained in a paper presented in Beijing in September 10–22, 2014 by He Wenping, "China also dispatches many Chinese experts to African countries to give lectures at universities, visit medical facilities and hospitals and advise farmers on agricultural production techniques." This quote shows the wide scope of such relations.

Chapter 6

1. For more on China's public diplomacy and how Confucius Institutes fit into it, see Hartig (2012, 2019) and Wu (2016).

2. Hanban offices, http://english.hanban.org/node_10971.htm

3. I explain these differences in more detail below, but the general gist is that CIs in Europe and North America have a balanced relation between host universities and the Confucius Institute. In Africa, the Chinese headquarters provide most of the funding, make hiring decisions, and control the curricula with a lot more autonomy than their counterparts in Europe.

4. Perhaps a rare exception is bringing language teachers from African countries to teach African languages courses at Chinese universities.

5. For works examining China's soft power, its mechanisms, and its effects in Africa, see Bodomo (2009); Ding (2008); Li (2009); Liang (2012).

6. Interview with the director of Confucius Institute in Addis Ababa University in Ethiopia in March 2015.

7. Aside from the occasional language immersion programs or short-term summer internships.

8. I asked a civil servant in the Chinese Ministry of Education about faculty exchange programs with African countries and the response was that the ministry does not have any programs for African faculty to teach in China. All the programs are for Chinese faculty to do "volunteer" teaching in African institutions or for Africans to get training in China. Interview in Jinhua, Zhejiang Province, June 2014.

9. Aside from the occasional Swahili teachers who are from East Africa, there is almost never any African faculty to teach subject matter on African literature, history, or other content classes.

10. For more on the Academy's mission statement, see http://yenchingacad emy.org

11. This map shows the representation of admitted scholars, http://yenchin gacademy.org/yenchingscholars

12. I interviewed the four African students who have been admitted to the Yenching Academy and asked about their impressions and experiences. All four students expressed very positive impressions of the program and about their career prospects as young female entrepreneurs based on the connections that they developed during their time at Yenching. The interview was conducted via Skype in May 2015.

13. Li Keqiang 2014, http://www.fmprc.gov.cn/mfa_eng/wjdt_665385/ zyjh_665391/t1154397.shtml

14. The financial crisis of 2008 caused a slash of funding in the United Kingdom, Germany, and other countries' scholarship programs for African academics. The rise of right-wing political movements in Europe and in the US has also contributed to a closing up and a weakness in attracting African students to Western universities.

15. FOCAC Sharm El Sheikh Action Plan (2010–12), http://www.focac.org/ eng/ltda/dsjbzjhy/hywj/t626387.htm

16. Full text at https://www.fmprc.gov.cn/zflt/eng/dwjbzjjhys/t954274.htm

17. FOCAC 2018 action plan, https://www.focac.org/eng/zywx_1/zywj/ t1594297.htm

18. FOCAC III action plan.

19. When I visited the ECPC and spoke to a few students about the quality of training they had received, they were generally satisfied. The faculty who work at the ECPC said that the institute is improving the quality of its services as Chinese and Ethiopian partners gain more experience working with each other.

20. Podcast episode with Frank Youngman, "Chinese Studies at the University of Botswana," 2015. http://www.chinafile.com/library/china-africa-project/chi nese-studies-university-botswana

21. These details were obtained from interviewing the director of the CI of Addis Ababa University about her institute but also about CIs in Africa more generally. The interview was in March 2015.

22. This is not a surprising finding but it's interesting to recall at this point that China is the single largest provider of such capacity-building programs for Africans. The net is cast much wider in terms of attracting young Africans to go to China and perceive China as a place for business opportunities, higher education, and a better life.

23. Interviews with students at the Confucius Institute at Addis Ababa University, March 2015.

24. SACE Foundation, http://www.sacefoundation.org/welcome/

25. For more on this model, refer to http://www.sacefoundation.org/techni cal-training-initiative/

26. For more on the Pentagon's decision to cut funding for universities that host a Confucius Institute, deeming it not in the US national interest to do so, see Chan 2019.

Chapter 7

1. The US, France, and Japan have military bases in Djibouti.

2. China Military Online 2018b.

3. United States Africa Command, "U.S. Soldiers Present Donated Educational Supplies to Cameroonian School Children," 2016, https://www.africom. mil/media-room/article/28109/u-s-soldiers-present-donated-educational- supplies-to-cameroonian-school-children

4. BRI was announced during Xi's keynote speech in Astana, Kazakhstan, in September 2013.

5. See, e.g., discussions in Benabdallah 2018.

6. Xi Jinping's speech at the Belt and Road Forum in May 2017, accessed April 2018, http://www.xinhuanet.com/english/2017-05/14/c_136282982.htm

7. For discussions on pre-Westphalian China, its diplomatic relations, Confucian thought and its role in Ancient China's perception of international order, see Kang 2013.

8. Afrobarometer Round 6, 2016, "China's Growing Presence in Africa Wins Largely Positive Popular Reviews," http://afrobarometer.org/sites/default/files/ publications/Dispatches/ab_r6_dispatchno122_perceptions_of_china_in_af rica1.pdf

Bibliography

Abbott, Kenneth, and Duncan Snidal. 1998. "Why States Act through Formal International Organizations." *Journal of Conflict Resolution* 42 (1): 3–32.

Abdenur, Adriana, and Carlos Frederico Pereira da Silva Gama. 2015. "Triggering the Norms Cascade: Brazil's Initiatives for Curbing Electronic Espionage." *Global Governance: A Review of Multilateralism and International Organizations* 21 (3): 455–474.

Abrahamsen, Rita. 2004. "The Power of Partnerships in Global Governance." *Third World Quarterly* 25 (8): 1453–1467.

Abrahamsen, Rita. 2016. "Africa and International Relations: Assembling Africa, Studying the World." *African Affairs* 116 (462): 125–139.

Abrahamsen, Rita, and Michael Williams. 2011. *Security beyond the State: Private Security in International Politics.* Cambridge: Cambridge University Press.

Acharya, Amitav. 2014. "Who Are the Norm Makers? The Asian-African Conference in Bandung and the Evolution of Norms." *Global Governance* 20 (3): 405–417.

Acharya, Amitav, and Barry Buzan, eds. 2010. *Non-Western International Relations Theory: Perspectives from Asia.* London: Routledge.

Afrobarometer Round 6. 2016. "China's Growing Presence in Africa Wins Largely Positive Popular Reviews." Accessed July 27, 2019. http://afrobarometer.org/sites/default/files/publications/Dispatches/ab_r6_dispatchno122_perceptions_of_china_in_africa1.pdf

Agathangelou, Anna M., and L. H. M. Ling. 2003. "Power and Play through Poisies: Reconstructing Self and Other in the 9/11 Commission Report." *Millennium: Journal of International Studies* 33 (3): 827–853.

Agathangelou, Anna M., and L. H. M. Ling. 2004. "The House of IR: From Family Power Politics to the Poisies of Worldism." *International Studies Review* 6 (4): 21–49.

Agathangelou, Anna M. 2017. "From the Colonial to Feminist IR: Feminist IR Studies, the Wider FSS/GPE Research Agenda and the Questions of Value, Valuation, Security and Violence." *Gender and Politics*, 13 (4): 739–746.

Aidoo, Richard, and Steve Hess. 2015. "Non-interference 2.0: China's Evolving

Foreign Policy towards a Changing Africa." *Journal of Current Chinese Affairs* 44 (1): 107–138.

Alden, Chris. 2007. *China in Africa.* London: Zed Books.

Alden, Chris. 2009. "China and Africa's Natural Resources: The Challenges and Implications for Development and Governance." *Occasional Paper,* South African Institute of International Affairs, no. 41 (September): 1–26. Accessed July 27, 2019. https://www.voltairenet.org/IMG/pdf/China_and_Africa_s_Natural_Resources.pdf

Alden, Chris. 2014. "Seeking Security in Africa: China's Evolving Approach to the African Peace and Security Architecture." *Report for NOREF—Norwegian Peacebuilding Resource Centre.* Accessed July 27, 2019. https://www.saiia.org.za/wp-content/uploads/2014/04/SAIIA_Alden_2014_Seeking-security-in-Africa-Chinas-evolving-approach-to-APSA-NOREF.pdf

Alden, Chris, and Daniel Large. 2015. "On Becoming a Norms Maker: Chinese Foreign Policy, Norms Evolution and the Challenges of Security in Africa." *China Quarterly* 221: 123–142.

Alden, Chris, and Yu-Shan Wu. 2014. "South Africa and China: The Making of a Partnership." *Occasional Paper,* South African Institute of International Affairs, no. 199 (August): 1–39.

AllAfrica. 2015. "Botswana: China-Botswana Military Exchanges Contribute to Bilateral Relationship." Accessed July 27, 2019. http://allafrica.com/stories/201509071212.html

Allen, Amy. 1998. "Rethinking Power." *Hypatia* 13 (1): 21–40.

Alves, Ana Cristina. 2010a. "A Brief Analysis of China's Oil Interests in Angola." *China Monitor* (August): 4–10.

Alves, Ana Cristina. 2010b. "The Oil Factor in Sino-Angolan Relations at the Start of the 21st Century." *Occasional Paper,* South African Institute of International Affairs, no. 55 (February): 1–32.

Andersen, Morten Skumsrud, and Iver B. Neumann. 2012. "Practices as Models: A Methodology with an Illustration Concerning Wampum Diplomacy." *Millennium,* 40 (3): 457–481.

Anderson, Ben. 2011. "Population and Affective Perception: Biopolitics and Anticipatory Action in US Counterinsurgency Doctrine." *Antipode* 43 (2): 205–236.

Anderson, Ben. 2012. "Affect and Biopower: Towards a Politics of Life." *Transactions of the Institute of British Geographers* 37 (1): 28–43.

Ang Yuen Yuen. 2018. "The Real China Model, It's Not What You Think." *Foreign Affairs,* June 29. Accessed July 27, 2019. https://www.foreignaffairs.com/articles/asia/2018-06-29/real-china-model?cid=int-now&pgtype=hpg&region=br1

Arduino, Alessandro. 2018. *China's Private Army Protecting the New Silk Road.* Singapore: Palgrave Macmillan.

Atkinson, Carol. 2006. "Constructivist Implications of Material Power: Military Engagement and the Socialization of States, 1972–2000." *International Studies Quarterly* 50 (2): 509–537.

Atkinson, Carol. 2014. *Military Soft Power: Public Diplomacy through Military Education Exchanges.* Lanham, MD: Rowman and Littlefield.

Ba, Oumar. 2017. "International Justice and the Postcolonial Condition." *Africa Today* 63 (4): 45–62.

Bachrach, Peter, and Morton S. Baratz. 1962. "Two Faces of Power." *American Political Science Review* 56 (4): 947–952.

Baldwin, David. 1985. *Economic Statecraft.* Princeton, NJ: Princeton University Press.

Baldwin, David. 1989. *Paradoxes of Power.* Oxford: Blackwell.

Baldwin, David. 2013. "Power and International Relations." In *Handbook of International Relations*, 2nd ed. Edited by Walter Carlsnaes, Thomas Risse, and Beth A. Simmons, 273–297. Thousand Oaks, CA: SAGE Publications.

Bandurski, David. 2017. "The Fable of the Master Storyteller." *China Media Beat*, September 27. Accessed July 27, 2019. http://chinamediaproject. org/2017/09/29/the-fable-of-the-master-storyteller/

Barnes, Trevor. 2016. "U.S. Soldiers Present Donated Educational Supplies to Cameroonian School Children." *Africom.mil*, April 19. Accessed July 27, 2019. https://www.africom.mil/media-room/article/28109/u-s-soldiers-present-donated-educational-supplies-to-cameroonian-school-children

Barnett, Michael N., and Raymond Duvall. 2005. "Power in International Politics." *International Organization* 59 (1): 39–75.

Barnett, Michael N., and Martha Finnemore. 1999. "The Politics, Power, and Pathologies of International Organizations." *International Organization* 53 (4): 699–732.

Beijing Review. 2012. "China, Africa Join Hands in Media Cooperation" Accessed October 7, 2019. http://www.bjreview.com/special/2012-08/24/con tent_478033.htm

Benabdallah, Lina. 2015. "Political Representation of China-Africa: The Tale of a Playful Panda, or a Threatening Dragon?" *Africa Review* 7 (1): 28–41.

Benabdallah, Lina. 2016. "China's Peace and Security Strategies in Africa: Building Capacity Is Building Peace?" *African Studies Quarterly* 16 (3–4): 17–34.

Benabdallah, Lina. 2017. "Explaining Attractiveness: Knowledge Production and Power Projection in China's Policy for Africa." *Journal of International Relations and Development* 22 (2): 495–514.

Benabdallah, Lina. 2018. "China-Africa Military Ties Have Deepened: Here Are 4 Things to Know." *Washington Post*, July 6. Accessed July 27, 2019. https://www.washingtonpost.com/news/monkey-   cage/wp/2018/07/06/china-africa-military-ties-have-deepened-here-are-4- things-to-know/

Benabdallah, Lina. 2019. "Contesting the International Order by Integrating It: The Case of China's Belt and Road Initiative." *Third World Quarterly* 40 (1): 92–108.

Benabdallah, Lina, and Daniel Large. 2018. "China and African Security." In *New Directions in Africa-China Studies*, edited by Daniel Large and Chris Alden, 312–325. London: Routledge.

Berber, Laura. 2018. "Lesson Learning in the Case of China-Sudan and South Sudan Relations (2005–2013) in In *New Directions in Africa-China Studies*, edited by Daniel Large and Chris Alden, 179–208. London: Routledge.

Bian Yanjie. 2018. "The Prevalence and the Increasing Significance of Guanxi." *China Quarterly* 235: 597–601.

Bing Ngeow Chow. 2017. "Barisan Nasional and the Chinese Communist Party: A Case Study in China's Party-Based Diplomacy." *China Review* 17 (1): 53–82.

Bloomfield, Allan. 2016. "Norm Antipreneurs and Theorizing Resistance to Normative Change." *Review of International Studies* 42 (2): 310–333.

Bodomo, Adams. 2009. "Africa-China Relations: Symmetry, Soft Power and South Africa." *China Review* 9 (2): 169–178.

Börzel, Tanja A., and Thomas Risse. 2010. "Governance without a State: Can It Work?" *Regulation & Governance* 4 (2): 113–134.

Brautigam, Deborah. 2009. *The Dragon's Gift: The Real Story of China in Africa*. Oxford: Oxford University Press.

Brautigam, Deborah. 2011. "Aid 'with Chinese Characteristics': Chinese Foreign Aid and Development Finance Meet the OECD-DAC Aid Regime." *Journal of International Development* 23 (5): 752–764.

Brautigam, Deborah. 2015. *Will Africa Feed China?* New York: Oxford University Press.

Brautigam, Deborah. 2018. "Loan Pledges Reduced in China's FOCAC Financial Package for Africa 2018: Four Facts." *China-Africa Research Initiative*, September 3. Accessed July 27, 2019. http://www.chinaafricarealstory.com/2018/09/chinas-focac-financial-package-for.html?spref=tw

Brautigam, Deborah, and Tang Xiaoyang. 2011. "Africa Shenzhen: China's Special Economic Zones in Africa." *Modern African Studies* 49 (1): 27–54.

Brown, Tanner. 2018. "University of Michigan to Close Confucius Institute." *CX Live News*, December 11. Accessed July 27, 2019. https://www.caixinglobal.com/2018-12-11/university-of-michigan-to-close-confucius-institute-101357941.html

Butterfield, Rya. 2014. "Reviving the 'Confucius' in Confucius Institute diplomacy." *China Media Research* 10 (1): 13–21.

Buzan, Barry. 2010. "China in International Society: Is 'Peaceful Rise' Possible?" *Chinese Journal of International Politics* 3 (1): 29–33.

Buzan, Barry. 2016. "Confusing Public Diplomacy and Soft Power." *Asia Dialogue*, March 10. Accessed July 27, 2019. https://theasiadialogue.com/2016/03/10/confusing-public-diplomacy-and-soft-power/

Byrne, Bradley. 2018. "Expresses Concern about Chinese Actions in Africa." Press release, March 6. Accessed July 27, 2019. https://byrne.house.gov/media- cen ter/press-releases/byrne-expresses-concern-about-chinese-actions-in-africa

Campbell, David. 1998. *Writing Security: United States Foreign Policy and the Politics of Identity*. Rev. ed. Minneapolis: University of Minnesota Press.

Campbell, Horace. 2008. "China in Africa: Challenging US Global Hegemony." *Third World Quarterly* 29 (1): 89–105.

Campbell, Horace, and Sreeram Chaulia. 2009. "Unequal Equals: Angola and China." *World Affairs* 13 (1): 44–83.

Carr, Edward Hallett. (1940) 2001. *The Twenty Years' Crisis, 1919–1933: An Introduction to the Study of International Relations*. New York: Palgrave.

Carrozza, Ilaria. 2019. "China's Multilateral Diplomacy in Africa: Constructing the Security-Development Nexus." In *New Perspectives on China's Relations with the World*, edited by Daniel Johanson, Jie Li, and Tsunghan Wu, 142–158. Bristol, UK: E-International Relations Publishing.

Chan, Tara Francis. 2019. "Pentagon to End Language Funding for Universities That Host Chinese Communist Party–Funded Confucius Institutes." *Newsweek*, April 30. Accessed July 27, 2019. https://www.newsweek.com/confucius-institute-pentagon-communist-chinese-1406772

Chaziza, Mordechai. 2018. "China's Military Base in Djibouti." *Mideast Security and Policy Studies*, no. 153: 1–27. Accessed July 27, 2019. https://besacenter.org/wp-content/uploads/2018/08/153-Chaziza-Chinas-Military-Base-in-Djibouti-web.pdf

Chen Dingding, Pu Xiaoyu, and Alastair Iain Johnston. 2014. "Debating China's Assertiveness." *International Security* 38 (3): 176–183.

China Military Online. 2016. "Malian Defense Minister Meets with Chinese Military Delegation." August 16. Accessed July 27, 2019. http://english.chinamil.com.cn/news-channels/china-military-news/2016–08/16/content_7210210.htm

China Military Online. 2018a. "Defense Ministry's Regular Press Conference on Dec. 27." December 27. Accessed July 27, 2019. http://eng.chinamil.com.cn/view/2018–12/27/content_9390144.htm

China Military Online. 2018b. "Djibouti Pupils Visit PLA Support Base in Djibouti." May 15. Accessed July 27, 2019. http://eng.chinamil.com.cn/view/2018–05/15/content_8032773.htm

China's International Department. 2017a. "EPRDF Cadre Study Group to Visit China." http://www.idcpc.org.cn/english/forenotice/201706/t20170609_90433.html

China's International Department. 2017b. "EPRDF Mayor Study Group to Visit China." June 6. Accessed July 27, 2019. http://www.idcpc.org.cn/english/forenotice/201704/t20170420_89396.html

China Times. 2012. "President Hu Jintao's Speech at Opening Ceremony of Fifth Ministerial Conference of Forum on China-Africa Cooperation." July 18. Accessed July 27, 2019. http://thechinatimes.com/online/2012/07/4356.html

Chinese Central Government. 2009. "State Council Order No. 564." September 28. Accessed July 27, 2019. http://www.gov.cn/zwgk/2009–10/19/content_1443395.htm

Chowdhury, Arjun. 2017. "International Norms in Postcolonial Time." In *Against International Relations Norms: Postcolonial Perspectives*, edited by Charlotte Epstein, 106–122. New York: Routledge.

Christensen, Thomas. 2011. "The Advantages of an Assertive China: Responding to Beijing's Abrasive Diplomacy." *Foreign Affairs* 90 (2): 54–67.

Clark, Ian. 2012. "International Society and China: The Power of Norms and the Norms of Power." *Chinese Journal of International Politics* 7 (3): 315–340.

Clover, Charles. 2017. "Chinese Private Security Companies Go Global." *Financial Times*, February 26. Accessed July 27, 2019. https://www.ft.com/content/2a1ce1c8-fa7c-11e6-9516-2d969e0d3b65

Cohen, Warren. 2010. *America's Response to China: 5th Edition*. New York: Columbia University Press.

Comaroff, Jean, and John L. Comaroff. 2012. "Theory from the South: Or, How Euro-America Is Evolving toward Africa." *Anthropological Forum* 22 (2): 113–131.

Connolly, William. 2002. *Neuropolitics: Thinking, Culture, Speed*. Minneapolis: University of Minnesota Press.

Cooke, Jennifer. 2009. "China's Soft Power in Africa." In *Chinese Soft Power and Its Implications for the United States: Competition and Cooperation in the Developing World*, edited by Carola McGiffert, 27–44. Washington, DC: Center for Strategic and International Studies.

Coons, Christopher, and Marco Rubio. 2018. "A Letter of Concern about China's Investments in Africa." November 13. Accessed July 27, 2019. https://www.coons.senate.gov/newsroom/press-releases/sens-coons-rubio-write-letter-to-secs-pompeo-mattis-expressing-concern-about-chinas-expanding-influence-in-the-horn-of-africa

Cooper, Davina. 1994. "Productive, Relational and Everywhere? Power and Resistance within Foucauldian Feminism." *Sociology* 28 (2): 435–454.

Corkin, Lucy. 2008a. "AERC Scoping Exercise on China-Africa Relations: The Case of Angola." Report prepared for the African Economic Research Consortium. January. Accessed July 27, 2019. https://www.africaportal.org/documents/5614/Angola.pdf

Corkin, Lucy. 2008b. "Competition or Collaboration? Chinese and South African Transnational Companies in Africa." *Review of African Political Economy* 35 (115): 128–134.

Corkin, Lucy. 2009. "Unpacking Angola's Beijing Connection." *Pambazuka News*, January 31. Accessed July 27, 2019. www.pambazuka.org/en/category/africa_china/53758

Corkin, Lucy. 2011. "China and Angola: Strategic Partnership or Marriage of Convenience?" *Angola Brief* 1 (1): 1–4.

Corkin, Lucy. 2013. *Uncovering African Agency: Angola's Management of China's Credit Lines*. Surrey, UK: Ashgate.

Cull, John, David Culbert, and David Welch. 2003. *Propaganda and Mass Persuasion: A Historical Encyclopedia, 1500 to the Present*. Santa Barbara: ABC-CLIO.

Dahir, Abdi Latif. 2018. "A Kenyan Painter's Art Questions China's Deepening Reach in Africa," *Quartz Africa*, July 29. Accessed July 27, 2019. https://qz.com/africa/1343155/michael-soi-china-loves-africa-paintings-question-chinas-influence-in-africa/

Dahl, Robert. 1957. "The Concept of Power." *Behavioral Science* 2 (3): 201–215.

Dahl, Robert. 1961. *Who Governs? Democracy and Power in an American City*. New Haven, CT: Yale University Press.

Davis, Noela. 2012. "Subjected Subjects? On Judith Butler's Paradox of Interpellation." *Hypatia* 27 (4): 881–897.

Deng Yanting. 2012. "Sino-African Ties Dissected." *China Daily*, February 1. Accessed July 27, 2019. http://www.chinadaily.com.cn/opinion/2012–02/01/content_14514767.htm

Deutsche Welle. 2019. "Can Chinese Weapons Contribute to Peace in Africa?" July 14. Accessed July 27, 2019. https://amp.dw.com/en/can-chinese-weapons-contribute-to-peace-in-africa/a-49588144

Development Reimagined. 2018. "FOCAC—Just How Unique Is It?" Accessed July 27, 2019. https://developmentreimagined.com/wp-content/uploads/2018/08/focac-7-briefing-final.pdf#page=3

Digeser, Peter. 1992. "The Fourth Face of Power." *Journal of Politics* 54 (4): 977–1007.

Ding Shen. 2008. *The Dragon's Hidden Wings: How China Rises with Its Soft Power*. Plymouth, UK: Lexington Books.

Doty, Roxanne. 1993. "Foreign Policy as Social Construction: A Post-Positivist Analysis of US Counterinsurgency Policy in the Philippines." *International Studies Quarterly* 37 (3): 297–320.

Doty, Roxanne. 1996. *Imperial Encounters: The Politics of Representation in North-South Relations*. Minneapolis: University of Minnesota Press.

Dreher, Axel, Andreas Fuchs, Roland Hodler, Bradley C. Parks, Paul A. Raschky, and Michael J. Tierney. 2019. "African Leaders and the Geography of China's Foreign Assistance." *Journal of Development Economics* 140: 44–71.

Dunn, Kevin, and Iver B. Neumann. 2016. *Undertaking Discourse Analysis for Social Research*. Ann Arbor: University of Michigan Press.

Eisenman, Joshua. 2018a. "Contextualizing China's Belt and Road Initiative." Written testimony for the U.S.-China Economic and Security Review Commission, submitted on January 19. Accessed July 27, 2019. https://www.uscc.gov/sites/default/files/Eisenman_USCC%20Testimony_20180119.pdf

Eisenman, Joshua. 2018b. "Comrades-in-Arms: The Chinese Communist Party's Relations with African Political Organizations in the Mao Era, 1949–76." *Cold War History* 18 (4): 429–445.

Enloe, Cynthia. 1989. *Bananas, Beaches, and Bases: Making Feminist Sense of International Politics*. Berkeley: University of California Press.

Epstein, Charlotte. 2008. *The Power of Words in International Relations: Birth of an Anti-Whaling Discourse*. Cambridge: Massachusetts Institute of Technology Press.

Epstein, Charlotte. 2012. "Stop Telling Us How to Behave: Socialization or Infantilization? Stop Telling Us How to Behave." *International Studies Perspectives* 13 (2): 135–145.

Epstein, Charlotte. 2014. "The Postcolonial Perspective: An Introduction." *International Theory* 6 (2): 294–311.

Epstein, Charlotte, ed. 2017. *Against International Relations Norms: Postcolonial Perspectives*. London: Routledge.

Erickson, Andrew, and Gabe Collins. 2012. "Enter China's Security Firms." *Diplomat*, February 21. Accessed July 27, 2019. http://thediplomat.com/2012/02/enter-chinas-security-firms/

Essa, Azad. 2018. "China Is Buying African Media's Silence." *Foreign Policy*, September 14. Accessed July 27, 2019. https://foreignpolicy.com/2018/09/14/china-is-buying-african-medias-silence/

Fairbank, John. 1974. *The Missionary Enterprise in China and America*. Cambridge, MA: Harvard University Press.

Fang Yang. 2011. "The Importance of Guanxi to Multinational Companies in China." *Asian Social Science* 7 (7): 163–168.

Feige, Johannes. 2016. "Why China's Djibouti Presence Matters." *Diplomat*, April 13. Accessed July 27, 2019. http://thediplomat.com/2016/04/why-chinas-djibouti-presence-matters/

Ferrie, Jared. 2016. "China's Dangerous Double Game in the Sudans." *IRIN News*, July 27. Accessed July 27, 2019. http://www.irinnews.org/news/2016/07/27/china's-dangerous-double-game-sudans

Findlay, Stephanie. 2014. "South Africa: ANC Looks to Learn from Chinese Communist Party." *Time*, November 24. Accessed July 27, 2019. http://www.time.com/3601968/anc-south-africa-china-communist-party/

Finnemore, Martha. 1996. *National Interests in International Society*. Ithaca, NY: Cornell University Press.

Finnemore, Martha, and Kathryn Sikkink. 1998. "International Norm Dynamics and Political Change." *International Organization* 52 (4): 887–917.

FOCAC. 2012. "President Hu Proposes Measures in Five Priority Areas to Boost China-Africa Ties in Beijing." July 19. Accessed July 27, 2019. http://www.focac.org/eng/dwjbzjjhys/t953114.htm

FOCAC. 2015a. "AU Chairperson Lauds Chinese President's Speech at FOCAC Summit." December 5. Accessed July 27, 2019. http://africa.chinadaily.com.cn/2015-12/05/content_22637260.htm/

FOCAC. 2015b. "President Jacob Zuma: Closing Remarks to the Johannesburg Summit of the Forum on China-Africa Cooperation." December 5. Accessed July 27, 2019. https://www.gov.za/speeches/president-zuma-closing-remarks-johannesburg-summit-forum-china-africa-cooperation-5-dec

FOCAC. 2015c. "Full Text of the Action Plan, Johannesburg, South Africa." December 25. Accessed July 27, 2019. https://www.focac.org/eng/zywx_1/zywj/t1327961.htm

FOCAC. 2018. "Full Text of the Action Plan, Beijing, China." September 12. Accessed July 27, 2019. https://www.focac.org/eng/zywx_1/zywj/t1594297.htm

Forum on China-Africa Cooperation (FOCAC). 2009. Sharm El Sheikh Action Plan (2010-2012). November 8-9. Accessed October 7, 2019. http://bw.china-embassy.org/eng/zt/zfhz/t628555.htm

Foucault, Michel. 1980. "Truth and Power." In *Power/Knowledge: Selected Inter-*

views and Other Writings (1972–1977), edited by Colin Gordon. London: Tavistock.

Foucault, Michel. 1982. "The Subject and Power." *Critical Inquiry* 8 (4): 777–795.

Foucault, Michel. 1991. "Questions of Method." In *The Foucault Effect: Studies in Governmentality*, edited by Graham Burchell, Colin Gordon, and Peter Miller, 73–86. Chicago: University of Chicago Press.

Foucault, Michel. 2003. *Society Must Be Defended: Lectures at the Collège de France, 1975–76*. New York: Picador.

Foucault, Michel. 2004. *Securité, Territoire, Population (Cours au Collège de France, 1977–1978)*. Paris: Gallimard, Seuil Hautes Etudes.

Fourie, Elsje. 2015. "China's Example for Meles' Ethiopia: When Development 'Models' Land." *Journal of Modern African Studies* 53 (3): 289–316.

Fournier, Philippe. 2011. "Welfare and Foreign Aid Practices in Contemporary America: A Governmental Study." *Foucault Studies* 12 (October): 147–170.

Fung, Courtney. 2016. "What Explains China's Deployment to UN Peacekeeping Operations?" *International Relations of the Asia-Pacific* 16 (3): 409 – 441.

Garwood-Gowers, Andrew. 2012. "China and the 'Responsibility to Protect': The Implications of the Libyan Intervention." *Asian Journal of International Law* 2 (2): 375–393.

Gill, Stephen, and David Law. 1988. *The Global Political Economy: Perspectives, Problems, and Policies*. Baltimore, MD: Johns Hopkins University Press.

Gill, Stephen, and David Law. 1989. "Global Hegemony and the Structural Power of Capital." *International Studies Quarterly* 33 (4): 475–499.

Gilpin, Robert. 1981. *War and Change in World Politics*. Cambridge: Cambridge University Press.

Glaser, Charles. 2011. "Will China's Rise Lead to War? Why Realism Does Not Mean Pessimism." *Foreign Affairs*, March/April. Accessed July 27, 2019. https://www.foreignaffairs.com/articles/asia/2011-03-01/will-chinas-rise-lead-war

Glynos, Jason, and David Howarth. 2007. *Logics of Critical Explanation in Social and Political Theory*. London: Routledge.

Godehart, Nadine. 2016. "No End of History: A Chinese Alternative Concept of International Order?" *SWP Research Paper* 2016/RP 02 (January). Accessed July 27, 2019. http://www.swp-berlin.org/en/publications/swp-research-papers/swp-research-paper-detail/article/no_end_of_history.html

Goh, Brenda, Michael Martina, and Christian Shepherd. 2017. "Local, Global Security Firms in Race along China's 'Silk Road.'" *Reuters Business News*, April 23. Accessed July 27, 2019. https://www.reuters.com/article/us-china-silkroad-security-analysis-idUSKBN17P10Y

Goldstein, Avery. 2005. *Rising to the Challenge: China's Grand Strategy and International Security*. Stanford, CA: Stanford University Press.

Goldstein, Avery. 2013. "First Things First: The Pressing Danger of Crisis Instability in U.S.-China Relations." *International Security* 37 (4): 49–89.

Graham, Linda. 2005. "Discourse Analysis and the Critical Use of Foucault." Paper presented at Australian Association for Research in Education Annual

Conference, Sydney, November 27–December 1. Accessed July 27, 2019. https://eprints.qut.edu.au/2689/

Grovogui, Siba N. 2013. "Deferring Difference: A Postcolonial Critique of the "Race Problem" in Moral Thought." In *Postcolonial Theory and International Relations: A Critical Introduction*, edited by Sanjay Seth, 106–123. London: Routledge.

Guthrie, Doug. 1998. "The Declining Significance of Guanxi in China's Economic Transition." *China Quarterly* 154: 254–282. https://eprints.qut.edu.au/2689/

Guzzini, Stefano. 2000. "A Reconstruction of Constructivism in International Relations." *European Journal of International Relations* 6 (2): 147–182.

Guzzini, Stefano. 2011. "Relational Power." In *Encyclopedia of Power*, edited by Keith Dowding, 564–567. Thousand Oaks, CA: SAGE Publications.

Guzzini, Stefano. 2013. "The Ends of International Relations Theory: Stages of Reflexivity and Modes of Theorizing." *European Journal of International Relations* 19 (3): 521–541.

Guzzini, Stefano. 2016. "Power." In *Concepts in World Politics*, edited by Felix Berenskoetter, 23–40. London: SAGE Publications.

Guzzini, Stefano, and Iver B. Neumann. 2012. *The Diffusion of Power in Global Governance: International Political Economy Meets Foucault*. Houndmills, UK: Palgrave Macmillan.

Haas, Peter. 1992. "Introduction: Epistemic Communities and International Policy Coordination." *International Organization* 46 (1): 1–35.

Haas, Peter. 2001. "Policy Knowledge: Epistemic Communities." In *International Encyclopedia of the Social and Behavioral Sciences*, edited by Neil J. Smelser and Paul B. Baltes, vol. 17, 11578. Oxford: Elsevier Science.

Hackenesch, Christine. 2015. "Not as Bad as It Seems: EU and US Democracy Promotion Faces China in Africa." *Democratization* 22 (3): 419–437.

Hafner-Burton, Emilie, Miles Kahler, and Alex Montgomery. 2009. "Network Theory in International Relations." *International Organization* 63 (3): 559–592.

Hagström, Linus. 2005. *Japan's China Policy: A Relational Power Analysis*. London: Routledge.

Hagström, Linus, and Astrid H. M. Nordin. 2019. "China's 'Politics of Harmony' and the Quest for Soft Power in International Politics." *International Studies Review* (May): doi: 10.1093/isr/viz023.

Hall, Stuart. 1985. "Signification, Representation, Ideology: Althusser and the Post-Structuralist Debates." *Critical Studies in Mass Communication* 2 (2): 91–114.

Hanauer, Larry, and Lyle J. Morris. 2014. *Chinese Engagement in Africa: Drivers, Reactions, and Implications for U.S. Policy*. Santa Monica, CA: RAND Corporation.

Hansen, Lene. 2006. *Security as Practice: Discourse Analysis and the Bosnian War*. New York: Routledge.

Hartig, Falk. 2012. "Confucius Institutes and the Rise of China." *Journal of Chinese Political Science* 17 (1): 53–76.

Hartig, Falk. 2016. *Chinese Public Diplomacy: The Rise of the Confucius Institute.* London: Routledge.

Hartig, Falk. 2019. "A Review of the Current State of Research on China's International Image Management." *Communication and the Public* 4 (1): 68–81.

Hawkins, Amy. 2018. "Beijing's Big Brother Tech Needs African Faces." *Foreign Policy*, July 24. Accessed July 27, 2019. https://foreignpolicy.com/2018/07/24/beijings-big-brother-tech-needs-african-faces/

He Huifeng. 2018. "China Is Training Foreign Officials to Spread Its Political Model, Including How to 'Guide Public Opinion' Online." *South China Morning Post*, July 14. Accessed July 27, 2019. https://www.scmp.com/news/china/economy/article/2155203/remote-corner-china-beijing-trying-export-its-model-training#IJgP3kyytjEOR7rK.99

He Wenping. 2007. "The Balancing Act of China's Africa Policy." *China Security* 3 (3): 23–40.

He Wenping. 2009. "China's African Policy: Driving Forces, Features and Global Impact." *Africa Review* 1 (1): 35–53.

Hemmings, Clare. 2005. "Invoking Affect: Cultural Theory and the Ontological Turn." *Cultural Studies* 19 (5): 548–567.

Holslag, Jonathan. 2008a. "China's Diplomatic Maneuvering on the Question of Darfur." *Journal of Contemporary China* 17 (54): 71–84.

Holslag, Jonathan. 2008b. "China's Next Security Strategy for Africa." Brussels Institute of Contemporary China Studies. *Asia Paper* 3 (6): 1–26.

Holslag, Jonathan. 2009a. "China's New Security Strategy for Africa." *Parameters* 39 (2): 23–37.

Holslag, Jonathan. 2009b. "Embracing Chinese Global Security Ambitions." *Washington Quarterly* 32 (3): 105–118.

Howarth, David. 2000. *Discourse.* Buckingham, UK: Open University Press.

Hwang Kuan Go. 1987. "Face and Favor: The Chinese Power Game." *American Journal of Sociology* 92 (4): 944–974.

Jabri, Vivienne. 2014. "Disarming Norms: Postcolonial Agency and the Constitution of the International." *International Theory* 6 (2): 372–390.

Jackson, Patrick Thaddeus. 2005. "Relational Constructivism: A War of Words." In *Making Sense of International Relations Theory*, edited by Jennifer Sterling-Folker, 139–155. Boulder, CO: Lynne Rienner.

Jackson, Patrick Thaddeus, and Daniel Nexon. 1999. "Relations before States." *European Journal of International Relations* 5 (3): 291–332.

Jacques, Martin. 2009. *When China Rules the World: The End of the Western World and the Birth of a New Global Order.* New York: Penguin Press.

Jensen, Andrew. 2015. "Bridling the Black Dragon: Chinese Soft Power in the Russian Far East." Master's thesis, Harvard Extension School. Accessed July 27, 2019. https://dash.harvard.edu/handle/1/26519856

Johnston, Alastair Iain. 1996. "Cultural Realism and Strategy in Maoist China." In *The Culture of National Security*, edited by Peter Katzenstein, 216–269. New York: Columbia University Press.

Johnston, Alastair Iain. 2003. "Is China a Status Quo Power?" *International Security* 27 (4): 5–56.

Johnston, Alastair Iain. 2008. *Social States: China in International Institutions, 1980-2000*. Princeton, NJ: Princeton University Press.

Johnston, Alastair Iain. 2013. "How New and Assertive Is China's New Assertiveness." *International Security* 37 (4): 7–48.

Jordan, Javier, and Nicola Horsburgh. 2005. "Mapping Jihadist Terrorism in Spain." *Studies in Conflict and Terrorism* 28 (3): 169–191.

Jorge, Njal. 2012. "The 'Chinese Connection' in Mozambique's Hosting the 2011 Maputo All-Africa Games." *China Monitor* 72 (June): 4–19.

Joseph, Jonathan. 2009. "Governmentality of What? Populations, States and International Organizations." *Global Society* 23 (4): 413–427.

Joseph, Jonathan. 2012. *The Social in the Global: Social Theory, Governmentality and Global Politics*. Cambridge: Cambridge University Press.

Junbo Jian. 2012. "China in the International Conflict-Management: Darfur as a Case." *Global Review* (Winter): 7–11. Accessed July 27, 2019. https://www.saferworld.org.uk/resources/publications/719-chinas-role-in-international-conflict-management-sudan-and-south-sudan-global-review

Kang, David. 2003. "Getting Asia Wrong: The Need for New Analytical Frameworks." *International Security* 27 (4): 57–85.

Katzenstein, Peter, ed. 1996. *The Culture of National Security: Norms and Identity in World Politics*. New York: Columbia University Press.

Katzenstein, Peter, ed. 2009. *Civilizations in World Politics: Plural and Pluralist Perspectives*. London: Routledge.

Kavalski, Emilian. 2013. "The Struggle for Recognition of Normative Powers: Normative Power Europe and Normative Power China in Context." *Cooperation and Conflict* 48 (2): 247–267.

Kavalski, Emilian. 2014. "Recognizing Chinese IR Theory." In *Asian Thought on China's Changing International Relations*, edited by Niv Horesh and Emilian Kavalski, 230–248. London: Palgrave.

Kavalski, Emilian. 2017. *The Guanxi of Relational International Theory*. New York: Routledge.

Kavalski, Emilian. 2018. "Guanxi or What Is the Chinese for Relational Theory of World Politics?" *International Relations of the Asia-Pacific* 18 (3): 397–420.

Keck, Margaret E., and Kathryn Sikkink. 1999. "Transnational Advocacy Networks in International and Regional Politics." *International Social Science Journal* 51 (1): 89–101.

Kelly, Robert. E. 2012. "A 'Confucian Long Peace' in Pre-Western East Asia?" *European Journal of International Relations* 18 (3): 407–430.

Kgosana, Caiphus. 2018. "ANC Looks to China for Election Strategy and Tactics." *Times Live*, July 29. Accessed July 27, 2019. https://www.timeslive.co.za/news/2018-07-28-anc-looks-to-china-for-election-strategy-and-tactics/

King, Kenneth. 2013. *China's Aid and Soft Power in Africa: The Case of Education and Training*. Martlesham, UK Boydell & Brewer.

King, Kenneth. 2014. "China's Higher Education Engagement with Africa" In *Education, Learning, Training: Critical Issues for Development. International Development Policy Series*, 5, edited by Gilles Carbonnier, Michael Carton, and Kenneth King. Leiden: Brill Nijhoff.

Kishi, Roudabeh, and Clionadh Raleigh. 2015. "Chinese Aid and African Pariah States." Working Paper, Department of Geography, University of Sussex. Accessed July 27, 2019. https://www.semanticscholar.org/paper/Chinese-Aid-and-Africa-%E2%80%99-s-Pariah-States-Kishi-Raleigh/9f4e8ab4089e09bbf-39beb4044cac3e18ee3a74e

Kuan, Teresa. 2014. "Banking in Affects: The Child, a Landscape, and the Performance of a Canonical View." In *The Political Economy of Affect and Emotion in East Asia*, edited by Jie Yang, 65–81. New York: Routledge.

Kuo, Lily. 2016. "China's Model of Economic Development Is Becoming More Popular in Africa than America's." *Quartz Africa*, October 28. Accessed July 27, 2019. https://qz.com/africa/820841/chinas-model-of-economic-development-is-becoming-more-popular-in-africa-than-americas/

Kuo, Lily. 2017. "Beijing Is Cultivating the Next Generation of African Elites by Training Them in China." *Quartz Africa*, December 14. Accessed July 27, 2019. https://qz.com/africa/1119447/china-is-training-africas-next-generation-of-leaders/

Kurlantzick, Joshua. 2007. *Charm Offensive: How China's Soft Power Is Transforming the World*. New Haven, CT: Yale University Press.

Laclau, Ernesto, and Chantal Mouffe. 1985. *Hegemony and Socialist Strategy: Towards a Radical Democratic Politics*. London: Verso.

Large, Daniel. 2008a. "Beyond 'Dragon in the Bush': The Study of China-Africa Relations." *African Affairs* 107 (426): 45–61.

Large, Daniel. 2008b. "China and the Contradictions of 'Non-interference' in Sudan." *Review of African Political Economy* 35 (115): 93–106.

Large, Daniel. 2009. "China's Sudan Engagement: Changing Northern and Southern Political Trajectories in Peace and War." *China Quarterly* 199: 610–626.

Large, Daniel. 2012. "Between the CPA and Southern Independence: China's Post-Conflict Engagement in Sudan." *Occasional Paper*, South African Institute for International Affairs, no. 115 (April): 1–25.

Larkin, Bruce. 1971. *China and Africa 1949–1970: The Foreign Policy of the People's Republic of China*. Berkeley: University of California Press.

Larsen, Henrik. 2013. "Discourses of State Identity and Post-Lisbon National Foreign Policy: The Case of Denmark." *Cooperation and Conflict* 49 (3): 368–385.

Leander, Anna. 2005. "The Power to Construct International Security: On the Significance of Private Military Companies." *Millennium: Journal of International Studies* 33 (3): 803–826.

Lee, Karthie. 2014. "Chinese Private Security Firms for Overseas: Crossing the River by Feeling the Stones." *Africa Monitor*, September 8. Accessed July 27, 2019. http://iissonline.net/chinese-private-security-firms-go-overseas-crossing-the-river-by-feeling-the-stones/

Legro, Jeffery. 1997. "Which Norms Matter? Revisiting the 'Failure' of Interna-
tionalism." *International Organization* 51 (1): 31–63.

Lemke, Thomas. 2001. "'The Birth of Bio-Politics': Michel Foucault's Lecture at
the College de France on Neo-liberal Governmentality." *Economy and Society*
30 (2): 190–207.

Lemos, Anabela, and Daniel Ribeiro. 2007. "A New Colonial Power in Mozambique." *International Rivers*, September 17. Accessed July 27, 2019. https://
www.internationalrivers.org/resources/a-new-colonial-power-in-
mozambique-2591

Le Pere, Garth, and Garth Shelton. 2007. *China, Africa and South Africa: South-
South Co-operation in a Global Era*. Midrand, South Africa: Institute for Global
Dialogue.

Li Anshan. 2005. "African Studies in China in the Twentieth Century: A Historio-
graphical Survey." *African Studies Review* 48 (1): 59–87.

Li Anshan. 2009. "What's to Be Done after the Fourth FOCAC?" *China Monitor* 12
(November): 7–9. Accessed July 27, 2019. https://www.fmprc.gov.cn/zflt/eng/
dsjbzjhy/t647036.htm

Li Anshan. 2012. *A History of Overseas Chinese in Africa to 1911*. New York: Dia-
sporic Africa Press.

Li Anshan. 2013. *The Politics of Human Resource Development*. Accessed July 27,
2019. http://awsassets.panda.org/downloads/the_forum_on_china_africa_
cooperation_1.pdf

Li Keqiang. 2014. "Bring about a Better Future for China-Africa Cooperation."
May 5. Accessed July 27, 2019. http://et.china-embassy.org/eng/zt/123qwe/
t1154908.htm

Li Mingjiang. 2009a. "Soft Power in Chinese Discourse: Popularity and Prospect."
In *Soft Power: China's Emerging Strategy in International Politics*, edited by Li
Mingjiang, 21–44. Plymouth, MA: Lexington Books.

Li Mingjiang. 2009b. "China's Gulf of Aden Expedition and Maritime Cooperation in East Asia." *China Brief* 9 (1): 5–8.

Li Na, and Meng Wang. 2016. "Mali's Former PM: Chinese Peacekeepers Win Ma-
lians' Hearts." *China Military Online*, June 6. Accessed July 27, 2019. http://
eng.mod.gov.cn/Opinion/2016–06/06/content_4670851.htm

Liang Wei. 2012. "China's Soft Power in Africa: Is Economic Power Sufficient?"
Asian Perspective 36 (4): 667–692.

Liu Guangyuan. 2013. "Deepen China-Africa Media Cooperation and Enrich the
China-Africa Community of Shared Destinies." Speech delivered at the Seminar on China-Africa Media Cooperation on November 18 at the Chinese Embassy in Kenya. Accessed October 7, 2019. http://ke.china-embassy.org/eng/
xw/t1100582.htm

Liu Guijin. 2004. "China-Africa Relations: Equality, Cooperation and Mutual Development." Presentation at a seminar organized by the Institute for Security
Studies in South Africa. November 9. Previously accessible at https://issafrica.
org/seminars/2004/0911chinaspeech.pdf

Liu Guijin. 2005. "All-Weather Friends in Need and Indeed: China-Africa Relations Seen from the Eyes of a Chinese Diplomat." *African Renaissance* 2 (4): 10–19.

Liu Yumei. 2007. "China's Soft Power and the Development of China-Africa Relations." *China International Studies* 7 (Summer): 81–96.

Lobell, Steven E., Norrin M. Ripsman, and Jeffrey Taliaferro. 2009. *Neoclassical Realism, the State and Foreign Policy.* Cambridge: Cambridge University Press.

Lui, Andrew. 2012. "China Rising, Human Rights and 'Hard Times': The Foreign Policy and Network Implications of an Asian Century." *APSA 2010 Annual Meeting Paper.* Available at SSRN: https://ssrn.com/abstract=1644365

Lukes, Steven. 1974. *Power: A Radical View.* London: Macmillan.

Lukes, Steven. 2005. "Power and the Battle for Hearts and Minds." *Millennium: Journal of International Studies* 33 (3): 477–493.

Lynch, Colum. 2012. "China's Arms Exports Flooding Sub-Saharan Africa." *Washington Post,* August 25. Accessed July 27, 2019. https://www.washington-post.com/world/national-security/chinas-arms-exports-flooding-sub-saha ran-africa/2012/08/25/16267b68-e7f1-11e1-936a-b801f1abab19_story. html?utm_term=.68da0740c444

March, James, and Johan Olsen. 1984. "The New Institutionalism: Organizational Factors in Political Life." *American Political Science Review* 78 (3): 734–749.

Massumi, Brian. 2002. *Parables for the Virtual: Movement, Affect, Sensation.* Durham, NC: Duke University Press.

Mattern, Janice Bially. 2005. "Why 'Soft Power' Isn't So Soft: Representational Force and the Sociolinguistic Construction of Attraction in World Politics." *Millennium: Journal of International Studies* 33 (3): 583–612.

Mbachu, Dulue. 2006. "Nigerian Resources: Changing the Playing Field." *South African Journal of International Affairs* 13 (1): 77–82.

McClurg, Scott D., and Joseph K. Young. 2011. "Political Networks: Editors' Introduction: A Relational Political Science." *PS: Political Science & Politics* 44 (1): 39–43.

McEwan, Cheryl. 2001. "Postcolonialism, Feminism and Development: Intersections and Dilemmas." *Progress in Development Studies* 1 (2): 93–111.

Mearsheimer, John J. 2001. *The Tragedy of Great Power Politics.* New York: W. W. Norton.

Miller, Arthur H. 2006. "Promoting Democratic Values in Transitional Societies through Foreign Aid." Presented at the Midwest Political Science Association Annual Meeting, Chicago.

Milliken, Jennifer. 1999. "The Study of Discourse in International Relations: A Critique of Research and Methods." *European Journal of International Relations* 5 (2): 225–254.

Ministry of Foreign Affairs of the People's Republic of China. 2006. "First Africa Strategy Paper, Beijing." January. Accessed July 27, 2019. http://en.people. cn/200601/12/eng20060112_234894.html

Ministry of Foreign Affairs of the People's Republic of China. 2012. "Address at the Joint Conference of Confucius Institutes in Africa by Amb. Tian Xuejun." September 11. Accessed July 27, 2019. http://za.china-embassy.org/eng/sgxw/Achive/t968980.htm

Ministry of Foreign Affairs of the People's Republic of China. 2015a. "Fifth Ministerial Conference of FOCAC Opens Further China-Africa Cooperation." July 23. Accessed July 27, 2019. https://www.fmprc.gov.cn/zflt/eng/dwjbzjjhys/t954274.htm

Ministry of Foreign Affairs of the People's Republic of China. 2015b. "Second Africa Strategy Paper, Beijing." December 5. Accessed July 27, 2019. http://africa.chinadaily.com.cn/2015-12/05/content_22632880.htm

Ministry of Foreign Affairs of the People's Republic of China. 2015c. "Remarks by H. E. Chinese Ambassador Hu Dingxian at the Seminar on 2015 China-Aid Human Resource Development Cooperation Program." December 16. Accessed July 27. 2019. http://ls.china-embassy.org/eng/dsxx/dsjh/t1326221.htm

Ministry of Foreign Affairs of the People's Republic of China. 2016. "Chinese Foreign Policy and Its Impact on Africa." May 20. Accessed July 27, 2019. http://gh.china-embassy.org/eng/zjgx/zzwl/t1365142.htm

Ministry of National Defense of the People's Republic of China. 2015a. "Chinese Peacekeepers in DR Congo Open Chinese Language Class for Orphans." May 8. Accessed July 27, 2019. http://eng.mod.gov.cn/DefenseNews/2015-05/08/content_4583900.htm

Ministry of National Defense of the People's Republic of China. 2015b. "Chinese Peacekeepers Play 'Significant' Role for Liberia Peace: UN Official." October 30. Accessed July 27, 2019. http://eng.mod.gov.cn/DefenseNews/2015-10/30/content_4626701.htm

Ministry of National Defense of the People's Republic of China. 2016a. "Chinese Military Expert Team Returns from Ethiopia." January 14. Accessed July 27, 2019. http://eng.mod.gov.cn/TopNews/2016-01/14/content_4636448.htm

Ministry of National Defense of the People's Republic of China. 2016b. "Foreign Military Attaches to China Visit PLA General Hospital." May 12. Accessed July 27, 2019. http://eng.mod.gov.cn/DefenseNews/2016-05/12/content_4657092.htm

Ministry of National Defense of the People's Republic of China. 2016c. "China to Provide 10% of UN Peacekeeping Budget." May 31. Accessed July 27, 2019. http://eng.mod.gov.cn/Peacekeeping/2016-05/31/content_4667753.htm

Ministry of National Defense of the People's Republic of China. 2016d. "China Trains UN Peacekeeping Officers." June 6. Accessed July 27, 2019. http://eng.mod.gov.cn/DefenseNews/2016-06/06/content_4670932.htm

Mohan, Giles, Ben Lampert, May Tan-Mullins, and Daphne Chang. 2014. *Chinese Migrants and Africa's Development: New Imperialists or Agents of Change?* London: Zed Books.

Monson, Jamie. 2009. *Africa's Freedom Railway: How a Chinese Development Project*

Changed Lives and Livelihoods in Tanzania. Bloomington: Indiana University Press.

Morgan, Matthew. 2008. "China-Africa When the Going Gets Tough." *African Business* 346 (3): 60–62.

Morgenthau, Hans. (1948) 1985. *Politics among Nations: The Struggle for Power and Peace*. 6th ed. Edited by Kenneth Thompson. New York: McGraw-Hill.

Musgrave, Paul, and Daniel Nexon. 2018. "Defending Hierarchy from the Moon to the Indian Ocean: Symbolic Capital and Political Dominance in Early Modern China and the Cold War." *International Organization* 72 (3): 591–626.

Mutethya, Edith. 2018. "Communist Party of China Shares Tips with Kenya's Jubilee Party." July 15. Accessed July 27, 2019. http://europe.chinadaily.com.cn/a/201807/15/WS5b4af4caa310796df4df67fe.html

Nakkazi, Esther. 2018. "China Ramps Up Support for African Higher Education." *University World News*, September 7. Accessed July 27, 2019. https://www.universityworldnews.com/post.php?story=20180907083412817

Narlikar, Amrita. 2011. "Is India a Responsible Great Power?" *Third World Quarterly* 32 (9): 1607–1621.

Nathan, Andrew, and Jonathan Scobell. 2012. *China's Search for Security*. New York: Columbia University Press.

Nayyar, Deepak. 2008. "The Rise of China and India: Implications for Developing Countries." In *Issues in Economic Development and Globalization: Essays in Honour of Agit Singh*, edited by Philip Arestis and John Eatwell, 73–94. Houndsmills, UK: Palgrave Macmillan.

Negi, Rohit. 2008 "Beyond the 'Chinese Scramble': The Political Economy of Anti-China Sentiment in Zambia." *African Geographical Review* 27 (4): 41–64.

Neumann, Iver B., and Ole Jacob Sending. 2010. *Governing the Global Polity: Practice, Mentality, Rationality*. Ann Arbor: University of Michigan Press.

Nijal, Jorge. 2012. "Chinese Aid to Education in Mozambique" Conferência Internacional do Iese. Moçambique: Acumulação E Transformação Em Contexto De Crise Internacional. Niu, Changsong. 2015. "Confucius Institutes and China's Cultural Diplomacy in Africa" Presented at the International Conference on China-Africa Communications: Media Development, Cross-cultural Communication, and Public Diplomacy, June 12–13 in Beijing.

Nordin, Astrid. 2012. "How Soft Is 'Soft Power'?" Unstable Dichotomies at Expo 2010." *Asian Perspective* 36 (4): 591–613.

Nordin, Astrid. 2016. *China's International Relations and Harmonious World: Time, Space and Multiplicity in World Politics*. New York: Routledge.

Nye, Joseph. 1990. "Soft Power." *Foreign Policy*, no. 80 (Autumn): 153–171.

Nye, Joseph. 2004. *Soft Power: The Means to Success in World Politics*. New York: Public Affairs.

Olander, Eric, Cobus van Staden, and Frank Youngman. "Chinese Studies at the University of Botswana." *Chinafrica Project China File Podcast*, January 18. Accessed July 27, 2019. http://www.chinafile.com/library/china-africa-project/chinese-studies-university-botswana

Oren, Ido. 2009. "The Unrealism of Contemporary Realism: The Tension between Realist Theory and Realists' Practices." *Perspectives on Politics* 7 (2): 283–301.

Pan, Chengxin. 2012. *Knowledge, Desire, and Power in Global Politics: Western Representations of China's Rise.* Cheltenham, UK: Edward Elgar.

Pan, Chengxin. 2018. "Toward a New Relational Ontology in Global Politics: China's Rise as Holographic Transition." *International Relations of the Asia Pacific* 18 (3): 339–367.

Park, Yoon Jung. 2009. "Chinese Migration in Africa." *Occasional Paper*, South African Institute of International Affairs, no. 24 (February): 1–18.

Persaud, Randolph. 2002. "Situating Race in International Relations: The Dialectics of Civilizational Security in American Immigration." In *Power, Postcolonialism and International Relations: Reading Race, Gender and Class*, edited by Geeta Chowdhry and Sheila Nair, 56–81. London: Routledge.

Piedalue, Amy, and Susmita Rishi. 2017. "Unsettling the South through Postcolonial Feminist Theory." *Feminist Studies* 43 (3): 548–70.

Pouliot, Vincent. 2016. *International Pecking Orders: The Politics and Practice of Multilateral Diplomacy.* Cambridge, MA: Cambridge University Press.

Prashad, Vijay. 2001. *Everybody Was Kung Fu Fighting: Afro-Asian Connections and the Myth of Cultural Purity.* Boston: Beacon Press.

Prasso, Sheridan. 2019. "China's Digital Silk Road Is Looking More Like an Iron Curtain." *Bloomberg Businessweek*, January 10. Accessed July 27, 2019. https://www.bloomberg.com/news/features/2019-01-10/china-s-digital-silk-road-is-looking-more-like-an-iron-curtain

Pu Xiaoyu. 2019. *Rebranding China: Contested Status Signaling in the Changing Global Order.* Stanford, CA: Stanford University Press.

Qin Yaqing. 2010. "International Society as a Process: Institutions, Identities, and China's Peaceful Rise." *Chinese Journal of International Politics* 3 (2): 129–153.

Qin Yaqing. 2011. "Rule, Rules, and Relations: Towards a Synthetic Approach to Governance." *Chinese Journal of International Politics* 4 (2): 117–45.

Qin Yaqing. 2012. "Culture and Global Thought: Chinese International Theory in the Making." *Revista CIDOB d'Afers Internacionals* 100: 67–89.

Qin Yaqing. 2014. "Continuity through Change: Background Knowledge and China's International Strategy." *Chinese Journal of International Politics* 7 (3): 285–314.

Qin Yaqing. 2016. "A Relational Theory of World Politics." *International Studies Review* 18 (1): 33–47.

Qin Yaqing. 2018. *A Relational Theory of World Politics.* Cambridge: Cambridge University Press.

Ramo, Copper. 2004. *The Beijing Consensus: Notes on the New Physics of Chinese Power.* London: Foreign Affairs Policy Center.

Read, Brigitte. 2014. "Angola's Chinese-Built Rail Link and the Scramble to Access the Region's Resources." Africa-China Reporting Project, University of Wit-

watersand, February 26. Accessed July 27, 2014. http://china-africa-reporting.
co.za/2014/02/angolas-chinese-built-rail-link-and-the-scramble-to-access-
the-regions-resources/

Redden, Elizabeth. 2017. "New Scrutiny for Confucius Institutes." *Inside Higher
Ed*, April 26. Accessed July 27, 2019. https://www.insidehighered.com/
news/2017/04/26/report-confucius-institutes-finds-no-smoking-guns-
enough-concerns-recommend-closure

Reuters. 2006. "Mugabe Says Army Will 'Pull Trigger' on Opponents." August 15.
Accessed July 27, 2019. https://www.zimbabwesituation.com/old/aug16
_2006.html

Reuters. 2015. "China Condemns Mali Attack with Three Chinese among the
Dead." November 21. Accessed July 27, 2019. https://www.reuters.com/arti
cle/us-mali-attacks-china-xi/china-condemns-mali-attack-with-three-chi
nese-among-the-dead-idUSKCN0TA07P20151121

Reuters. 2018. "Confucius Institute Closed at US University amid Concerns about
Chinese Influence on Campuses." *South China Morning Post*, August 15. Accessed July 27, 2019. https://www.scmp.com/news/world/united-states-can
ada/article/2159888/confucius-institute-closed-us-university-amid

Richmond, Yale. 2005. "Cultural Exchange and the Cold War: How the West
Won." *Polish Review* 50 (3): 355–360.

Robertson, Winslow, and Lina Benabdallah. 2016. "China Pledged to Invest $60
Billion in Africa: Here's What That Means." *Washington Post*, January 7. Accessed July 27, 2019. https://www.washingtonpost.com/news/monkey-cage/
wp/2016/01/07/china-pledged-to-invest-60-billion-in-africa-heres-what-
that-means/

Ronning, Helge. 2014. "How Much 'Soft Power' Does China Have in Africa?" Un-
published paper presented at the International Conference on China and
Africa Media, Communications, and Diplomacy. September 10. Accessed
July 27, 2019. https://www.cmi.no/file/2916-.pdf

Rose, Gideon. 1998. "Neoclassical Realism and Theories of Foreign Policy." *World
Politics* 51 (1): 144–172.

Rose, Nicholas. 1999. *Powers of Freedom: Reframing Political Thought.* Cambridge:
Cambridge University Press.

Rose, Nicholas, Pat O'Malley, and Mariana Valverde. 2006. "Governmentality."
Annual Review of Law and Social Science 2 (1): 82–104.

Saferworld. 2011. "China's Growing Role in African Peace and Security." January.
Accessed July 27, 2019. https://www.saferworld.org.uk/resources/
publications/500-chinas-growing-role-in-african-peace-and-security

Sageman, Marc. 2004. *Understanding Terror Networks.* Philadelphia: University of
Pennsylvania Press.

Sautman, Barry, and Yan Hairong. 2014. "Bashing 'the Chinese:' Contextualizing
Zambia's Collum Coal Mine Shooting." *Journal of Contemporary China* 23 (90):
1073–1092.

Sawicki, Jana. 1998. "Feminism, Foucault, and Subjects of Power and Freedom."

In *The Later Foucault: Politics and Philosophy*, edited by Jeremy Moss, 93–107. London: SAGE Publications.

Schaller, Michael. 2015. *The United States and China*. New York: Oxford University Press.

Schimmelfennig, Frank, and Ulrich Sedelmeier. 2004. "Governance by Conditionality: EU Rule Transfer to the Candidate Countries of Central and Eastern Europe." *Journal of European Public Policy* 11 (4): 669–687.

Schmidt, Brian. 1998. *The Political Discourse of Anarchy: A Disciplinary History of International Relations*. Albany: State University of New York Press.

Schmidt, Heather. 2015. "The Politics of Affect in Confucius Institutes: Reorienting Foreigners towards the PRC." *New Global Studies*. 8 (3): 353–375.

Selg, Peter. 2016. "Two Faces of the 'Relational Turn.'" *PS: Political Science & Politics* 49 (1): 27–31.

Sending, Ole Jacob. 2002. "Constitution, Choice and Change: Problems with the `Logic of Appropriateness' and Its Use in Constructivist Theory." *European Journal of International Relations* 8 (4): 443–470.

Seth, Sanjay. 2013. "'Once Was Blind but Now Can See': Modernity and the Social Sciences." *International Political Sociology* 7 (2): 136–151.

Shambaugh, David. 2013. *China Goes Global: The Partial Power*. New York: Oxford University Press.

Shambaugh, David, and Ren Xiao. 2012. "China: The Conflicted Rising Power." In *Worldviews of Aspiring Powers: Domestic Foreign Policy Debates in China, India, Iran, Japan, and Russia*, edited by Henry R. Nau and Deepa M. Ollapally, 36–72. New York: Oxford University Press.

Shih Chih-yu, and Chiung-Chiu Huang. 2015. "China's Quest for Grand Strategy: Power, National Interest, or Relational Security?" *Chinese Journal of International Politics* 8 (1): 1–26.

Shih Chih-Yu, and Chiung-Chiu Huang. 2016. "Balance of Relationship and the Chinese School of IR: Being Simultaneously Confucian, Post-Western, and Post-Hegemonic." In *Constructing a Chinese School of International Relations: Ongoing Debates*, edited by Yongjin Zhang and Teng-Chi Chang, 177–191. New York: Routledge.

Shinn, David H. 2009. "China and the Conflict in Darfur." *Brown Journal of World Affairs* 16 (1): 85–100.

Shinn, David H. 2011. "The Impact of China's Growing Influence in Africa." *European Financial Review* (April 25), 16–19. Accessed July 27, 2019. https://www.europeanfinancialreview.com/the-impact-of-chinas-growing-influence-in-africa/

Shinn, David H. 2014. "Ethiopia and China: Two Former Empires Connect in the 20th Century." In *Africa's Growing Role in World Politics*, edited by Tatiana Deych, 187–199. Moscow: Institute of African Studies, Russian Academy of Sciences.

Shinn, David H., and Joshua Eisenman. 2012. *China and Africa: A Century of Engagement*. Philadelphia: University of Pennsylvania Press.

Shouse, Eric. 2005. "Feeling, Emotion, Affect." *M/C Journal* 8 (6). http://journal. mediaculture.org.au/0512/03shouse.php

Sohn, Injoo. 2012. "After Renaissance: China's Multilateral Offensive in the Developing World." *European Journal of International Relations* 18 (1): 77–101.

Solomon, Ty. 2013. "Time and Subjectivity in World Politics." *International Studies Quarterly* 58 (4): 671–681.

Solomon, Ty. 2014. "The Affective Underpinnings of Soft Power." *European Journal of International Relations* 20 (3): 720–741.

Spegele, Brian, Peter Wonacott, and Nicholas Bariyq. 2012. "China's Workers Are Targeted as Its Overseas Reach Grows." *Wall Street Journal*, February 1. Accessed July 27, 2019. http://www.wsj.com/articles/SB1000142405297020465 2904577194171294491572

Steele, Brent J. 2010. *Defacing Power: The Aesthetics of Insecurity in Global Politics.* Ann Arbor: University of Michigan Press.

Stockholm International Peace Research Institute (SIPRI). 2018. "Trends in International Arms Transfers." SIPRI Fact Sheet, March. Accessed July 27, 2019. https://www.sipri.org/sites/default/files/2018-03/fssipri_at2017_0.pdf

Stohl, Cynthia, and Michael Stohl. 2007. "Networks of Terror: Theoretical Assumptions and Pragmatic Consequences." *Communication Theory* 17 (2): 93–124.

Strauss, Julia. 2009. "The Past in the Present: Historical and Rhetorical Lineages in China's Relations with Africa." *China Quarterly* 199: 777–795.

Sudan Tribune. 2014. "South Sudanese Rebels Downplay the Deployment of Chinese Troops." September 6. Accessed July 27, 2019. http://www.sudantribune. com/spip.php?article52308

Sun, Yun. 2016. "Political Party Training: China's Ideological Push in Africa?" Brookings Institute. July 5. Accessed July 27, 2019. https://www.brookings. edu/blog/africa-in-focus/2016/07/05/political-party-training-chinas-ideo-logical-push-in-africa/

Suzuki, Shogo. 2009. *Civilization and Empire*. London: Routledge.

Suzuki, Shogo. 2014. "Journey to the West: China Debates Its 'Great Power' Identity." *Millennium: Journal of International Studies* 42 (3): 632–650.

Swedlund, Haley. 2017a. *The Development Dance: How Donors and Recipients Negotiate Foreign Aid*. Ithaca, NY: Cornell University Press.

Swedlund, Haley. 2017b. "Is China Eroding the Bargaining Power of Traditional Donors in Africa?" *International Affairs* 93 (2): 389–408.

Tang Shiping. 2018. "China and the Future International Order(s)." *Ethics & International Affairs* 32 (1): 31–43.

Taylor, Ian. 2006. "China's Oil Diplomacy in Africa." *International Affairs* 82 (5): 937–959.

Taylor, Ian. 2011. *The Forum on China-Africa Cooperation (FOCAC)*. New York: Routledge.

Taylor, Ian. 2014. *Africa Rising? BRICS—Diversifying Dependency*. Oxford: James Currey.

Thies, Cameron, and Mark David Nieman. 2017. *Rising Powers and Foreign Policy Revisionism: Understanding BRICS Identity and Behavior through Time*. Ann Arbor: University of Michigan Press

Thrall, Lloyd. 2015. *China's Expanding African Relations: Implications for U.S. National Security*. Santa Monica, CA: RAND Corporation.

Thrift, Nigel. 2004. "Intensities of Feeling: The Spatial Affect." *Geografiska Annaler: Series B, Human Geography* 86 (1) 57–78.

Tickner, Arlene B. 2013. "Core, Periphery and (Neo)imperialist International Relations." *European Journal of International Relations* 19 (3): 627–646.

Tiezzi, Shannon. 2014. "In South Sudan Conflict, China Tests Its Mediation Skills." *Diplomat*, June 6. Accessed July 27, 2019. https://thediplomat.com/2014/06/in-south-sudan-conflict-china-tests-its-mediation-skills/

Tiezzi, Shannon. 2015. "UN Report: China Sold $20 Million in Arms and Ammunition to South Sudan." *Diplomat*, August 27. Accessed July 27, 2019. https://thediplomat.com/2015/08/un-report-china-sold-20-million-in-arms-and-ammunition-to-south-sudan/

Tugendhat, Henry. 2014. "Chinese Training Course for African Officials: A 'Win-Win' Engagement?" *SAIS China-Africa Research Initiative*, no. 3 (December). Accessed July 27, 2019. https://saiscari.files.wordpress.com/2014/10/sais-cari-brief-3-2014-tugendhat.pdf

Ukaejiofo, Rex. 2014. "China-Africa Agricultural Co-operation: Mutual Benefits or Self-Interest?" Centre for Chinese Studies, Stellenbosch University Working Paper. Accessed July 27, 2019. https://www.eldis.org/document/A69655

United National Office for South-South Cooperation (UNSOSSC). 2017. "What Is South-South Cooperation?" http://unossc1.undp.org/sscexpo/content/ssc/about/what_is_ssc.htm

United States Africa Command (AFRICOM). 2019. "About the Command." Accessed July 27, 2019. http://www.africom.mil/about-the-command

Van Hoeymissen, Sara. 2010. "China's Support to Africa's Regional Security Architecture: Helping Africa to Settle Conflicts and Keep the Peace?" *China Monitor* 49 (March): 10–14.

Vasquez, John. 1997. "The Realist Paradigm and Degenerative versus Progressive Research Programs: An Appraisal of Neotraditional Research on Waltz's Balancing Proposition." *American Political Science Review* 91 (4): 899–912.

Walt, Stephen. 1987. *The Origins of Alliances*. Ithaca, NY: Cornell University Press.

Waltz, Kenneth N. 1986. "Reflections on *Theory of International Politics*: A Response to My Critics." In *Neorealism and Its Critics*, edited by Robert O. Keohane, 322–346. New York: Columbia University Press.

Wang Hongying. 2003. "National Image Building and Chinese Foreign Policy." *China: An International Journal* 1 (1): 46–72.

Wang Xuejun. 2012. "Review on China's Engagement in African Peace and Security." *China International Studies* 32 (January/February): 72–91.

Wanga, Justus. 2016. "Jubilee Looks to the Communist Party for Lessons." *Daily Nation*, September 18. Accessed July 27, 2019. https://www.nation.co.ke/

news/politics/Jubilee-looks-to-the-Communist-Party-for-lessons/1064–3385490-yy2x8x/index.html

Wasserman, Hermann, and Daniel Madrid-Morales. 2018. "How Influential Are Chinese Media in Africa? An Audience Analysis in Kenya and South Africa." *International Journal of Communication* 12 (2): 2212–2231.

Wekesa, Bob. 2014. "Whose Event? Official versus Journalistic Framing of the Fifth Forum on China-Africa Cooperation (FOCAC V)." *Journal of African Media Studies* 6 (1): 57–70.

Weldes, Jutta. 1999. Constructing National Interests: The United States and the Cuban Missile crisis. viii ed. Minneapolis: University of Minnesota Press.

Were, Anzetse. 2018. "Debt Trap? Chinese Loans and Africa's Development Options." *South African Institute for International Affairs Policy Insight*, no. 66 (September): 1–12.

Wilcox, Lauren. 2014. *Bodies of Violence: Theorizing Embodied Subjects in International Relations.* New York: Oxford University Press.

World Press Freedom Index. 2018. Accessed July 27, 2019. https://rsf.org/en/ranking/2018

Wu Qian. 2018. "Defense Ministry's Regular Press Conference on Dec. 27." *China Military*, December 27. Accessed July 27, 2019. http://eng.chinamil.com.cn/view/2018–12/27/content_9390144.htm

Wu Xinbo. 2001. "Four Contradictions Constraining China's Foreign Policy Behavior." *Journal of Contemporary China* 10 (27): 293–301.

Wu Yu-Shan. 2016. "China's Media and Public Diplomacy Approach in Africa: Illustrations from South Africa." *Chinese Journal of Communication* 9 (1): 81–97.

Wu Zhengyu, and Ian Taylor. 2011. "From Refusal to Engagement: Chinese Contributions to Peacekeeping in Africa." *Journal of Contemporary African Studies* 29 (2): 137–154.

Xi Jinping. 2013. "President Xi's Speech at Nazarbayev University." June 11. Accessed July 27, 2019. http://china.org.cn/business/2014–06/11/content_32634034.htm

Xi Jinping. 2014. "New Asian Security Concept for New Progress in Security Cooperation." Remarks at the Fourth Summit on the Conference on Interaction and Confidence Building Measures in Asia. May 21. Accessed July 27, 2019. http://www.cica-china.org/eng/zxghd/yxdscfh/t1170132.htm

Xi Jinping. 2015a. "Address to the United Nations General Assembly." *Quartz Africa*, September 29. Accessed July 27, 2019. http://qz.com/512886/read-the-full-text-of-xi-jinpings-first-un-address/

Xi Jinping. 2015b. "Opening of a New Era of China-Africa Win-Win Cooperation and Common Development." Remarks at FOCAC, Johannesburg. December 4. Accessed July 27, 2019. http://www.dirco.gov.za/docs/speeches/2015/xi1204.htm

Xi Jinping. 2017. "Full Text of President Xi's Speech at Opening of the Belt and Road Forum." *XinhuaNet*, May 14. Accessed July 27, 2019. http://www.xinhuanet.com/english/2017–05/14/c_136282982.htm

Xiaoyun Li. 2005. *China's Foreign Aid and Aid to Africa*. Paris: Organization for Economic Cooperation and Development.

Xiaoyun Li. 2009. "China's Foreign Aid and Aid to Africa: Overview." Unpublished paper presented at the College of Humanities and Development, China Agricultural University, no. 100094.

Xiaoyun Li, Qi Gubo, Tang Lixia, Zhao Lixia, Jin Leshanl, Guo Zhanfeng, and Wu Jin. 2012. *Agricultural Development in China and Africa: A Comparative Analysis*. New York: Routledge.

Xinbo Wu. 2001. "Four Contradictions Constraining China's Foreign Policy Behavior." *Journal of Contemporary China* 10 (27): 293–294.

Xinhua News Agency. 2004. "Military Institute Set Up for Training Foreign Officers." August 7. Accessed July 27, 2019. http://www.china.org.cn/english/2004/Aug/103238.htm

Xinhua News Agency. 2012. "Exploring China Tianjiao Tewi: The Goal Is to 'Target' the Overseas Security Market." Last accessed August 14, 2016; no longer available. http://news.xinhuanet.com/photo/2012-10/01/c_123783959_3.htm

Xinhua News Agency. 2015. "Backgrounder: China's Major Overseas Evacuations in Recent Years." *ChinaDaily.com.cn*, March 30. Accessed July 27, 2019. http://www.chinadaily.com.cn/china/2015-03/30/content_19954649.htm

Xinhua News Agency. 2018. "Ugandan Students to Pursue Studies in China." *Xinhuanet*, August 26. Accessed July 27, 2019. http://www.xinhuanet.com/english/2018-08/26/c_137418938.htm

Xu Wei. 2012. "More Consideration Given to Guards for Overseas Workers." *China Daily*, February 22. Accessed July 27, 2019. http://www.chinadaily.com.cn/china/2012-02/22/content_14662657.htm

Xuetong Yan. 2014. "From Keeping a Low Profile to Striving for Achievements." *Chinese Journal of International Politics* 7 (2): 153–184.

Yang Jie, ed. 2014. *The Political Economy of Affect and Emotion in East Asia*. New York: Routledge.

Yang Mei-Hui Mayfair. 1994. *Gifts, Favors, and Banquets: The Art of Social Relationships in China*. Ithaca, NY: Cornell University Press.

Yu T. George. 1980. "The Tanzania-Zambian Railway: A Case Study in Chinese Economic Aid to Africa." In *Soviet and Chinese Aid to African Nations*, edited by Warren Weinstein and Thomas H. Henriksen, 117–144. New York: Praeger.

Yu T. George. 2009. "China, Africa, and Globalization: The 'China Alternative.'" Institute for Security and Development Policy Asia Paper. June. Accessed July 27, 2019. http://isdp.eu/content/uploads/publications/2009_yu_china-africa-and-globalization.pdf

Zaharna, Rhonda. 2014. "China's Confucius Institutes: Understanding the Relational Structure and Relational Dynamics of Network Collaboration." In *Confucius Institutes and the Globalization of China's Soft Power*, edited by Jain Wang, 9–32. Los Angeles: Figueroa Press.

Zarakol, Ayşe. 2014. "What Made the Modern World Hang Together: Socialization or Stigmatisation?" *International Theory* 6 (2): 311–332.

Zhang Feng. 2015. "China as a Global Force." *Asia & the Pacific Policy Studies* 3 (1): 120–128.

Zhang Yongjin, and Barry Buzan. 2012. "The Tributary System as International Society in Theory and Practice." *Chinese Journal of International Politics* 5 (1): 3–36.

Zhao Lei. 2015. "Academy Helps Bolster Overseas Terrorism Fight." *China Daily*, April 8. Accessed July 27, 2019. http://www.chinadaily.com.cn/china/2015-08/04/content_21494804.htm

Zeng Aiping. 2015. "China-Africa Governance Exchanges and Experiences." *China Institute of International Studies*, December 3. Accessed July 27, 2019. http://www.ciis.org.cn/english/2015-12/03/content_8424552.htm

Index

Addis Ababa, 12, 24, 114, 115, 117, 126, 127, 129, 135, 152, 158, 159
African National Congress (ANC), 2, 34, 38
African Union, 12, 67, 72, 76, 78
Afrobarometer, 147, 160
agency, 20, 48, 58, 107, 110, 111, 116, 131, 133, 146, 148
agriculture, 7, 28, 33, 39, 40, 74, 131, 134, 144, 151, 156
Algeria, 28, 29, 77, 83, 100
Alliance Française, 113, 125, 126, 127
Angola, 38, 76, 79
anticolonial, 26, 28, 29, 108
    See also decolonial; postcolonialism
arms, 23, 67, 68, 69, 78, 84
Asian Infrastructure and Investment Bank (AIIB), 153, 155
Atkinson, Carol, 86, 87, 88

balance of power, 65
Bandung, 22, 28, 29, 154
Bangladesh, 80, 90
Banquet, 16, 41, 51, 53, 56
Barnett, Michael, 45, 49, 50
Beijing Consensus, 144, 153
Belt and Road Initiative (BRI), 56, 61, 81, 91, 121, 144, 145, 146, 153, 160
Botswana 34, 37, 76, 125, 159
branding ,21, 27, 73, 92, 113, 117, 139, 140
BRICS, 20, 58, 155

cadre, 2, 3, 32, 36, 37, 38, 39, 66, 77, 89
Cameroon, 36, 122, 128, 143, 160
Capacity Building, 2, 9, 26, 40, 63, 74, 94, 95, 96, 123, 132, 138, 146, 151, 159
Chad, 24, 36, 37

China model, 1, 2, 3, 11, 15, 16, 20, 43, 51, 56, 77, 82, 83, 96, 101, 109, 130, 138, 140, 144, 146, 147, 148
China's Communist Party (CCP), 2, 3, 22, 32, 33, 34, 38, 39, 82, 146, 147, 148
China's Communist Party School, 2, 32, 63, 148
China Daily, 76, 83, 91, 93, 99, 100
China Export-Import Bank, 62, 65
China's Global TV Network (CGTN), 93, 98, 99, 100, 101, 103, 105, 108, 157, 158
China's Ministry of Foreign Affairs (MOFA), 12, 23, 24, 27, 156
China's People's Liberation Army (PLA), 74, 76, 82
colonialism, 18, 20, 21, 26, 27, 28, 30, 32, 60, 71, 92, 107, 108, 115, 131, 132, 133, 139, 149
combat, 76, 78, 81, 89, 90
    See also conflict
conditionality, 1, 20, 25, 32
conflict, 22, 23, 24, 29, 45, 46, 67, 71, 72, 73, 81, 90, 154
    See also combat
Confucianism, 9, 53, 76, 155, 160
Confucius Institutes, 61, 63, 111, 112, 113, 114, 115, 117, 118, 119, 120, 121, 122, 123, 124, 125, 126, 125, 126, 127, 128, 129, 130, 131, 132, 133, 134, 135, 136, 140, 144, 147, 158
constructivism, 49, 54, 87
cooperation
    bilateral, 74
    multilateral, 67, 71
    south-south, 20, 21, 31, 32, 40, 152
counterterrorism, 65, 74, 90, 143, 157

Printed and bound by CPI Group (UK) Ltd, Croydon, CR0 4YY

10/06/2025

14686727-0001